THE GEORGE GUND FOUNDATION
IMPRINT IN AFRICAN AMERICAN STUDIES

The George Gund Foundation has endowed this imprint to advance understanding of the history, culture, and current issues of African Americans.

The publisher and the University of California Press Foundation gratefully acknowledge the generous support of the George Gund Foundation Imprint in African American Studies.

Acts of Love

Acts of Love

BLACK PERFORMANCE AND THE KISS THAT CHANGED FILM HISTORY

Allyson Nadia Field

UNIVERSITY OF CALIFORNIA PRESS

University of California Press
Oakland, California

© 2026 by Allyson Nadia Field

All rights reserved.

Library of Congress Cataloging-in-Publication Data

Names: Field, Allyson Nadia, author
Title: Acts of love : Black performance and the kiss that changed film history / Allyson Nadia Field.
Description: Oakland, California : University of California Press, [2026] | Includes bibliographical references and index.
Identifiers: LCCN 2025038144 (print) | LCCN 2025038145 (ebook) | ISBN 9780520392922 hardback | ISBN 9780520392939 paperback | ISBN 9780520392946 ebook
Subjects: LCSH: African Americans in motion pictures—19th century
Classification: LCC PN1995.9.B585 F54 2026 (print) | LCC PN1995.9.B585 (ebook)
LC record available at https://lccn.loc.gov/2025038144
LC ebook record available at https://lccn.loc.gov/2025038145

Manufactured in the United States of America

GPSR Authorized Representative: Easy Access System Europe, Mustamäe tee 50, 10621 Tallinn, Estonia, gpsr.requests@easproject.com

35 34 33 32 31 30 29 28 27 26
10 9 8 7 6 5 4 3 2 1

Dedicated to the memory of Henry T. Sampson, Jr. (1934–2015)
Historian of Black theater and film, nuclear engineer, inventor

CONTENTS

Introduction

OUT OF THE ARCHIVE

WHEN SAINT SUTTLE AND GERTIE Brown visited William Selig's moving-picture studio at 43 Peck Court on a spring day in 1898, they may have been apprehensive about the meeting. Located on a seedy side street in Chicago's notorious Levee District, Peck Court was best known as a site of prostitution, gambling, and murder. After the Great Chicago Fire of 1871, the red-light district moved from downtown to what is now the South Loop, and that area thrived during the 1893 World's Columbian Exposition with the influx of visitors looking to complement the wholesome fairground attractions with more carnal experiences. Teeming with sex workers and gamblers, the Levee was also home to many of the city's entertainers on the popular stage and the backdrop to its nascent moviemaking enterprise.

Suttle and Brown had worked together as a "colored act" in vaudeville, performing as a singing-and-dancing romantic duo. Charisma, elegance, and chemistry fueled their stage routine and led to this opportunity. But Peck Court wasn't an Opera House, and the Levee was a far cry from the city's respectable theaters. Was young Gertie, still a teenager, nervous at visiting the most disreputable part of the city? Or was she used to keeping her guard up, having been on the stage since she was nine years old? Perhaps Suttle—a tall, confident, twenty-eight-year-old actor—offered a reassuring presence. After all, he lived just two blocks from Selig's studio, on the equally dodgy Harmon Court.

Walking those infamous cobblestoned alleyways, the actors were willing to take a chance for the opportunity to promote their act. Seasoned professionals, Suttle and Brown were accustomed to the varied milieus of show people and a world that skirted the edge of respectability. Work was work, and they needed it.

As a producer, Selig surely seemed legit. Like them, he had traveled on the minstrel circuit. He had even partnered—as an equal—with a Black man in show business. It's possible they had heard of him or knew folks who had worked with him. True, he was capitalizing on Black talent, but most white showmen of the time were cashing in on the vogue for blackness in some form or another. It's reasonable to think that while Suttle and Brown had a long-cultivated distrust of white theater executives and white managers of Black entertainers, they performed a calculation familiar to many working performers of their time: the chance for publicity outweighed the potential for debasement. And maybe the Polyscope, Selig's novel camera-projector contraption, would be their ticket to fame.

Whispers were spreading among vaudevillians about the machine that performed for them even when they were offstage. There wasn't a clear consensus on whether it was a boon or a threat to an actor's livelihood. Few new technologies are unreservedly embraced, and the moving picture had its detractors. But the movies couldn't (yet) convey song or the dazzle of multicolored costumes, so stage folk looked on it more with curiosity than concern. Suttle and Brown might have thought of performing for this strange apparatus as a possible promotion for their act, not much different than sitting for a portrait at a photography studio like J. B. Wilson, which catered to Chicago's theatrical performers. Selig's headquarters even resembled a photography studio with its sets and backdrops, though it was lit entirely with natural light rather than hot lamps. At least they wouldn't have to stand completely still. And so, misgivings checked at the door, they went in as professionals and treated the Polyscope as an audience of one.

I imagine they almost walked out. Brown was a pro and prepared to perform her part, but as the camera operator kept coaxing Suttle to kiss her—beyond the choreographed embrace of their act—she may have worried about respectability in front of the camera. She was young but not naïve. Brown would have worked hard to stay off indecent stages and out of bawdy rooms, and she was surely resolved not to go in that direction now. And yet, surrounded by Selig and his all-male, all-white production crew, was Gertie ill at ease? Did she feel bashful at the producer's repeated entreaties to kiss? Perhaps Suttle laughed off her misgivings. She and Suttle kissed nightly on stage, so why not in front of this mustachioed Bohemian and his curious machine? I imagine she relaxed, her professionalism overcoming apprehension. *I'm an actress. It's a love scene. I am in love.*

Her skirt swished as Suttle enfolded her in his arms with valiant assurance. She withdrew only to be drawn back again and again, kisses smothering laughter.

. . .

I enter the story in January 2017. It was a dark winter, and I was scared. The nation was weeks away from a presidential inauguration portending an uncertain future, and I had been admitted to the hospital to be induced into labor with my second child, more than a month before her due date. I was in labor when an email arrived from Dino Everett, the moving-image archivist at the University of Southern California, writing to me as a scholar of early African American cinema. The subject line read, "Tell me I am overreacting." I skimmed the message—short rolls, couple kissing, African Americans, pre-1900—and though I'd thought looking at my phone might be a good distraction from pain, I was wrong. I could not concentrate, and I put the phone away.

Two weeks later, home and with a healthy newborn, I finally opened his message. The email included astonishing images from an unidentified nitrate print Everett had acquired from a collector in New Orleans, along with his straightforward question: "Does this seem important?"

This time I answered immediately: "Yes!" Everett had found a near-complete, fifty-foot nitrate print from circa 1900, in remarkable condition for its age. Even more surprising was the subject of the film: an African American couple joyously embracing. To Everett, these images seemed incongruous with the stereotypes, racist tropes, and comedic ridicule that tend to characterize early cinema's portrayal of Black people. I shared his astonishment. Looking at a set of digitally scanned enlargements of the nitrate reel, I was also taken by the seemingly naturalistic performance. The frames revealed a man, dressed in a suit with wide lapels and defined piping that appeared to be from a theatrical costume, holding hands with a woman in a dress with wide, ruffled shoulders and flounced sleeves. Smiling and laughing, they kiss four times throughout the film.

Unlike early cinema's rampant portrayal of Black subjects in demeaning, racist caricatures, these performers are not the butt of a joke and their kiss is not a punch line. Rather than a portrayal of lasciviousness, caricature, or buffoonery, the display of affection between the couple is striking in its tenderness and apparent sincerity. Even today, having looked at these images for almost a decade, this sense of naturalness is hard for me to overstate. Indeed,

FIGURE 1. Digital scans from the nitrate print of *Something Good—Negro Kiss* (Selig, 1898). Courtesy of Dino Everett, USC HMH Foundation Moving Image Archive.

what makes the film so distinctive is the utter candor of the actors who seem to genuinely find amusement in the scene. These performers laugh and seem to be having fun with their flirtation, expressing joy and earnest affection with each other.

I'd never seen anything like it from this era, and the frame enlargements presented a tantalizing archival mystery: what was this film and who were these performers?

It took a year of careful research, but eventually we could identify Everett's nitrate print as *Something Good—Negro Kiss*, made by William Selig in Chicago in 1898 and featuring vaudeville performers Saint Suttle and Gertie Brown.

Once Everett and I were confident in our identification and dating of the artifact, he digitally restored the film and we nominated it to the National Film Registry, an annual list of twenty-five films deemed culturally, historically, or aesthetically significant by the Librarian of Congress. As a rare nineteenth-century artifact of Black affection, *Something Good* met a contemporary hunger for moving images of Black love, especially from a period of film history known for its animosity toward Black humanity. Moreover, the format of early films—very short, easily digestible scenes—ideally suited the current media landscape, dominated by social media's snippet-sized videos. What is old turns out not only to be new again but definitional to the circulation of moving images in our digital present.

When the film was named to the National Film Registry in 2018, it garnered tremendous attention, accelerated by its remediation from nitrate film (accessible only to archival specialists) to a digitized short film easily viewed and shared across social media. Netflix counsel and Twitter personality Kyle Alex Brett set the film to Nicholas Britell's score for Barry Jenkins's *If Beale Street Could Talk* (2018), and The Oprah Winfrey Network (OWN) series *Black Love* posted it to Instagram with sobbing emojis: "We're not crying you are!" The resulting exposure created an impassioned response through social media with shares and comments from significant Hollywood figures like Jenkins, Viola Davis, Tracee Ellis Ross, Lena Waithe, Jada Pinkett Smith, MJ Rodriguez, Tambay Obenson, and Janelle Monáe. Poet and president of the Andrew W. Mellon Foundation Elizabeth Alexander shared it; the creator of #OscarsSoWhite, April Reign, retweeted it; and The Black List founder Franklin Leonard commented, "Absolutely broke me." To date, Brett's initial post has been viewed more than a million times and has been shared by celebrities with tens of millions of followers.

But social media comments have also reflected a bittersweet response. "There is something so sweet yet so sad about this footage," one viewer wrote, while Brett himself said, "Ok. So, I've been crying watching that on loop. And I think it's because they seem so happy and I feel so fucking angry wondering what 1900 America did with that happiness." Many commenters shared moving stories of parents and grandparents falling in love, and others pointed to the historical erasure and misrepresentation of African American love and affection in American cinema. One viewer wrote on Twitter, "The nation could've had this all along, and still it gets cursed with D. W. Griffith's *Birth of a Nation*." Others celebrated the power that cinema has to assert such an electrifying image against the systematic rejection of Black humanity: "Imagine if our grandparents and parents were able to see this in their prime!," and "This is like opening a time capsule and seeing love in its purest form. It's beautiful to see, but hard to know the hateful times they were living in." As Tracee Ellis Ross noted, "Seeing images of Black love and Black joy is special. We do not get enough of this. And this is from 1898."

Along with other social media users, artists also encountered the rediscovered *Something Good* in its viral circulation. This archival rediscovery inspired contemporary African American artists, including filmmakers Kevin Jerome Everson, Kahlil Pedizisai, Ina Archer, and Amina Ross, and poets Christian Campbell and Gabrielle Daniels. Most recently, Lauryn Hill projected *Something Good* during her twenty-fifth anniversary tour for *The Miseducation of Lauryn Hill*. In the context of Hill's personal reflections on the power of L.O.V.E., *Something Good* emblematized the endurance of Black love across generations, a resilient force of resistance in a climate of hate.

The electrifying response to *Something Good* in our moment has been a major impetus for the writing of this book. This rediscovery restores a piece of American film history that impacts not only how scholars understand that history, but also reminds us that contemporary audiences seek images and histories that can serve as a usable past. And no matter the audience, the rediscovery of *Something Good* establishes that Black affection on film has a legacy as long as the medium itself. It may have been out of sight for more than a century, but it existed.

120 years later, as we celebrate the rediscovery of *Something Good*, we must confront the suppression, for most of the twentieth century, of this image of African American affection on screen. The film's obscurity is likely the result of a confluence of factors: extremely low survival rates for early films, archival priorities, and resource allocation (rendering many early films that are lucky enough to be stored in archives nevertheless uncatalogued), and collective—justifiable—embarrassment over our nation's cultural heritage and its mistreatment of nonwhite subjects. If we see the film as having been hidden, it was not at the hands of a singular nefarious actor but by the values, investments, and concerns of motion-picture producers, archivists, and scholars, shaped by the social and political climates in which the film was made, circulated, neglected, and rediscovered.

At the same time, the rediscovery and viral circulation of the film are inextricably imbricated in the desires, practices, and responses of archivists, historians, and viewers in our own moment. As film historian Jacqueline Stewart has cautioned in her work on the "narratives of loss and recovery" surrounding the Tyler, Texas Black Film Collection at Southern Methodist University, "In contemporary efforts to recover marginalized histories, we may be so heavily inclined to read such materials as authentic, self-evidently valuable documents that we do not attend to the many layers of physical and intellectual work that make them available to us, that convert their status from lost to found."[1] In this book, I foreground the research process both to show the work of creating historical meaning—always an interpretive practice—and to resist the tendency to presume films can be self-evident. In the case of Suttle and Brown's filmed kisses, there are myriad layers beneath the surface appearance of carefree flirtation. Their rediscovered moving images concretize their historical presence, but they also prompt more questions around race and performance onstage and on-screen at the turn of the century, the way archives create meaning, and the creative work historians do with fragments and traces of lives long past. Their filmic image also raises questions about the medium of moving images, its relation to forms of live performance, and its circulation far and wide, across time and media formats.

Of course, when Suttle and Brown entered Selig's studio, they had no idea that motion pictures would gain such significance over the next century. And they certainly could not have anticipated that, 120 years later, people would marvel at the short movie they made. How could they fathom the idea that their playful kisses would be the subject of widespread awe and acclaim? One might wonder, as well, what would have happened if *Something Good* had achieved popularity in its time. As working performers with long experience on the professional circuits, Suttle and Brown no doubt would have sought to capitalize on their newfound fame.

Suttle and Brown were savvy entertainers at the center of popular culture's latest fads. In 1898, they pegged their aspirations to the national—indeed, international—craze for a dance called "the cakewalk." A form of promenade, in which the dancers process in pairs and take solo turns, the cakewalk developed from the antebellum Southern plantation to become a worldwide phenomenon performed by professionals (Black and white) and amateurs alike. Ubiquitous on stages and in parlors at the turn of the century, the cakewalk even formed a cycle of early film subjects, including American Mutoscope and Biograph's *Cake Walk* (US, 1897), Georges Méliès's *Le cakewalk infernal* (The Infernal Cakewalk, France, 1903), Robert W. Paul's *Kiddies' Cakewalk* (UK, 1903), Pathé's *Le cake-walk chez les nains* (The Dwarfs' Cakewalk, France, 1903), and Alexander Shiryaev's animated

Cakewalk (Russia, 1906). Even when they had no Black dancers, cakewalk films globalized African American performative culture on international screens.

The cakewalk made up the bread and butter of many popular acts—Black and non-Black—as performers peppered their stage time with the audience-pleasing dance. Suttle and Brown, for their part, were half of a cakewalking quartet, along with John and Maud Brewer. Together, the two couples were known as the Rag-Time Four, a singing-and-dancing comedic group billed on the vaudeville stage as "the Blackville twins and their Best Gals." Likely on the same day that Suttle and Brown recorded *Something Good*, the Rag-Time Four also danced the cakewalk for Selig's Polyscope. Remarkably, moving images of the Rag-Time Four's cakewalk have survived.

This book tells the story of this astonishing film and its performers, contending that *Something Good* complicates the familiar history of an American cinema founded on horribly racist caricatures and reveals an alternative, obscured history of Black representation on screen, one based on genuine delight and joyful embrace. The rediscovery of *Something Good* also gifts us its two remarkable actors, Saint Suttle and Gertie Brown. The film beckons us to search for them, and I took what felt like an invitation—even a responsibility—to seek out these forgotten actors and restore them to the histories they were so vital in shaping. This book thus presents *Something Good* as a prism from which multiple stories refract: the history of the film and its myriad meanings then and now; Black performance on stage and screen at the turn of the twentieth century; the lives, careers, and ambitions of its performers; and the act of archival rediscovery and the research and writing of history.

This book also reveals the extraordinary fact that *Something Good* was part of a constellation of subsequently unearthed early films featuring the same performers. Together, this group of films constitutes a powerful counter-image to the insidious antiblack tropes pervading American popular culture. Looking across stage and screen, this book restores an image of Black affection and joy to film history; expands our archive of crucial artifacts of early cinema; and uncovers the fascinating lives of Saint Suttle and Gertie Brown, finally establishing their rightful place in the history of American culture.

• • •

No records survive to tell us what kind of arrangement structured the Rag-Time Four's visit to Selig's Peck Court studio, how long the filming took, or even if the performers visited on more than one session. We don't know what they thought about their experience, motion pictures, or their recorded performance. We don't know if they even saw their own films. Like many almost-famous figures, they left relatively few traces of their professional and personal lives. The scene I conjured at the opening of this Introduction is speculation informed by extensive research, surviving evidence, and my training as a film historian. I don't presume my account to be totally authoritative; no history can be. Indeed, I foreground the research process to demonstrate the constructedness of narratives of the past and the tenuousness of our grasp of lives and experiences so far removed from our own. Our inquiries into the past often symptomatize the anxieties afflicting our present. While my research began at the start of a global rightward political lurch, it concluded as the enactment of fascistic, white supremacist policies began to unravel decades of civil rights advances and protections in the US. Reckoning with the lives and trajectories of Saint Suttle and Gertie Brown at the end of the first quarter of the twenty-first century meant acknowledging the arc of the moral universe might not actually bend toward justice, no matter how much we may want it to. However, viewing their time through the lens of my own, especially as a non-Black scholar of African American film history, motivated me to treat the act of research as a form of care. I recognize the contours and limits of historical approaches to vexed questions of race and representation, the legacies of American antiblackness, and the ingrained operations of power that scholarship risks reinforcing. Antiracist history is not merely about centering marginalized subjects—as important as that work is—but also rethinking the very function, forms, and purposes of scholarship. My commitment to scholarship that works toward a more just and equitable society finds its locus of struggle in instances of the emergence of media practices that can both codify and challenge racial hegemonies.

With the story of *Something Good* and its performers, empirical evidence meets informed speculation in the crafting of historical narratives, and this story necessarily involves my own interpretive analysis. I hope this work will be followed by that of many others. Indeed, the rediscovery of film artifacts that were once considered lost invites the engagement of anyone who watches these films, whether they encountered them on-screen, in an archive, or through social media. My hope is that the research and interpretive frameworks I lay out in this book will inspire readers to view these—and other—films through their own lenses, proffering alternative interpretations and attending to their own affective responses to surviving evidence.

That evidence has expanded over the course of this project. It now includes two films Selig recorded with Suttle and Brown in 1898: *Something Good—Negro Kiss* and a longer, full-figure version found in Leksvik, Norway, after the shorter film went viral. Also extant are the two cakewalk films the Rag-Time Four performed for Selig. *A Night in Blackville*, another Selig film shot at about the same time as the cakewalk and kiss films, likely also includes the Rag-Time Four performers. Adding to the mystery of these artifacts of early cinema, a fragment survives of a kiss film made slightly later than *Something Good* and by a different producer, in which Saint Suttle kisses an unidentified partner. These artifacts are girded by disparate records of production and exhibition, themselves fragmentary and largely opaque.

As much as this is a story about films and performers, it is also a story about material artifacts and the process of making sense out of scattered traces of an under-recorded history of under-documented people, whose "own individual stories," as historian Natalia Molina notes, "are not well served by printed records."[2] As I show in this book, these two strands interconnect and weave a story about Black film and theatrical performance in the ragtime era. Written history tends to downplay evidence in favor of narrative, focusing on what we presume to know of the past rather than how it is that we arrive at our deductions. Here, I center the material traces of Suttle, Brown, and the Rag-Time Four, from the written record to surviving nitrate prints, for several reasons. The first is to detail how history is written and how, in the wake of archival absences, we might find ways of accessing under-documented voices and stories. Second, because of the imbrication of material evidence and the creation of meaning, attention to artifacts' materiality can prove key to determining how we make sense of these traces, as I detail in Chapter One. The third reason is that attention to material artifacts invites associations and connections otherwise left untraced due to archival absence, underscoring another benefit of focusing on issues of provenance (the origin, circulation, and trajectory of a particular print), materiality (its physical characteristics), form (the formal aspects of the moving images), and metadata (the data that describes and gives information about other data: i.e., how it is we know what we presume to know).

Material print history tells us much about the films and performers, and how audiences received them. A surviving reel can also unlock aspects of the history of under-documented figures—like Suttle and Brown—whose careers left scant and scattered traces, requiring us to connect faded dots to chart the ephemeral contours of their professional lives. In the case of Suttle, the two ends of his trajectory as a performer—from the 1890s to the 1920s—resound in a curious echo. As I'll show in Chapter Five, in his later career he draws from themes and tropes of his earlier years, reframing and thereby reclaiming them in a gesture of creative autonomy in his ambitious dreams for Black musical theater. Brown's professional life extends to the Harlem Renaissance, and her performing partner and husband Tim Moore's career goes even further, to midcentury television. Considered together, Suttle's and Brown's biographies include all formats of Black public performance in the early to mid-twentieth century. And in their performance in *Something Good*, Suttle and Brown instantiate an alternative genealogy of Black affection on-screen. Given the material precarity of early film, that such histories might be lost should not be as surprising as it is. And yet, it's a reminder of the fragility of history itself.

I take the opacity of the historical record not as a barrier to understanding but an invitation to seek out Suttle and Brown and their world, mindful that every history is a construction built half blind and from inadequate tools. Definitiveness, therefore, cannot be the goal. Rather, this book treats the search as integral to the subject. It tells the story of Suttle and Brown's films: the rediscovery of their nitrate doubles and circulation of their digital images in our century, one so removed from their own. It also tells the story of Suttle, Brown, and the community of performers in their orbit. Centered on these working entertainers, this book posits them as different kinds of stars, not with the financial success of fame, but still possessing their own radiance. Their luminance is like a beacon across time, helping us see the conditions that largely stymied mainstream success in their era but could not dim their brilliance across the century.

THE PERFORMERS

The members of the Rag-Time Four are enigmatic figures. Despite years of research, their early lives and upbringing remain largely a mystery to me. The occasional federal census or city directory captures them in rare moments of relative domestic stability, but apart from a few marriage licenses, ship manifests, and death certificates, little documentation survives to sketch the contours of their personal lives outside their theatrical careers.

Suttle, Brown, and the Brewers were part of the first generation of African Americans born after Emancipation. Slavery's fractured family structures marked each of their genealogies, with three of them born to couples from vastly different regions (only Saint Suttle's parents were from neighboring states). As fascinating as the performers are, we can only imagine the lives—straddling both sides of Emancipation—forged by their parents. Pain, resilience, drama, joy, and love certainly shaped their lives as performers, though how and in what ways we can only infer from the histories in which they were enmeshed. The little we do know shows that each performer in the Rag-Time Four came from a different background, geographically and socially distinct. Their experiences illustrate the diversity of African American lives, too often treated as a monolith.

Gertie Brown: The Creole Gal

Gertie Brown was born Gilberta Gertrude Chevalier in August 1878 in Louisiana. She began her stage career when she was nine, though I have found no records to indicate what her acts entailed at that age. Given her early start on the stage, she likely came from a musical family. Brown's father, John Chevalier, was from Louisiana, and his name suggests he was Creole or French. He may have been the man listed in military records as John Cavilieir, conscripted into the Confederate Army as a musician, or a free—or freed—Black man undocumented by that name. He might have been a white man. Gertie's mother, Catherine King, was from Ohio, and that background was prominent enough in Brown's upbringing to be mistaken for her own by the time of her death in 1934.

Sometime between her birth and her appearance in the Rag-Time Four at nineteen, she started going by the name Gertie Brown. The 1900 census lists her as married, but apparently not living with her spouse (named Brown or otherwise). Whether the marriage was real or a ruse to deter unwanted suitors, secure a room in a respectable boardinghouse, or another reason—it may have been a mistake of the census taker—she seems to have adopted Brown as her official name up to her marriage to fellow actor Harry Roscoe "Tim" Moore in 1915.

Like many actors, Brown seems to have been concerned with her age, especially after her marriage. Official documents vary her birth year from 1878 in the 1900 census, to 1882 on her passport application in 1917 (making her only a year younger than her husband, who shaved six years off his age on the same application), to 1884 on her death certificate in 1934 (listing her as forty-nine but leaving her date of birth blank). The difference is slight, so perhaps vanity isn't to blame for the discrepancies. Still, the inexactitudes in official ledgers remind us of the fallibility of historical records; in addition to their endemic biases that efface and misrepresent Black lives, historical documents are rife with mundane errors. Yet with few surviving evidentiary traces, unreliable records become the precious foundation for careful assessment and critical adjudication.

Brown's career was enviable for its consistency if modest in scope; from childhood to middle age, she worked unflaggingly. When she died, her obituary recognized her tenacity and dependability proclaiming, "She was a trouper."[3]

Saint Suttle: The Black Millionaire

While Brown enjoyed a long stage career and remained active until her death, Suttle struggled to sustain an acting career after the 1910s. It was not for want of trying. He danced and sang under tents and on stages in venues ranging from the humblest to the most ornate. He also published original songs, contributing to the ragtime era with his singular interpretations of Black sociality set to syncopated rhythms. On stage and through his ragtime compositions, Suttle cultivated his persona as the "Black Millionaire."

Saint Suttle was born Douglas Suttle—or Saint Douglas Suttle—in Elkton, Kentucky, in 1870, the second of eight children. His father, Moses Suttle, was born in 1843 in Tennessee, and his mother, Peggy Hogan, was born in 1846 in Kentucky. His entry into theatrical life is unknown, though according to Reginald Robinson, the ragtime pianist and composer (and MacArthur "genius grant" Fellow), Suttle's original compositions demonstrate musical mastery and tutelage. Where Suttle would have received that training is uncertain, though some ragtime composers acquired musical skills from their families, in schools or churches, or from more experienced musicians who took promising youngsters under their wings.

By 1900, Suttle had been married for four years to English-born housekeeper Mary L. Suttle, then twenty-one. They had four children, only one of whom was still living by the time the 1900 census taker came to Harmon Court. After 1900, Mary and the baby fall from the historical record. In 1909, Suttle, at age thirty-nine, had another child with eighteen-year-old Goldie Payne. The child, Ruth Suttle, was born in Madison, Indiana. Two years later, the couple had a second child—a son who died in infancy[4]—

followed by Marjorie, born in 1912, and Iola, born in 1914. After that, Goldie and the children slip from any official records involving Suttle.

Suttle worked consistently, it seems, through the 1900s and then intermittently in the 1910s and 1920s. His career extends from the cakewalk circuit to the vaudeville stage to musical theater, with his tireless initiative driving various schemes and ventures. Suttle's ambition outweighed his successes, however. By the early 1930s, he was struggling to support himself independently. He died from a carcinoma in 1932. His death certificate lists his occupation as "laborer."[5]

John and Maud Brewer

John Brewer and Maud Brown, who married in December 1898, spent years building their careers before joining Suttle and Brown to make up the Rag-Time Four. John Brewer was born in 1869 in Marshall, Texas, to a Texan father and a mother from Pennsylvania.[6] Maud Brown (no known relation to Gertie) was born in 1875 and was originally from the Hawaiian Islands. Her mother was from Honolulu and her father was from Kentucky.

John Brewer was the professional backbone of the group. He began his career in the early 1880s and was steadily employed in different troupes across the country. A lead comedian, Brewer was known as "the Black Eddie Foy" of comic opera, after the popular Irish American vaudevillian.[7] With a long face, prominent forehead, and thin lips, Brewer shared physical characteristics, as well as comedic affinities, with Foy.

In 1890, while performing with McCabe and Young's Minstrels in Cuba, the twenty-one-year-old John Brewer married a woman identified in the *New York Clipper* as Rato Martinie (perhaps a Cuban named Rita Martinez?) and returned to the US with the troupe "in a full supply of fine clothes and diamonds."[8] At that point, Martinie/Martinez falls out of the historical record and within eight years Brewer was single again, or at least in a position to remarry. If they weren't already acquaintances, John likely met Maud Brown in 1897 when she joined *The Black Trilby* (starring John), a spectacular minstrel version of the popular, long-running play *Trilby* about a young woman abducted by a hypnotist named Svengali—the origin of the term for a scheming manipulator—and made into a famous singer.[9]

Their distinct backgrounds shaped the members of the Rag-Time Four's personal styles and skills, but it was the cakewalk that brought them together as a quartet and minstrelsy that extended them a platform.

Minstrelsy

The theatrical world into which the Rag-Time Four entered was dominated by minstrelsy. A capacious category, minstrelsy has meant different things in different eras, but it stems from the nineteenth-century practice of white male performers donning blackface makeup, usually made from a paste of burnt cork, to perform an impression of blackness born from the imagination of white anxieties, fears, and desires. Whites (particularly Irish immigrants) were anxious about their precarity in a changing America, feared and reviled perceived difference, and nonetheless were drawn to what they projected as the transgressive potentialities of blackness. Blackface offered, in American Studies scholar W. T. Lhamon Jr.'s words, "protective camouflage" to license "scandalous actions."[10]

The minstrel show typically comprised three broad sections, including comedic banter, songs, and dances (including the cakewalk); a variety of routines; and a sketch or playlet. Stock characters provided archetypes for performers to enact, including variations on enslaved figures, a mixed-race "wench," a dandy, and other types that functioned to undermine Black people's claims to full citizenry. The forms and tropes of minstrelsy thus depended on racist caricature. However divorced from reality, these caricatures took psychic hold of a nation navigating complex formations of race, class, immigration, migration, gender, and the social transformations affecting these categories and the people represented and misrepresented by them.

Given the outright racism of minstrelsy, one of the most confounding plot twists in the grand narrative of American popular culture certainly would be the rise—and celebrity—of Black performers working within the genre. Twenty-first-century viewers confronted with images of Black performers in blackface are often perplexed, dismayed, and outright shocked. These reactions indicate blackface's symbolic strength as a highly visible marker of American antiblack racism. The persistence of the practice to this day—its ability to evolve and take on new forms adaptive to new technologies, such as digital blackface—evinces the relentlessness of racism.

But doing the work of history requires understanding why Black actors from the mid-nineteenth to the early twentieth century occupied a form so evidently hostile to their humanity. The answer is not hard to fathom. In addition to offering access to the entertainment sphere and its potential for fame and success, minstrelsy afforded Black performers the freedom to mock.

Wearing the mask, Black actors could do and say things unthinkable in normal theatrical—much less everyday—contexts. For many Black performers, minstrel conventions were ones not just to adopt but also to exploit and appropriate.

The appropriation of an appropriation is what makes Black blackface minstrelsy so intriguing as a performance practice. Part of minstrelsy's instability and ambivalence lies in its ability to simultaneously encompass vile antiblackness and subversive potentials inherently critical of the claims of antiblackness. How quickly we slip into a hall of mirrors where the original referent is no longer—if it ever was—solid. It's ironic yet fitting that this "peculiarly unstable form," as cultural historian Eric Lott characterizes blackface minstrelsy, has become a synecdoche for the most reviling antiblack racism, when it also gave rise to the Black superstars of the nineteenth and early twentieth centuries.[11] In the production of an idea of race through performance, Lott writes, blackface minstrelsy helped formulate "the cultural commodity 'blackness'" that Black performers took up in their own acts.[12]

Celebrated Black performers who took the stage under burnt cork or figurative blackface (performing as a minstrel character even absent the mask) included Billy Kersands, Ernest Hogan, Bert Williams, and George Walker. Each was among the most popular Black comedians of their day and each, like most Black minstrels, negotiated stereotype and caricature in their racialized comedy. Black minstrel performers appealed to audiences as offering authenticity, savvily capitalizing on their identities to undercut white performers' claims to expertise via proximity to blackness. However, authenticity functioned less as a barometer of accuracy and more as an ironic discourse. When Williams and Walker, for example, advertised as "Two Real Coons," it seemed to point to their status as Black men in contradistinction to white minstrels. Yet "real" just as readily modified "coons," suggesting their enactment of a stock type signifying performative blackness. In a move theater historian David Krasner terms "reinscription," Black performers like Williams and Walker "gained access to the theatre by imitating a misrepresentation of blackness constructed by whites."[13] In minstrelsy, there can be no operative "real." Inescapable due to its ubiquity and popularity, minstrelsy nonetheless gave Black performers access to the stage and the license to subversively clown.

Minstrelsy's reach was long and extended beyond the practice of blackface. Its performance structures and forms persisted, carrying stock figures and tropes beyond the traditional minstrel show. As far as we know, Saint Suttle and Gertie Brown never "blacked up" on stage, though they were considered minstrel performers. Yet Suttle was sometimes compared to fellow Black performers who did perform in blackface, suggesting the lines between those who did and didn't weren't so fixed. And Brown's last stage partner (and husband) Tim Moore made a career out of clowning under cork, even when performing alongside his wife.

Vaudeville

Minstrelsy helped feed vaudeville, where discrete attractions were collected in variety programs. For example, the olio of minstrelsy—a short dance, song, or act—led to the variety show, and both white and Black performers appropriated minstrel tropes. Ethnic acts, comedians, singers, and dancers would share bills with acrobats, magicians, animal acts, ventriloquists, and other novelty performers and teams. These spectacles were modular, offering "Something for Everybody" in the aim at broad appeal.[14]

For the variety stage of vaudeville, it was common for booking agents to limit Black acts to one per bill for theaters catering to predominantly white patrons. On just one 1901 program, for example, as a vaudeville duo Suttle and Brown shared bills with eclectic acts such as Hacker and Lester (comedy bicycle riders), Monsieur Torcat (a French novelty actor), Ranos Bull Dogs (trained canines), the Two Nibbes (a "Jewish Act," one of many acts trading on the mockery of ethnic types), John Zimmer (a juggler), and a variety of singers and dancers.[15] On such bills, the sole Black act was posited as safe novelty to white audiences.

Things were different on the Black vaudeville circuits catering to Black audiences in the 1910s and 1920s, as entire bills could be made up of Black performers. One 1911 program saw Otto Mayo (a dancer), the Shattuck Comedy Four (a singing quartet), the McCarvers (comedians), Wise and Milton ("travesty artists," performers in drag and ethnic masquerade), and Alonzo Moose (an illusionist).[16] Until that time, Black vaudeville performers were largely isolated from one another on mainstream popular stages unless they constituted a minstrel company or a dedicated musical theater revue. The members of the Rag-Time Four worked across these forms, from the vaudeville stage to touring Black musical-theater companies, taking advantage of any and all opportunities to advance—or at least sustain—their careers.

At the turn of the century, vaudeville theaters became a main venue for the public projection of motion pictures as they embraced the latest entertainment novelty and, as a result, unwittingly welcomed what would become the agent of their decline.

Cinema

Initially, moving images found audiences in fairgrounds, Vitascope parlors, and ersatz exhibition venues. These were short subjects, typically one shot of about twenty to thirty seconds in length. Termed "attractions" by film historians Tom Gunning and André Gaudreault, these films were characterized by direct display to spectators, echoing the appeals of live performance. Dancers, strongmen, and magicians appealed to the camera. Travelogues and scenic views presented audiences with spectacles of far-off locales. Parades, processions, and military scenes brought current events to disparate places. And on top of the projected views, the spectacle of the moving-image apparatus constituted its own attraction for audiences drawn to the latest feat in illusory entertainment.

Before 1905, when the rise of the nickelodeon era saw dedicated spaces for the public consumption of moving images, motion pictures were integrated into existing theatrical entertainments. Movies joined live acts to create spectacles for a novelty-seeking audience. Like live acts, early motion pictures were discrete attractions collated in a variety program to appeal to a broad audience. These early motion pictures reflected the variety of vaudeville programs. For example, *Something Good* screened at various venues alongside parade footage, scenes related to the Spanish-American War, a trick film involving a haunted dining room, a scene of girls pillow fighting in a seminary, a comedy involving lovers being interrupted, a comedy set in a butcher shop, and the funeral procession of Queen Victoria.[17]

Movies rapidly developed over the course of Suttle's and Brown's careers. From short subjects less than a minute long, motion pictures soon became feature-length dramas, comedies, melodramas, adventures, and historical spectacles. By the late 1910s, films had more in common with our contemporary understanding of "movies" than they did with the early films of the turn of the century. Remarkably, Gertie Brown starred in a now-lost feature film in 1923 (discussed in Chapter Six), making her possibly the only Black actress—indeed, one of the few actors at all—to appear in both early cinema and the heyday of silent-era comedy.

Across these eras, Black performers shuttled between theater and cinema, negotiating minstrel forms in both arenas. They no doubt carried strong feelings about the dominance of the mask of blackness in entertainment, but one thing is certain: they were performers. We need not think of Suttle and Brown's kiss as a sincere expression of affection to appreciate the powers of their performance. One of my most emphatic contentions in this book is that their cinematic kiss must be understood as a performance of love enacted by professional actors. Performing is work, and performing love is an act. And this act of love has moved millions.

Fueling the affective impact of *Something Good* among contemporary viewers is a hunger for images of Black love. Cinematic depictions of Black people expressing joy, pleasure, affection, courtship, and love have been woefully under-represented in film history from early cinema through the studio era. The known instances of Black couples kissing in narrative films occur overwhelmingly in an intra-racial context: in Black-cast films made for mainstream audiences, and in race films produced for primarily Black audiences.

In the silent era, the dominant tendency was to depict Black affection as an object of ridicule. For example, two surviving Black-cast films made for mainstream audiences, *A Fool and His Money* (dir. Alice Guy-Blaché, Solax, 1912) and *Lime Kiln Club Field Day* (dir. Edwin Middleton and T. Hayes Hunter, Biograph, 1913, unreleased), include couples that court and kiss in the context of comedy and caricature: romance is treated as fickle affection in *A Fool and His Money* and as childlike naiveté in *Lime Kiln Club*.

Compounding the presumed comedy that attended blackness since minstrelsy, producers combined Black affection with other antiblack racist tropes, from chicken stealing to razor fights. Keystone's blackface farce *A Colored Girl's Love* (dir. Mack Sennett, 1914) was advertised with the unabashedly racist query, "Did you ever see a negro kiss his wife? You must see this." The industry trade press described the comedy by conflating the black(face) protagonists and the racist trope of chickens: "The antics of two colored swains for the hand of a dark brown chicken, with a lot of feathered chickens on the side are very funny as interpreted by the able comedians who appear in the principal parts. This comedy will not give offense and will afford a number of laughs."[18] Of course, the imagined spectator is white; the magazine had little concern for the possible offensiveness of the film to Black

FIGURE 2. Bert Williams and Odessa Warren Grey share a smooch in the rushes for *Lime Kiln Club Field Day* (Biograph, 1913).

audiences, especially in its relating its Black figures to chickens. (Yet we might also pause: the description's emphatic assertion that the film will not offend reveals that the theme of Black courtship, even if portrayed comically, risks offending white sensibilities.) Keystone's *The Darktown Belle* (dir. Henry Lehrman, 1913) combines razor fights, Black promiscuity, and "disgust" at the sight of a Black man and woman kissing.[19] As with *The Darktown Belle*, most of these comedies were performed by white actors in blackface, though it's possible that Black actors were enlisted for some roles. Keystone's *A Dark Lover's Play* (1915) was advertised as featuring "real negroes and negresses," however the notion of "real" might be as fictive as the depiction of exaggerated affection.[20] In each of these cases, the comedy seems to have turned on the ridicule of Black romance.

As films became longer and narratively multidimensional, we find depictions of Black affection functioning in more complex ways. For example, the demonstrative affection of a Black couple motivates the narrative action in Buster Keaton's *The Navigator* (dir. Buster Keaton and Donald Crisp, Metro-Goldwyn, 1924). Keaton's character, the wealthy "sap" Rollo Treadway, looks out his window to the street below, where a chauffeured car carrying a newlywed

FIGURE 3. The newlyweds who inspire Rollo to get married in *The Navigator* (dir. Buster Keaton and Donald Crisp, 1924).

Black couple comes to a stop and we are given a medium close-up of the couple as they embrace. The scene cuts back to Rollo, who looks at a photo of the girl next door and declares to his butler, "I think I'll get married."

I linger on these few shots in *The Navigator* because of their sheer oddity that is at once singular and naturalized. On the surface, the inclusion of the Black newlyweds as catalyst for Rollo's intentions seems to illustrate his capriciousness and immaturity, as the couple's ebullience serves as foil for Keaton's deadpan. The Black couple is certainly meant to serve as a point of comedy, but Rollo's resolve—even if delivered in his characteristic style—revises the absurdity of the images and treats them, in effect, at face value. However, their narrative function goes beyond comic ornament; the newlyweds become impetus for his desire to marry and thus the motivation for the film's plot, in which Rollo mistakenly boards *The Navigator*. His love interest unwittingly follows and antics ensue.

The film's treatment of blackness would be notable even if it stopped at the newlyweds. It doesn't. In the film's climax, Rollo and his would-be bride find themselves stranded off the shore of a remote island inhabited by the most stereotypical of "native cannibals." While Rollo attempts to fix the ship by

FIGURE 4. Rollo and his sweetheart at the end of *The Navigator* (dir. Buster Keaton and Donald Crisp, 1924).

donning a diving suit and tending to the submerged damage, the girl is abducted by the natives, brought to shore, and thrown before the cannibal chief.[21] The camera pans across a row of menacing dark bodies, made up with ersatz chalk marks and adorned with beaded necklaces. She recoils in horror as she stares up at the cannibal chief looming over her. Of course, she's saved by Rollo emerging from the water (he was merely saving himself when his oxygen line was cut). Dressed in the diving suit, he scares away the easily frightened "primitives." In the end, she is finally won over and the film concludes shortly after its second kiss, this time between Rollo and his intended bride.

Bookending the film, the two kisses both echo and invert each other. In her white sailor suit, the girl becomes a makeshift bride to Rollo's black-clad groom, her sailor stripes mirroring the floral band of the bride's headdress. The sight of Black affection inspired Rollo to propose, but it was the fear of Black men that led the girl to relent. In this way, *The Navigator* enacts the double edge of representations of Black love on the (white) screen: depictions of affection (comedic or straight) are enmeshed with fears of Black sexuality.[22]

White viewers weren't the only ones watching these scenes. The representation of Black affection in mainstream Hollywood productions attracted the attention of African American entertainment columnists, who scrutinized productions for their treatment of Black actors and characters, not just in the main plots but also in films' incidental aspects, brief appearances, minor characters, uncredited roles, and even fleeting kisses.[23] Consider, for example, Black newspapers' attunement to the Black cinematic image in their coverage of Vincente Minnelli's 1945 wartime drama *The Clock*.

The Clock follows the whirlwind romance of an army corporal on a forty-eight-hour leave and a woman he meets in New York's Pennsylvania Station. Starring Judy Garland and Robert Walker, the film was shot entirely on the MGM lot in Culver City on sets designed to evoke New York City. The setting motivated the hiring of a number of African American actors and extras, a fact reported on in the Associated Negro Press (ANP), which frequently commented on the employment opportunities of Black performers in the film industry. Most notably, however, the film concludes with a long tracking shot of various lovers and families parting as soldiers prepare to return to service. One of these families is African American, perhaps as a gesture of inclusion and recognition of the broad impact of the war, and of progressive acknowledgment of the service of Black soldiers. After the soldier tells his son to take good care of his mother, the husband and wife briefly kiss goodbye. While the kiss amounts to a mere peck, they are the only couple to kiss in the entire sequence apart from Garland and Walker—and the Black press took note.

While wartime films often featured all-Black musical numbers (which could be excised for southern theaters), including suggestions of affection, they were largely comedic, like Hattie McDaniel's "Ice Cold Katie . . . Won't You Marry the Soldier" in *Thank Your Lucky Stars* (dir. David Butler, Warner Bros., 1943), or marked as performance within the fictional world of the film, like Ethel Waters' "Quick Sands" in *Stage Door Canteen* (dir. Frank Borzage, United Artists, 1943). Actual love scenes, courtship, or representations of sincere acts of kissing were rare. *Stormy Weather* (dir. Andrew L. Stone, 20th Century Fox, 1943), for example, even elided actual kissing between its main stars Lena Horne and Bill Robinson (who struck many fans as unconvincing "onscreen sweethearts"; Horne herself balked at their nearly forty-year age gap).[24] Hollywood films tiptoed around Black desire. As film historian Ellen C. Scott notes, even in Black-cast films, "The reality of black touch is excluded."[25]

During filming of *The Clock*, as Black critic Harry Levette reported in his syndicated column "Gossip of the Movie Lots" for the ANP, Minnelli directed actors Bobby Johnson and Jean Douglas to "make that kiss longer." Levette wrote, "Declared by many to have been the first time in their long experience as motion picture players to have seen a real embracing and kissing scene by colored actors in a major picture, a sequence was filmed last week in 'The Clock,' at M.G.M. studios. As if to prove to the movie public that he was bold enough to dare the unfavorable reaction of southerners who might not like it, Director Minnelli planned a fine episode of a colored lieutenant bidding his family goodbye." Levette reports on the shooting of the scene: "The scene was laid at the gates of the Pennsylvania station with Judy Garland, the star, there to bid goodbye to her soldier sweetheart played by Robert Walker. Just before the camera was to catch them, Jean and Bobby were to embrace and tender words of parting exchanged between the lieutenant and his dear ones he was leaving behind. Apparently under the impression that he was to make it as short as possible, Bobby only pressed a hurried kiss on the lips of his screen wife, but Mr. Minnelli stopped the camera and coming over to the group said: 'Now, listen, you're going a long ways overseas. So make that kiss longer.' He did."[26]

When *The Clock* was released, the ANP reported, "A larger number of colored players worked through it than in any other feature shooting at that time." And they celebrated the fact that "Several important bits fell to a number of these players, especially a romantic scene between Bobby Johnson and Jean Douglas in [an] as equally tender goodbye scene as that between Judy Garland and Robert Walker, who followed them into the camera immediately afterwards."[27] The ANP's emphasis on the "equally tender" moment of affection between the Black couple and the stars echoes the film's wartime appeal to universalism, emblematized by the long tracking shot linking diverse figures in a collective national embrace. The couple's kiss is presented as on par with its white counterpart; the camera constructs their kiss as part of a continuum of heterosexual love wrenched apart by war. Not only is Black love given screen time, but it is also treated in the same cinematic breath as that of its white stars, a rarity—if not singularity—in studio-era cinema.[28]

RACE FILM: THE EXCEPTION THAT PROVES THE RULE

Race films—made with nearly all-Black casts for Black audiences in segregated theaters—are a different story. Independent, low-budget, and in direct competition with highly capitalized and widely advertised Hollywood films, race films constituted a Sisyphean effort to provide an appealing alternative for Black moviegoers.

FIGURE 5. *Birthright* (dir. Oscar Micheaux, 1938).

The presumption of an intra-racial exhibition experience licensed producers and performers to depict Black people in a broader range of situations than seen in mainstream movies: at the center of dramas, comedies, actions, and romances. African American filmmakers like Oscar Micheaux and Spencer Williams, as well as white producers of race films like Richard E. Norman, had their characters court, flirt, fall in love, marry, and express affection in a far greater ambit than mainstream productions allowed. Oscar Micheaux's *The Exile* (1931), *Ten Minutes to Live* (1932), *The Girl from Chicago* (1932), *God's Step Children* (1938), and *Birthright* (1938) all include heterosexual kissing, ranging from chaste pecks to ardent embraces.

Even though race films' relatively meager resources sometimes made for awkward filming and acting, they allowed for a fuller expression of human situations than Hollywood permitted Black actors. However, as Hollywood featured more Black subjects in the postwar era and theaters became increasingly integrated, independent race-film producers couldn't compete. With the decline of race filmmaking by the late 1940s went the expansive range of cinematic portrayals of Black characters and experiences. It would be several decades before Hollywood's depiction of Black people matched the range of race films. Indeed, the Black press's emphasis on the brief glimpse of a Black couple's kiss in *The Clock* testifies to the scarcity of representations of Black affection in Hollywood movies. It wouldn't be until the 1970s that mainstream audiences would see a proliferation of Black-cast films, with romance forming the plots and subplots of Hollywood-distributed movies such as *Lady Sings the Blues* (dir. Sidney J. Furie, 1972), *Claudine* (dir. John Berry, 1974), and *Mahogany* (dir. Berry Gordy, 1975) that portrayed Black lead characters experiencing all of love's complexity.

SOMETHING GOOD—NEGRO KISS

More than seventy years after the fleeting kiss in *The Clock* elicited headlines in the Black press, the social media response to *Something Good* made clear that Black audiences still hunger for representations of Black romance and love. Suttle and Brown's kiss still counteracts pervasive unidimensional depictions of blackness, wresting the depiction of flirtation and affection away from the monopoly white couples have on images of romance in mainstream media.

With this book, I look at the many facets of the performance of kissing in *Something Good*. Part of what I want to show is that far from a self-contained work of art, the film invites us to examine its affective resonances and possible spectatorial responses, from the time of its production to contemporary engagements on social media and in independent film. Twenty seconds of affection, rediscovered only recently, serve as a surprising prism onto the valences of Black stage and screen performance, and the development of motion pictures alongside—and imbricated with—a popular culture enamored with Black performance during the same years that the US refused to recognize the full humanity and rights of Black people. *Something Good* offers something like a path not taken, a world in which Black affection could coexist with white romance on the screen.

This book is structured in two parts. The first offers a close look at *Something Good—Negro Kiss* itself, starting with the film's rediscovery and my own research into the world in which it was made and circulated. The long process of identification that followed the film's resurfacing in Dino Everett's collection at USC's film archive—detailed in Chapter One—challenged me, as a historian of African American film, to rethink my understanding of early cinema, race, and popular culture. The second chapter addresses the significance of the rediscovery, offering an interpretation of the film and its possible meanings in the context of its production and exhibition, to show the imbrication of minstrelsy, vaudeville, and cinema at the turn of the century. Ultimately, the first part shows how an archival rediscovery can change our understanding of film history.

The book's second part presents the results of historical recuperation: the writing into history of neglected figures and episodes brought about by the research detailed in the book's first part. Across four chapters, we follow the performers as they move from the late nineteenth century to the 1930s, from the South Side of Chicago, around the world, and to Harlem and its cultural Renaissance. Chapter Three traces the Rag-Time Four, the cakewalking quartet that initiated Suttle and Brown's collaboration along with John and Maud Brewer. Chapter Four looks at Suttle and Brown's vaudeville partnership after the dissolution of the Rag-Time Four. Chapters Five and Six attend to their subsequent respective careers and ambitions as they eked out a living in a grueling era for Black performers. Saint Suttle and Gertie Brown were part of a moment that, with hindsight, we can recognize as an early Black arts movement that constituted a dynamic, yet underappreciated, prelude to the Harlem Renaissance.

In between each chapter, I offer interstitial vignettes around sites of exhibition. We know very little about how and where *Something Good* was screened, who saw it, and what they thought about it. But the scant surviving archival traces suggest it reached a broad and eclectic audience across the country—indeed, the world. These vignettes explore how the film appeared in its time and the conditions under which its image of Black flirtation and kissing was projected.

To tell the stories of *Something Good*'s performers and their world I necessarily shift from the narration of my research process to the results of the research to center Saint Suttle, Gertie Brown, and their companions. This is a political gesture of giving the story over to the figures enabled by the rediscovery, identification, and historicization of *Something Good*. In forming a history of actors who left only ephemeral traces, I heed Black feminist historian Ashley D. Farmer's call to "do more with less," especially as it pertains to the lives of under-documented historical figures.[29] The imperative to "do more with less" involves sitting with scant surviving remnants and coaxing from them the suppressed stories they contain and, at times, obfuscate. This work also involves proffering informed speculation in the face of the paucity of historical evidence.

There are two interventions the book makes as it extends its scope from the film to the actors that appear in it and places where it was shown. First, *Something Good* affords us an opportunity to reconsider performance modes (minstrelsy and vaudeville), sites of spectatorship (both live and on-screen, for Black audiences and predominantly white audiences), and the appeals of performers (both Black performers and white performers working with tropes of blackness). It demonstrates, I argue, how archival rediscoveries change our basic understanding of the history of film, what kinds of films could be made at certain times, and what meanings early films could convey. Second, *Something Good* incites us to trace the lives of the performers recovered in this short film. Beyond a mere nitrate fragment, *Something Good* enables the recovery of entire lives, careers, and ambitions that had slipped through accounts in previous histories of twentieth-century American culture. Saint Suttle, Gertie Brown, and Maud and John Brewer represent a rich tradition of theatrical artistry that risks erasure if we don't go searching for it. For each of these figures, countless others await rediscovery. Likewise, our filmic heritage invites further investigation: if a book can be written based on one twenty-second nitrate fragment, what other histories might we craft from early cinema's ephemera?

If *Something Good* is important, it is not merely because of its significance for film history, as considerable as it is, but also because of its capacity to move viewers more than a century after filming. In the Conclusion, I return us to the present and reckon with the afterlives of the film's rediscovery, from its viral online circulation to its impact on contemporary filmmakers, poets, musicians, and other artists. I focus in particular on Kevin Jerome Everson and Kahlil Pedizisai's short film *Glenville* (2020). A direct homage to *Something Good*, *Glenville* prompts us to consider how early film serves as a mechanism for reckoning with cinema's vexed history of racist misrepresentation and systemic disenfranchisement. *Glenville* also illustrates one of the guiding orientations of this book: the rediscovery of *Something Good* does not merely change how we understand the emergence of American cinema; it also informs contemporary artistic practice and broader current investments in questions of race, representation, and cinema.

• • •

On that day in 1898, Suttle and Brown went to work as performers. They knew what they were doing and did it well, even if the machine they were performing for was only a couple of years old. The rest of their careers would take place in a world this machine would transform. How they came to make a movie, why this brief performance matters, how they then navigated the shifting landscape of American entertainment, and how we in turn make sense of the ephemera bequeathed to us across time are the stories this book tells.

ONE

Solving the Mystery of Archival Rediscovery

THE ROOTS OF BLACK REPRESENTATION in American cinema took hold in undeniably racist soil. The Supreme Court's decision in *Plessy v. Ferguson* (1896) upheld segregation; Jim Crow became enshrined in law; African Americans were systematically disenfranchised; white supremacist vigilantes freely marauded. Yet while antiblackness pervaded nineteenth-century culture, so did fascination with real and imagined Black subjects, whom audiences encountered on-screen as a kind of novelty that simultaneously rested on familiar, demeaning tropes. Some films presented Black performance as spectacle, as in *Dancing Darkies* (American Mutoscope Co., 1896) and *Dancing Darkey Boy* (Edison, 1897), essentializing dancing as something innate to Black people, especially children. Some trafficked in stereotypes of excessive appetite or criminality involving watermelons, chickens, and gambling, such as *A Watermelon Feast* (American Mutoscope Co., 1896); *Watermelon Contest* (Edison, 1900); *Who Said Watermelon?* (Selig, ca. 1900); *Chicken Thieves* (Edison, 1897); and *An Interrupted Crap Game* (American Mutoscope and Biograph Co., 1899), in which the gambling is interrupted for the pursuit of a chicken. Other films were structured around blackness itself as a joke, as in *A Hard Wash* (American Mutoscope Co., 1896) and *A Morning Bath* (Edison, 1896), where the implicit gag is that the mother cannot "clean" the skin color off her baby. Moving images also presented Black figures as de facto objects of curiosity in actualities such as the Spanish-American War film *Colored Troops Disembarking* (Edison, 1898), which featured a battalion of Black soldiers in the 24th Infantry Regiment disembarking from the steamer *Mascotte* in Tampa, Florida, in May 1898. Even if the film ostensibly celebrates the participation of Black soldiers in the US Army, Edison's catalog description nonetheless reverts to mockery, proclaiming the scene of cautious troops descending a steep gangplank at high tide "laughable."[1]

The heavy ugliness of these early film subjects and their framing of blackness as spectacle have long defined our understanding of early filmic depictions of Black people. All this meant that, when Dino Everett, the film archivist at USC, sent me images of the fragile nitrate print he'd obtained, I was shocked. Here was something new and extraordinary: a Black couple's joy captured by a camera more than a century ago. Astonished, I saw my screen brighten with images of love imbued with lightness and humor. Faced with black-and-white film frames of a man and woman laughing and repeatedly kissing, I stared in awe at something I had not thought existed, or even could have existed: an earnest portrayal of Black love in early cinema. It was like looking at a specter of an alternative history of American film in which Black people were portrayed with humanity and not as objects of ridicule. Was this print evidence of a path not taken?

The film was undoubtedly exceptional, but I had no idea what it was. The images presented a tantalizing archival mystery: Who were these charming lovers? What were they doing in an early motion picture? Solving the mystery—determining the producer and date of the film and naming the performers—entailed not only identification but also historical revision. The process of identifying the USC print as *Something Good—Negro Kiss* ultimately led me to rethink my understanding of early cinema to account for a production context that could enable the creation of such an extraordinary film.

Together, Everett and I set out to investigate the puzzle of this remarkable early film artifact. We gathered clues: material and immaterial, textual and extratextual, empirical and ephemeral. And we encountered pieces that stubbornly refused to fit the puzzle. Indeed, as some questions found answers, other enigmas emerged to muddy our picture. Rediscoveries of nineteenth-century film artifacts are rare, but as the story of *Something Good* suggests, there is still more to understand about cinema's early years and the culture it emerged into and, ultimately, transformed.

IDENTIFYING THE FILM

The initial scans of Everett's print raised a basic question: what might account for a seemingly uncaricatured portrayal of Black subjects from a period of cinema known for representational hostility to Black figures? Too early to

FIGURE 6. *The John C. Rice–May Irwin Kiss* (Edison, 1896).

have been produced by any known Black filmmaker and far earlier than the first known race films—films made with predominantly Black casts for African American audiences—this film seemed to defy recognizable categories. Yet the subject it portrayed was very familiar to early cinema. It seemed to be a riff on the famous *May Irwin Kiss*, a tightly framed, medium close-up shot of white stage actors May Irwin and John C. Rice talking, preparing to kiss, then kissing.

The May Irwin Kiss is a foundational film in the canon of American cinema. It was filmed by William Heise in the Black Maria, Thomas Edison's West Orange, New Jersey, studio, in April 1896 and known by various titles: *The Kiss*, *Kiss Scene*, *Picture of a Kiss*, *The May Irwin Kiss*, and *The John C. Rice–May Irwin Kiss*.[2] Edison's short film isolated the kissing scene from the stage production of *The Widow Jones*, featuring Rice and Irwin, and became a sensation upon its release in 1896. Irwin and Rice canoodle, flirt, prepare to kiss, and then finally kiss, all in less than twenty seconds. We know that, as with many popular films in early cinema, there were subsequent iterations with white actors, including at least one shot by Edison (in 1900, with different performers) that was known as *The Kiss* or *New Kiss*.[3] Presuming a direct (or even indirect) reference to *The May Irwin Kiss* offered a road map for the initial investigation of Everett's film.

With May Irwin's kiss in mind, the first task was to search for film titles that might reflect this subject in catalogs of film producers and distributors from about 1900 that are available in print, online databases, and microfilm. Catalogs are indispensable for compiling filmographies and, in the search for a version of *The May Irwin Kiss* made with Black actors, they enabled us to create a preliminary filmography of African American kiss film titles. The images Everett scanned seemed to me to be American, so although I had no hard evidence initially to support that impression, I started with motion-picture catalogs of American producers and followed that thread.[4] I searched physical catalogs, microfilm copies, and digital scans of motion-picture catalogs published by producers and distributors in cinema's first decade, combing for subjects related to Black figures kissing. I was stunned to find a significant number of titles suggesting early motion-picture subjects depicting Black affection. Was I encountering a cycle of Black kissing films?

Made for the industry, motion-picture catalogs offered exhibitors the choice of titles and subjects to create a full entertainment program. For film historians, they indicate the range of films produced for the exhibition market, a valuable list given that the vast majority of early films no longer survive. Catalogs are treasure troves, but they can be misleading. Since early films were sold over several years, thus often appearing in multiple catalogs, a film's listing in a particular catalog does not necessarily mean that it has the correct original date. Other problems abound. *Motion Picture Catalogs by American Producers and Distributors, 1894–1908*, a collection compiled by film historian Charles Musser, is based on surviving print catalogs in the Thomas Edison Papers, but most early catalogs are lost.[5] The catalogs used to compile the American Film Institute database, for example, might be the earliest available, but they still may not have correct production years or producers. Titles are often unavailable. Upon a film's release, its title often simply described the content, allowing exhibitors to purchase a subject and collate a series of films to create an entertaining program. In other words, titles indicate the subjects that were being produced on film but not discrete or proprietary objects. Further, before films were protected under copyright, producers notoriously copied from one another, not just in terms of recreating popular subjects but also the outright duping of prints. Early film production and exhibition was, in effect, the Wild West—what early film producer and historian Terry Ramsaye called in 1926 "the lawless film frontier."[6] Thus, we can't presume a title in the catalog of Siegmund Lubin—who was known as "the Pirate King" for his practice of rampant pirating of other manufacturer's films—was originally produced by him, even if the company sold it under the Lubin moniker. In short, catalogs provide clues, not definitive answers.

Still, the catalogs did reveal a small yet notable subset of the kiss film genre involving African Americans. None of these films was known to be extant (surviving in any material form), but the descriptions suggested a burlesque or parody of *The May Irwin Kiss* with Black performers (or white actors in blackface). The catalog descriptions also evoked a range of racist tropes, aligned with the stereotypes common in early filmic representations of blackness and that saturated US popular culture at the time.

On the subject of Black affection, turn-of-the-century American film catalogs yielded six distinct titles. One is *Something Good—Negro Kiss*, a fifty-foot film listed in the Selig Polyscope Company's *1903 Complete Catalogue of Films and Moving Pictures*, with a brief description: "Burlesque on the John Rice and May Irwin Kiss; is making a hit."[7] The title is listed again in 1907, carrying a more extended description: "It has never been denied that in his own way the 'Afro-American' brother is an adept in his own style of love-making. This film shows a swell 'coon' and his best girl making love and both evidently enjoy the situation, and are taking heaps of satisfaction out of it. The action is so lively and thoroughly amusing that the audience is as much pleased as the performers and apart from the fun in this picture the photography is of the best and never fails to please the audience."[8] A second title, *Colored Kissing Scene*, is listed in F.M. Prescott's 1899 *Catalogue of New Films* with a near verbatim description as *Something Good*, with the additional line, "One of the very funny incidents in this picture is the size of the colored man's mouth."[9] Third, in its September 1899 catalog, the New York City–based American Miror-Vitae Company sold a film for its distinct projector system under the title *Those Affectionate Darkies*, described simply as "An Ethiopian kissing match," invoking a common euphemism for Black subjects derived from minstrelsy.[10]

Along with these, Lubin—the "Pirate King"—listed three African American kiss films in his 1903 *Complete Catalogue*. The first, *Whose Baby Is You?* (1902), appears with the summary: "This is a very funny subject and shows 'Erastus' making love to his 'Dinah.' These darkies are of the 'Old Virginny' type and the figures being large, they can be seen from any part of the house, and will amuse every one [*sic*] who sees them."[11] Another film, *Darkies' Kiss*, is listed with the more extensive description identical to that of *Colored Kissing Scene*, with the addition of a concluding assessment: "Very laughable."[12] And *New Colored Kiss No. 2* is advertised in these terms: "This is rich. It is entirely different from the old colored kiss and shows a coon dude and his ladylove osculating in an interesting and improved style. The photography is perfect."[13]

These six titles suggested that there might have been a small yet significant cycle of "burlesques" on *The John C. Rice–May Irwin Kiss* featuring Black actors.[14] But I couldn't presume that these were necessarily six distinct films. Indeed, the description for *Colored Kissing Scene* in Prescott's 1899 catalog is nearly identical to Lubin's 1903 description of *Darkies' Kiss*. And both are, in turn, quite similar to the 1907 description of Selig's *Something Good—Negro Kiss*. Given rampant pirating of film prints and the duplicate wording of the catalog descriptions, I thought it was plausible that these titles were in fact the same film.

Still, with an initial filmography of titles and producers in place, Everett and I were able to turn to the evidence offered by the material object itself to match the potential production histories with what the object reveals. The print comprises 712 frames—about forty-five feet—and is likely missing about five feet at the beginning. Even without those frames, the film is impressively intact and the images exceptionally legible. Everett's print was a direct, first-generation, negative-to-positive film print and not a later duplicate—making it an especially rare early cinema artifact. Surviving early film prints are estimated to represent less than ten percent of films produced, and the films that survive are often remediated iterations, rarely original first-generation prints. For material qualities alone, this nitrate print constituted a significant discovery.

Everett and I knew that single round perforation holes, or "perfs," printed through from the negative on the lower third of each side of the frame, were also an important piece of evidence. The round perforation print-throughs are markings consistent with the Lumière Cinématographe films from about 1895 to 1900, as the Lumière brothers' combination camera-projector operated with a sprocket system requiring a pair of single round perforations on the side edges of each film frame.[15] Yet we do not know of any films on this subject by the Lumière brothers, whose oeuvre is well-documented. This is where the Wild West aspect of early film culture matters. In the same way that films were pirated and sold under different auspices, filmmaking technology was liberally copied, adapted, and appropriated. Lumière-style perfs did not mean the film was shot by the Lumières—or even that it had been shot on a Cinématographe.

But the Lumière-style perfs do provide an important clue—one that points back to the US, and to Chicago in particular. By early 1896, vaudevillian and traveling entertainer William Selig had returned to his native Chicago from touring the country, and upon arriving he set out to develop a motion-picture camera and projector to rival that of Edison. Attempting to get around the patent on the Armat-Edison machine, Selig enlisted Andrew Schustek, a mechanic from the Union Model Works machine shop, who had gotten his hands on an early Lumière Cinématographe.[16] Because of this, the Selig Standard Camera, also known as the "Schustek camera," and the Selig Polyscope projector were effectively knockoffs of the Lumière Cinématographe.[17] One result is that the early Selig films have the same perf marks as those of Lumière.

At the time, the only manufacturer of film stock in the United States was Eastman Kodak, which sold its film unperforated; Selig therefore had to hand-punch each perforation before designing his own perforation mechanism.[18] Early in the USC print, an errant perforation mark appears across several frames to the lower right of the woman, likely mispunched by mistake. The errant perforation mark had been covered over by hand-drawn scribbles on the positive, but it is a mistake that allows us a full view of the Lumière-style perf hole that is otherwise only visible on the edges of the frame. It also highlights the materiality of the film—its fragility, instability, construction, and painstaking preparation for exhibition at a time when the industry was still in its nascency.

Because there was no evidence that any Lumière film on this subject was ever made, we followed the more plausible explanation that it was a Selig film made with the Polyscope. Everett found that the perf print-throughs matched a sample Selig film of the same length from the same era, and his impression was that the film was similar to other Selig films with regard to texture and quality. Of the six titles we knew of from our catalog research, Selig's *Something Good—Negro Kiss* seemed the most likely match.

Working off this provisional identification also allowed us to pursue new leads, not least about when the film may have been made. While the Selig catalogs list that title as early as 1903, the William Selig papers give other information. The Selig papers are scant for the company's early film productions, but there is a high degree of documentation of company assets due to the litigious climate of early film manufacturing. Notes from a December 1900 meeting of the directors of the Selig Polyscope Company include an inventory and appraisal of all the firm's property, including films. Among the titles is *Something Good—Negro Kiss*, indicating that the film was produced in or before 1900.[19]

FIGURE 7. Errant perforation marks in frame. Frame enlargement courtesy of Dino Everett, USC HMH Foundation Moving Image Archive.

Selig sold his films through the Chicago-based Sears mail-order catalog aimed at professional and amateur film exhibitors, so the next step was to look through Sears catalogs from 1897 to 1900. The first mention of motion pictures in the Sears catalog appears in spring 1898. Two films, both titled *Kissing Scene*, seem to match the content of the print but have different lengths and catalog numbers: no. 21255 is a twenty-five-foot film listed as "Darky burlesque"; no. 21287, a fifty-foot film listed as "Oscullatory [*sic*] burlesque." "Osculatory," I learned, means "of, relating to, or characterized by kissing"; it was often misspelled.[20] Burlesque, in addition to derisive imitation and caricature, references the concluding portion of a minstrel show.[21] When combined, "osculatory burlesque" signifies a racialized, parodic kissing scene.

In the fall 1898 catalog, the twenty-five-foot film is described as "a burlesque on John Rice and May Irwin's famous kissing scene. This we consider one of the greatest side splitting scenes ever thrown on canvas." The fifty-foot film is listed as *Kiss Scene* and described as "a burlesque on the oscillatory performance of John Rice and May Irwin, as performed by two corpulent colored people. One of the funniest views on the market." The same catalog also sells Edison's Rice–Irwin film as *Kiss Scene*. The spring 1899 catalog has similar descriptions of each film, adding that the twenty-five-foot *Kissing Scene* "is good for an encore every time."

Strikingly, the fall 1898 catalog contained a frame enlargement that was also printed in the spring 1899 and spring 1900 catalogs. In each case, the image is positioned alongside the entry for the twenty-five-foot *Kissing Scene*. For an era represented by few filmic survivors, photos are rare and key pieces of visual evidence. A poor facsimile, this frame enlargement nonetheless shows a couple seated on something like a bench, occupying the lower half of the frame. The man is balding, and the woman does indeed seem corpulent. Their faces are indiscernible, but their medium close-up framing and seated position echo the format of *The May Irwin Kiss*. While details in the frame enlargement are difficult to make out, the image clearly has no correspondence to the USC print. Was this an impasse? A red herring? Tantalizingly, adjacent to the frame enlargement was a notice for customers to request a "special animated picture catalogue" with greater details on motion-picture products sold by Sears. In this catalog, *The Optigraph Moving Picture Machines* (1898), Sears lists no. 21255 *Kissing Scene* alongside a sketch iteration of the frame enlargement in the general catalog, confirming the dissimilarity between *Kissing Scene* and the USC print.[22]

The Sears catalogs confounded me. They presented two films of different lengths for sale, which might lead us to conclude that these were the same films, offered at different lengths. But since the image accompanying the twenty-five-foot film had no correlation to the USC print, it was tempting to read the fifty-foot offering as a distinct film, namely, *Something Good—Negro Kiss*. Indeed, in the spring 1900 catalog, the fifty-foot *Kiss Scene* is described as "a burlesque on the osculatory performance of John Rice and May Irwin. An encounter by two colored people in which a mutual good time is certainly enjoyed. One of the funniest views on the market." This wording is slightly different from the fall 1898 and spring 1899 descriptions that included the word *corpulent*. Could the omission be a correction made in the later catalog? Certainly, the USC print did not seem to show people who would fit that description.

FIGURE 8. *Kissing Scene* as advertised in the 1898 Sears, Roebuck and Co. catalog, *The Optigraph Moving Picture Machines*. Reproduction courtesy of Valerie Stenner, Special Collections, University of Delaware Library.

Our working hypothesis, then, was that Sears sold two different African American kiss films, one made by Selig (*Something Good—Negro Kiss*) and the other still unknown, likely produced by another manufacturer.[23] To be sure, it was possible that the Sears catalog descriptions were not entirely accurate and that the descriptor *corpulent* was meant to fit either the shorter *Kissing Scene* or the longer *Kiss Scene*; the catalog editor or even the films' manufacturers likely did not parse distinctions. *Corpulent* could simply be another signal toward comedy rather than a precise descriptor. And, of course, May Irwin herself could be described as corpulent, so any imitation of *The May Irwin Kiss* might conflate such details.

A later catalog helped us refine our hypothesis. In 1900, Sears stopped selling specific titles in their general catalog after being named by Edison in his patent lawsuit against Selig. However, Sears indicated that customers could request a special motion-picture catalog.[24] This catalog was first published in 1900 as *Public Exhibition Outfits: Moving Pictures, Magic Lanterns, Talking Machines* and updated annually for at least five years. Consulting

FIGURE 9. No. 21255 *Kissing Scene* as advertised in the 1900 Sears, Roebuck and Co. catalog, *Public Exhibition Outfits: Moving Pictures, Magic Lanterns, Talking Machines*. Reproduction courtesy of Valerie Stenner, Special Collections, University of Delaware Library.

this special catalog resolved two outstanding questions. First, Sears did indeed sell Selig's *Something Good—Negro Kiss*; and second, contrary to our initial presumption that only the fifty-foot film was Selig's, the twenty-five foot *Kissing Scene* (no. 21255) was clearly *Something Good—Negro Kiss* in a (presumably) abbreviated form.[25] In the special motion-picture catalog, this shorter film was described as "a scene interesting to the entire audience, young and old included. It is supposed to be a burlesque of an affectionate encounter between two coons, and there is no film shown which meets with more hearty appreciation, and which is more often redemanded than this one."[26] This entry is accompanied by a sketch of Suttle and Brown, likely drawn directly from a frame from a print given the fidelity to the filmed figures and the inversion of the image.

Indeed, while the 1900 special catalog sold the film as *Kissing Scene*, by the 1905 edition the film was listed under the title *Something Good—Negro Kiss* ("Burlesque on the John Rice and May Irwin Kiss").[27] The distribution of the film through Sears also helps in terms of definitive dating. Given that film no. 21255 appears in the Sears general catalog from the inauguration of their inclusion of motion pictures in spring 1898, it must have been produced before the catalog's publication.[28]

We also gleaned clues from other mail-order catalogs. Another Chicago-based catalog company, Montgomery Ward and Co., offered a fifty-foot film titled *Negro Kiss* with the brief description, "A colored gentleman and his lady indulge in numerous kisses and hugs. Very grotesque."[29] With a title closer to that of Selig's own inventory and a description that matches the USC print, it's likely that the film sold by Montgomery Ward was also *Something Good—Negro Kiss.*

While the term *grotesque* may sound misplaced to contemporary ears, by the late nineteenth century it had become a common descriptor to suggest comedy or satire based on race. Older associations of the term with the bizarre and fanciful had given way to allusions of the horrific, ugly, or repulsive; it also signaled caricature, comedy, or buffoonery—all of which was associated, in late nineteenth-century American popular entertainment, with blackness.[30] For example, the trade publication *The Phonoscope* in January 1899 noted that a film listed as *A Darktown Dance* was "full of fun and grotesque action."[31] In this era, antiblackness pervaded the entertainment scene, reflecting—and participating in—white rejections of Black freedom, coding blackness as unruliness, Black romance as ugliness, and Black people as unfit for citizenship. The term *grotesque* thus bore the weight of nineteenth-century white anxieties, reflecting the racist presumption that any presentation of Black affection must be comedic. To call *Negro Kiss* "grotesque" was to posit *The May Irwin Kiss* as a norm and *Negro Kiss* as its unnatural distortion. As with the other racist catalog descriptions of the African American kiss film cycle, the effect is to frame the product for the exhibitor and spectator, both irrespective of and likely deliberately countering the assertions of humanity conveyed by the film. Indeed, the catalog descriptions tell us more about the attitudes and anxieties of the theatrical and nontheatrical film market than they do about the film for sale.

Despite these inconsistencies and biases, when we considered the material evidence of the nitrate print alongside the film manufacturers' and mail-order catalog information, as well as the evidence contained in the Selig company papers, we had a very probable identification and dating of Everett's rediscovered print as *Something Good—Negro Kiss.* We now knew that this film was produced by William Selig and shot by his camera operator Thomas S. Nash in Chicago sometime prior to or in early spring 1898. No evidence has come to light to suggest a different identification.

IDENTIFYING THE PERFORMERS

What the film was, however, was not the only question we had about the USC print. Who were these actors who, advertising descriptors aside, made an elegant and loving pair? People in early films are notoriously difficult to identify, and African Americans in silent films were rarely—if ever—credited. How could we determine their identities?

Selig's background provided a starting point. *Something Good—Negro Kiss* features African Americans in minstrel costumes, and Selig was an experienced manager of minstrel shows. From 1893 to 1895, Selig co-owned two minstrel companies featuring Black performers. The first was owned with Lew Johnson, an African American barber from San Francisco with thirty years' experience running an itinerant "wagon show."[32] Their company, Selig and Johnson's Colored Minstrels, hired a young comedian named Bert Williams, and when Johnson quit, Selig formed a second company, the Mastodon Minstrels, with another young comedian, George Walker. Shortly after meeting, Williams and Walker would launch their own company and rise to become the most famous Black performers of the early twentieth century, pushing the minstrel tradition to more modern forms.

Selig had his first exposure to motion pictures while on the road with his Mastodon Minstrels: he encountered a kinetoscope in Dallas.[33] In April 1897, Selig opened a motion-picture studio at 43 Peck Court (later Eighth Street) between State Street and Wabash Avenue—or what film industry journal *Motography* euphemistically called "an obscure Chicago side street," as at the time this was the heart of Chicago's "brothel-strewn" tenderloin, the Levee District.[34] Cheap rent and proximity to the city's entertainers made it an ideal location for Selig's new venture, and given his stature and success as an owner of minstrel companies, local performers would have likely been eager to oblige a request for a performance in front of his new Polyscope.

Selig's position in the entertainment industry, along with the comportment and poise of the performers in *Something Good*, suggested these people were professionals. The man is costumed as "a swell," an elegantly attired dandy, and the woman wears a flounce-adorned dress. But that did not mean their identities would be easy to determine: many working minstrel and vaudeville performers left no photographic records or even reproduced illustrations. Serendipitously, curators at the Museum of Modern Art (MoMA) had recently had some success with analog facial recognition in the identification of actors in the Bert Williams's *Lime Kiln Club Field Day* (1913) project.[35]

FIGURE 10. *New Colored Kiss No. 2* (Lubin, ca. 1900), cataloged as "Sambo and Jemima Comedians," Library of Congress. Digital scan from nitrate print courtesy of George Willeman, Library of Congress.

I presented them with frame enlargements from the USC print, and our exchange led to two fascinating discoveries that changed the course of the investigation and rapidly accelerated the identification of the performers.

The first discovery was that MoMA was also working with a similar African American kiss film, held by the Library of Congress and cataloged as *Sambo and Jemima Comedians* (based on a title scratched into the print). This was almost certainly not the original title. Its nitrate print was not only a very short fragment of a few seconds but also a multiple-generation dupe—a copy of a copy of a copy, etc.—and therefore less clear than the print Everett found. The position of the couple is the reverse of *Something Good*, but the man wears the same costume in both films, albeit with the addition of an elaborate boutonniere in his left lapel in the Library of Congress print. The print was less clear, yet he was recognizable: it was the same actor as in the USC print, though paired with a different partner.

The second discovery was a positive identification of the man in both kiss films. MoMA researchers matched their print to an 1898 photograph of four minstrel performers on the sheet music cover for "Shake Yo' Dusters, or Piccaninny Rag," copyrighted by the S. Brainard's Sons Company, a Chicago-based popular-music publisher. The photograph's caption identifies the

FIGURE 11. Gertie Brown, Saint Suttle, Maud Brewer, and J. W. Brewer as the Rag-Time Four. Detail from sheet music cover for W. H. Krell, "Shake Yo' Dusters, or Piccaninny Rag" S. Brainard's Sons Co., 1898. Courtesy of the David M. Rubenstein Rare Book & Manuscript Library, Duke University.

performers as Maud Brewer, J. W. Brewer, Gertie Brown, and Saint Suttle—the last being recognizable as the man in both film prints. There was Saint Suttle!

It seemed likely that Brown was the woman in *Something Good*, but given the angle of her head in the photograph, we needed further photographic evidence to be sure. In the meantime, the identity of Saint Suttle was the key we needed to unlock the rest of the mystery. A discovery helped here: an image of Suttle in another extant photograph from the September 1899 *National Police Gazette* alongside the same woman, also identified as Gertie Brown. With this third vantage point, we felt confident she was the other actor in *Something Good*. Both photos were taken at the same studio—the backdrop is identical—named in the *National Police Gazette* portrait as J. B. Wilson, Chicago, a leading photographer catering to the theatrical profession.[36] Further, Suttle is wearing the same suit in the sheet music photo as he is in both films, though with different embellishments, suggesting that he was attired in his primary performance costume and that the films were

FIGURE 12. Saint Suttle and Gertie Brown, *National Police Gazette*, September 1899.

made about the same time the photo was taken—and thus about the same time as each other.

The two films, however, were almost certainly made by different producers. First, *Something Good—Negro Kiss* is listed as the only African American kiss film in the Selig inventory and in subsequent Selig film catalogs. Second, the Library of Congress print does not show any trace of the Lumière-style, single-round perf print-throughs that are prominent in the USC print. Third, the two films have a different mise-en-scène. While both films appear to have been shot in natural light, given the shadows, they have different backdrops—a dark canvas curtain in the USC print and a lighter backdrop (perhaps a white canvas curtain or a cement wall) in the Library of Congress print. They are likewise distinct in figure placement and movement, with Saint Suttle on the left in the USC print and the right in the one at the Library of Congress.[37]

So, what film did the Library of Congress have? Could the perfs be from Lubin's Cineograph? This would make sense given catalog titles like *Whose Baby Is You?* and *New Colored Kiss No. 2*.[38] Or could this be *Those Affectionate Darkies*, produced for the more obscure American Miror-Vitae of Eberhard Schneider and described as "an Ethiopian kissing match" in the manufacturer's catalog? To Everett, the Library of Congress print material seemed to have been produced later than the Selig film. Based on catalog and material evidence, my best guess is that the Library of Congress print cataloged as *Sambo and Jemima Comedians* is in fact Lubin's *New Colored Kiss No. 2*, first advertised in 1900 and listed as sixty-five feet.[39] But what we know with certainty is that Suttle appears in two different kiss films made at about the same time, with two different partners, produced by two different film companies.

With Suttle and Brown identified, one big mystery seemed solved. *Something Good—Negro Kiss* could be taken off the vast list of films believed to be nonextant. But larger questions remained. What accounts for such an exceptional early film artifact? How could it have come about? How do we make sense of it? And what might it suggest about how we think about early American films and the representation of race? The next chapter gives a fuller account of the film in the context of its mediascape and racialized representation at the turn of the century, based on the foundation of identification work laid here. First, though, we need to understand what Suttle and Brown may have been doing at Selig's studio on that spring day in 1898. To do this, we need to expand our historical methods.

SPECULATIVE PRODUCTION HISTORY

Suttle and Brown were based in Chicago, and likely the combination of their run at local vaudeville theaters and Selig's familiarity with the minstrel circuit led to them being invited to his studio. But what are they doing in *Something Good*? Did Selig intend to make a kiss film with Black performers as a parody of the Rice–Irwin kiss? In the next chapter I consider the implications of understanding the film as a parody of *The May Irwin Kiss*, but first I want to consider the possibility of another motivation.

The question of the impetus for the production of *Something Good* only emerged for me when I finally saw the restored version of the film. Up until that point, I only had access to the frame enlargements and an unstabilized scan of the unrestored print. In January 2018, Everett digitally restored the nitrate positive print, allowing for a clearer sense of the figures' movements and expressions.[40] Everett's restoration gave new life to figures that had been dormant for more than a century and gave me a different experience of the film. The restored version confirmed the impression of naturalism and joy that I had sensed at my first encounter with the scanned frames, and which the catalog entries emphasized. But it also added a new component. The scene felt *impromptu*; the performance felt improvised, caught up in the moment.

To be sure, this is intuition, speculation, and feeling. Marshaling impressions derived from being a spectator—not only a researcher—can open us to aspects of a film we might neglect if we only looked at it through an academic lens. *Something Good* moved me to think beyond its material evidence to be attuned to the power of the image to generate an affective response. Then, as a researcher, I was spurred to ask why the film might elicit such a feeling.

While my affective response is entirely subjective, it can serve as a form of evidence (albeit with different revelatory claims) when brought into productive contact with the other forms of evidence. Buttressed by a kind of formal analysis, my sense of the performers' improvisation is based on their gestures and how they appear to interact with the offscreen camera operator. After the first kiss and again right before the last, the performers seem to acknowledge a presence to the right of the camera, as if following the direction of a figure next to the recording apparatus. These fleeting glances are followed by a return to the kiss, perhaps suggesting an offscreen entreaty to kiss again. It might be tempting to dismiss such an impression as irrelevant, but this feeling can serve an important purpose in connecting the disparate pieces across an absent archive. As historian Carlo Ginzburg has asserted, "No one learns to be a connoisseur or diagnostician by restricting himself to practicing only preexistent rules. In knowledge of this type imponderable elements come into play: instinct, insight, intuition."[41] So, listening to intuition and allowing for speculation, we're left with a fascinating question. We may have needed the material evidence and extrafilmic archive to identify and date the film, but there are formal elements, particularly of mise-en-scène and performance, that we can only grasp in and through the moving image. What might account for Suttle and Brown's impromptu performance of intimacy before the Polyscope? What occasioned the film? As with the rest of this puzzle, answers to speculative questions are rooted in, though not exhausted by, the archive.

In the 1900 inventory of the Selig company's property, the item that follows *Something Good—Negro Kiss* is a film listed as *Cake Walk*. Selig's 1903 catalog describes *Cake Walk* as "one of the finest of its kind, portraying a number of swell darkies engaged in the popular past time of walking for the cake. The dance is well executed by people who have a reputation in this line, and the scene is a winner, and brings applause wherever exhibited."[42] This is a far more extensive description than that given, in the same 1903 catalog, to *Something Good—Negro Kiss* ("burlesque on the John Rice and May Irwin Kiss"). And it indicates that the cakewalk performers are professionals with "a reputation in this line," likely attired as "swells." The fall 1898 Sears catalog also offered a cakewalk film, *The Cake Walk*, with a description that echoes that of Selig's 1903 catalog: "This film is one of the finest of its kind, portraying a number of colored professionals in their favorite pastime. This is a winner and brings applause wherever exhibited." So these three titles—1898, 1900, 1903—likely all referred to the same cakewalk film. Considering the adjacency of *Cake Walk* to *Something Good—Negro Kiss* on the Selig property inventory, I thought it probable that Suttle and Brown were part of the cakewalk troupe that performed for Selig's *Cake Walk*, a film that had been considered lost.

This hunch was confirmed when Everett received an email from a German film scholar aptly named Dr. Robert J. Kiss. He had heard about our research and, as an expert in film identification, was working on some early Selig film fragments in several archives. Among these films was a ten-foot fragment (about seven seconds) of cakewalk footage archived at the Library of Congress. It's not a very sharp image, but the figures are clearly identifiable as the Rag-Time Four: Maud and John Brewer at the start of this footage, and Suttle and Brown at the end.

From this additional rediscovery, I imagine the following scenario: after the quartet filmed *Cake Walk*, Suttle and Brown shot a second film, a kind of impromptu parody of the famed Rice–Irwin kiss, at Selig's request. This could account for why, even though Suttle and Brown were seasoned performers, we have a strong sense of witnessing a candid moment of coy embarrassment, amusement, and genuine humor. They could be performing this act of intimacy for the camera and its offscreen operator as an afterthought to the more serious business of the day. But it would still be another film that the Selig Polyscope Company could sell.

FIGURE 13. *Cake Walk* (Selig, 1898). Maud Brown and John Brewer in the foreground, Saint Suttle and Gertie Brown in the background. Frame enlargement courtesy of the Library of Congress.

Identifying Suttle and Brown and arriving at a plausible theory for how *Something Good—Negro Kiss*'s burlesque of *The May Irwin Kiss* came about also helps explain the curious title of the film. While the titles of the (likely pirated) Lubin's *Darkies' Kiss* and the film sold by Prescott as *Colored Kissing Scene* are simply descriptive, Selig's title is doing more work on both sides of the dash. Unlike many Black-subject films of the time, the subtitle *Negro Kiss* abstains from deprecatory terms. Indeed, the Selig catalog refers to "the 'Afro-American' brother"—a rare usage in early film catalogs. Selig's experience in minstrelsy and his earlier partnership with an African American (Lew Johnson) might explain his eschewing of derogatory language, at least in the titles and catalog description of his Black-themed films.

The title *Something Good* is likewise noteworthy, recalling the showman's language of solicitation, which would have been familiar to Selig from his itinerant days. Here, the title serves as an entreaty to prospective viewers, beckoning with the promise of fulfilling entertainment. It also suggests an element of product differentiation. Suttle and Brown were traveling minstrels, but they were also vaudevillian minstrels—performers of a higher class of entertainment. *Something Good* signals to exhibitors that this film is high class and respectable, offsetting the potential lasciviousness suggested by *Negro Kiss*, for regardless of descriptor, the presumed association of African Americans with unbridled sexuality would be inherent to the title given the ubiquity of this stereotype. This interpretation is supported by the Sears catalog description pointing out the subject's interest "to the entire audience, young and old included."[43]

If the word *good* signals high class, what about *something*? It might be a gesture toward seriality—pointing to possible placement in an exhibitor's program. It also, interestingly, indicates a substantive scene (they kiss four times, after all). For example, Edison's synopsis of his 1900 version of *The Kiss* describes it as "nothing new. Just done over again and done well. Not a 'something made of nothing' kiss, but one of the old-fashioned 'home-made' kind that puts a whole audience into merriment and motion."[44] Of course the title *Something Good—Negro Kiss* appeared before Edison's second kiss film, but we can see how catalogs asserted a substantive "something" over its opposite, "nothing," when describing ardent kissing.

Could the title reflect an aspect of Suttle and Brown's stage act? I have yet to find anything to confirm this (such as a song or skit title), but the details that emerged in the process of identification make clear why we see the performers' apparent ease and familiarity with each other. Suttle and Brown were dancing partners, and the film shows their comfort with each other's bodies: the way they hold hands as if dancing, their small shimmies, and indeed their "osculation." Yet the performed intimacy seems genuine, a staged act that nonetheless feels impromptu—a kind of consummation of the chemistry performed on stage between Suttle and his "best girl." Indeed, this phrasing is one that Selig borrowed, taking it from the 1898 advertisements for the Rag-Time Four.[45]

The apparent amusement that Suttle and Brown take in their repeated kisses might also be due to the fact that they weren't romantic partners—at least not as far as we know. In 1898, Suttle had been married for two years to Mary L. Suttle, described in census records as a housekeeper.[46] We can't know what his personal relationship was to Brown, but the amusement with which they perform intimacy for the camera might be informed by a sense of sanctioned transgression. Selig's description of the "fun in this picture" is fitting: "both evidently enjoy the situation and are taking heaps of satisfaction out of it."[47]

All of this points to what makes the film incongruous with the range of catalog descriptions (from Sears, Lubin, and Prescott) that present it as a mere burlesque on the Irwin–Rice kiss, or that presume comedy because the subjects are African American. The broader background might even account for the addition in the Lubin and Prescott descriptions cited above that emphasizes humor: "One of the very funny incidents in this picture is the size of the colored man's mouth."[48] The film shows very few instances that might warrant this characterization, but it certainly referenced Suttle's minstrel persona, one that links him to other, more famous, minstrels like Ernest Hogan and Billy Kersands, two Black blackface performers known for their exaggerated facial expressions, especially involving their mouths. Kersands, for example, built comedy routines around his mouth, contorting it for laughs and filling it with improbable objects. The conflation of Suttle with minstrel stereotypes would in turn point to the power of the presumption of comedy embodied by the minstrel figure, in spite of the actual performance (just as *corpulent* may have operated as a comedic signifier in the Sears catalogs). Like his fellow minstrel performers, Suttle's body signified in excess of itself, one part of the multiple meanings, complex and contradictory, that are conveyed by *Something Good*.

. . .

I've been presenting the process of identifying *Something Good—Negro Kiss* as a roughly linear narrative of discovery. What actually happened is that each of these pieces of the puzzle overlapped, informed one another, opened up branches of inquiry, and closed off others. Presuming the print was Selig's raised the probability of Chicago-based performers; identifying Suttle and Brown confirmed this; the discovery of the Library of Congress print raised additional questions; the incongruence of sprocket holes confirmed some hypotheses; the Sears catalog allowed for dating but raised more unknowns. In the end, research gives a clearer picture of the context around this short film, but it can never be completely tidy.

Nor is it a closed book. The story of the rediscovery of *Something Good* prompted the recognition of previously unidentified artifacts. For example, in 2019, Norwegian archivists located an alternative version of *Something Good* at the National Library of Norway. The film had come to the library in the 1990s from the municipality of Leksvik and was cataloged as an unidentified Lumière film because of the single pair of round perforations. The film was apparently brought to Norway by exhibitor Hans Killingberg, who had traveled to the US in 1898, returning with prints and the apparatus for a

FIGURE 14. *Something Good—Negro Kiss* [Leksvik version] (Selig, 1898). Frame enlargement courtesy of the National Library of Norway.

motion-picture projector. It's possible that he purchased the alternate version directly from Selig and that Selig did not keep a copy (no such film is listed in the 1900 inventory of company property, for example). The Leksvik version was almost certainly filmed at the same time as *Something Good*, given that the set and costuming are identical. However, the print is inverted (possibly due to an error in the duplication from negative to positive), and the camera setup is further from the figures; filmed in long shot, both Brown and Suttle are shown in full figure. The film is longer than the USC print and consists of a prelude up to the couple's kissing, in which Suttle attempts to woo an unconvinced Brown who repeatedly rebuffs his advances, until he pulls her in for a kiss and wins her over. After they kiss six times, he spins her twice, finishing the act in a kiss and a twirl. It's probable that this was part of their stage routine as partners in the Rag-Time Four, possibly enacting the lyrics to a song (perhaps performed by John and Maud Brewer while Suttle and Brown pantomimed and kissed). What is clear from the Leksvik print is the degree to which Selig captures the couple as performers—professional actors at work before Selig's camera.

At its core, *Something Good* is a performance. Even as the cinematic kisses feel incredibly intimate, Suttle and Brown engaged the broader entertainment world of their time, not least with their "burlesque" on *The John C.*

Rice–May Irwin Kiss. What I have offered here is a procedural—the detailed process of discovery and revelation—that is the necessary groundwork for revisiting canonical texts and rethinking our collective understanding of early film history. Extending from the identification of *Something Good*, in the next chapter I situate the film in relation to the emergence of American cinema and demonstrate how a reconsideration of *The May Irwin Kiss* impacts how we understand racialized expressions in early film.

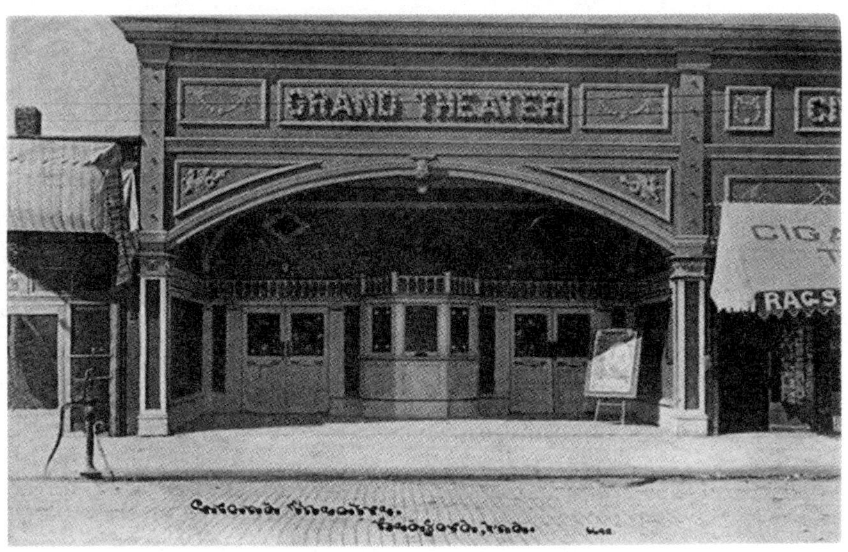
GRAND THEATER
RAGS

☞

Grand Theater

BEDFORD, INDIANA, 1899

WHEN J. W. HOGAN RETURNED from serving in Cuba in the Spanish-American War, he mounted a lecture tour to share his experiences, illustrating personal stories with moving pictures of the war procured from a distributor. Billed under the title "As Hogan Saw It," the show combined a descriptive lecture with moving pictures, songs, and violin accompaniment.

At the start of his tour in February 1899, Hogan booked the Grand Theater in Bedford, Indiana. The town of about six thousand, while small, was booming, with a population tripling in the previous decade due to the abundance of limestone in the area. Nearly all white, Bedford was probably a "sundown" town, enforcing racial segregation by intimidation and force.[1] *In a town likely hostile to African Americans and almost certainly with no Black spectators in the audience, Hogan's program of Spanish-American War pictures opened inexplicably with* Something Good—Negro Kiss, *which one Indiana paper described as "laughable."*[2]

The Spanish-American War marked the US's ascendance as a global power through expansionism. It was also the first American war recorded by moving-picture operators. Military films, which included both actualities and reenactments, played a significant role in generating and maintaining support for US expansionism. Images and stories of the war found eager audiences across the US. Film production companies flooded the market with a range of moving pictures depicting key episodes from the war and scenes of the daily lives of soldiers stationed in the Caribbean and the Pacific.

Tapping into the fervor for American military might, Hogan appealed to his audience's patriotism at the sight of "the boys in blue in battle." The local paper was not thrilled, deeming Hogan's lecture "a failure"—though it did not specify what was lacking in his presentation.[3] *Luckily, Hogan had packed the event* with other entertainments, including music, which the paper declared "all right," and a cakewalk performed by "the little people"—either dwarfs or children—whose dance "was pleasing to all."[4] Hogan's novelty performers received an enthusiastic response and obliged the audience with an encore.[5]

The cakewalking "little people" appeared in a section of the program depicting a "Day in Camp," meant to highlight "the amusing side of a soldier's life."[6] Comic songs and scenes provided levity from the actualities of troops, battleships, and war maneuvers, and a "Day in Camp" romanticized the soldiers' comradery while downplaying the gruesome aspects of war.

Even though segregated African American troops earned numerous Medals of Honor and Certificates of Merit for their valor in the Spanish-American War, and even though films of Black soldiers in the war existed, no records suggest that Hogan showed them.[7] Instead, his program circumscribed blackness to its all-too-common place in the era's popular spectacles: as comedy and entertainment. And yet, blackness also framed the program, from Suttle and Brown's kiss at the opening to the cakewalking "little people" at the close. How these components might have inflected the war pictures is unanswerable, especially without a fuller sense of how Hogan presented them. But as an outlier among the moving images, Something Good must have stood out to audiences, even if presented as comedic.

While we don't know the specific titles of each of the war films in Hogan's program, in the section of a "Day in Camp" he may have included scenes of soldiers at leisure. In one such film made at the time, the horrifying Tossing a Nigger in a Blanket (American Mutoscope Co., 1898), white American soldiers in Key West, Florida, amuse themselves by encircling a naked Black child and repeatedly tossing him high in the air with a blanket.[8] In the film's surviving frames, airborne limbs visually echo grotesque images of lynching victims, and the laughing soldiers recall the nameless masses of white vigilantes.

After a few weeks on the road, it appears as though Hogan sold his program to the Rummel & Martin Specialty Company, which mounted a very similar show in Indiana a few months later.[9] Rummel & Martin added new lecturers, musicians, and instruments (including a clarinet and xylophone) to the program. The cakewalk seems to have been cut, but Rummel & Martin kept Something Good as the prologue to the Spanish-American War films as they traveled across Indiana through the summer of 1899.[10] Love and war, both racialized, formed a curious program ostensibly balancing presumed *humor with patriotic valor. Did the charm of* Something Good *validate the racist program of US expansionism? Or did its humanizing depiction subvert the claims of the civilizing mission of the war? Or was it simply a pleasing attraction at the start of the show, intended to get the audience into a mood for entertainment?*

TWO

The Attraction of Affection

IN JULY 1896, A SAVVY showman named John Hopkins introduced a novelty amusement to his popular vaudeville house at 526 South State Street, thereby becoming the first to commercially exhibit motion pictures in Chicago.[1] Audiences crowded into the South Side theater to catch a glimpse of the Vitascope, a contraption developed by Thomas Edison that, they had heard, reproduced scenes from real life through a combination of electrical forces and then projected them on large screens before paying spectators.[2] What fantastic wizardry conjured shadows to lurch from the canvas screen, free from the bonds of perpetual stasis!

The vaudeville audience was used to variety, but the range of films on display and the vivid color, painstakingly painted by hand on each film frame, stunned even the most blasé amusement-seekers. As with the live stage, the Vitascope featured dancers, and Hopkins's audience was treated to three moving-picture dance acts. First, the Leigh Sisters, two smiling blondes, performed their famed umbrella dance. They twirled a large umbrella before the camera, hiding from the spectator's gaze in a kind of chaste striptease, then pulled it up to reveal a sudden costume change conveyed through new colors applied to their (noticeably short) skirts.[3] Annabelle Whitford then danced her famous serpentine, butterfly, and sun dances, with her (longer) skirts billowing around her, also adorned with meticulous hand-applied color. Then, painted to kaleidoscopic effect, Amy Muller performed her "toe dance," hopping around *en pointe* with one leg extended, before cartwheeling and spinning, skirts aswirl.[4]

The crowd at the Hopkins Theater also watched filmed scenes from a play staged the previous season in New York City, *A Milk White Flag*, a musical farce that brought thirty-four performers to Chicago without their having to travel. Then, with another change of film subject, the stage was left behind, and in what must have felt like a magical bending of time and space, the audience was transported to the northeast metropolis. New York City's Herald Square came to life with street cars, the elevated railway, and men and women converging at 6th Avenue and 35th Street. If these scenes weren't vertiginous enough, audiences next gaped at the gorge and whirlpool rapids at Niagara Falls, then cheered on uniformed firemen as they rescued people trapped in a burning building.

Finally, in the program's most popular portion, the audience heartily laughed at the "ludicrous" osculation of May Irwin and her *Widow Jones* co-star John C. Rice, who offered up a single stage kiss for the camera.[5]

Edison's Vitascope transfixed audiences at the Hopkins Theater. Attuned to his customer's desires, Hopkins saw that the future of entertainment was in moving pictures. He shrewdly offered a weekly bill of motion-picture subjects to keep spectators interested. Most films would change, though some popular subjects—like *The May Irwin Kiss*—would run over multiple weeks. The scheme worked. Just as the vaudeville and drama selections rotated to encourage regular attendance, so too would the motion-picture subjects vary weekly. Initially, Hopkins ordered films from Edison or a distributor, but by 1900 he was working exclusively with fellow Chicagoan William Selig to furnish motion pictures for the theater. Hopkins soon became Selig's biggest customer.[6] With this business arrangement, in 1898, *Something Good* undoubtedly joined *The John C. Rice–May Irwin Kiss* on the Hopkins screen.

Theaters depended on the availability of new motion-picture subjects to sustain the interest of novelty-chasing audiences. The subjects were short, typically less than thirty seconds, and heterogenous, but they shared a tendency to directly appeal to spectators. The Leigh Sisters, Whitford, and Muller all made eye contact with the camera, as if dancing before a theatrical audience; the New York City street scenes and the firemen enacting a rescue appealed to spectators' curiosity and thirst for views and experiences otherwise out of reach. May Irwin and John C. Rice, too, were filmed side by side, as if immediately facing the viewer, offering humorous intimacy for a gawking public. Each of these short subjects constituted what Tom Gunning and André Gaudreault have characterized as a film "attraction." The term reflects film's shared genealogy with the attractions of showmen at fairgrounds and circuses: forms of popular entertainment that used novelty to entice spectators and draw money from their pockets.[7] As a concept, "attraction" posits early cinema as a continuation of spectacular ways of relating to audiences that emphasized "direct stimulation," in Gunning's words, through "inciting visual curiosity, and supplying pleasure through an exciting spectacle," complemented by the appeal of the new technology itself.[8]

William Selig, the producer of *Something Good—Negro Kiss*, was well suited to making cinema "attractions": they were an extension of his showman's craft as a prestidigitator and manager of minstrel shows.[9] *Something Good* combined Selig's investment in monetizing Black performance with the display of kissing as an established filmic subject. An attraction of attraction, *Something Good* spectacularized Black kissing for film audiences. The film represents not just the cinema of attractions, but what I term the cinema of racialized attractions.[10]

For late nineteenth- and early twentieth-century spectators, part of the appeal of *Something Good* was its reference to *The May Irwin Kiss*, grounding its humor in the presumption of the inherent novelty of African American actors riffing off the popularity and ubiquity of the film of white actors. Indeed, *Something Good* was sold with catalog descriptions marketing it as a "burlesque on the John Rice and May Irwin Kiss," explicitly advertising it as a parody of its famous predecessor.[11] This positioning presumes that audiences would see these figures as imitators or as escalating the more chaste sexuality of Irwin and Rice with a greater degree of explicitness, even mocking the staid formality of the white lovers with what would have been understood as the natural licentiousness of the Black lovers. For presumed white audiences, Black bodies would have been coded as inherently sexual (threateningly so for the man, promiscuously so for the woman). At the same time, they would be presumed to be inherently humorous, as American folklorist Constance Rourke, writing in 1931, ascribed to the "primitive comic sense" of blackface minstrelsy: "to be black is to be funny."[12] Significantly, the threat and the humor would be bound up with each other. (This is explicit in the early set of films about crap games, prize fights, and razor skirmishes in "Blackville.")[13] Thus, the "burlesque" is both imitative and an exaggerated reimagining.

Something Good is doing something more than what is accounted for by the framework of attractions alone. The casting of Suttle and Brown, after all, is not merely a substitution for Rice and Irwin. The racialized fantasies that were conjured by early filmmakers and understood by spectators depended on a complex interplay of intertextual and extrafilmic associations for their legibility. In this context, race, especially blackness, whether visible or not, was a distinct attraction of early cinema, even where we do not expect to find it.

In fact, the cinema of racialized attractions is already present in *The John C. Rice–May Irwin Kiss*.

THE JOHN C. RICE–MAY IRWIN KISS: "A LYRIC OF THE STOCK YARDS"

The John C. Rice–May Irwin Kiss was filmed by William Heise in Edison's Black Maria studio in West Orange, New Jersey, in April 1896.[14] The theater stars performed their kiss scene from the hit play *The Widow Jones*, which had premiered the previous year. The resulting twenty-second film presents the couple seated side by side in medium close-up. They briefly banter, and then Rice tilts toward Irwin, who offers the side of her mouth as she presumably delivers her lines from the play. They then part and face one another. Rice adjusts his mustache, holds her face in his hands, and they kiss. The majority of the brief subject is the setup for the kiss, which is delivered with performative gestures and a range of motion cognizant of the camera's position and proximity. In short, this is a performance for the benefit of the motion-picture machine—an attraction—with no pretense of real-life intimacy.

The first kiss recorded by a motion-picture camera, *The May Irwin Kiss* was produced as a "publicity stunt" for the *New York World*, which reproduced the "forty camera winks of kiss" in a series of frame enlargements under the header "The Anatomy of a Kiss."[15] The *New York World* celebrated the film as a "revelation" for its technological achievement: "Such pictures were never before made. In the forty-two feet of kiss recorded by the kinetoscope every phase is shown with startling distinctness."[16] The newspaper rendered the act of kissing into a photographic motion study like that of Eadweard Muybridge or the chronophotography of Étienne-Jules Marey, while simultaneously sharing in the comedy of Fred Ott's sneeze in *Edison Kinetoscopic Record of a Sneeze* (Edison, 1894), also shot in the Black Maria, the individual frames of which had been reprinted in *Harper's Weekly* in 1894.[17]

This first filmic kiss was tremendously popular upon its release, yet it was likely seen by spectators as more humorous than "overtly sexy."[18] Recall the *Chicago Tribune*'s assessment of *The May Irwin Kiss* as "ludicrous." The humor of the film may have also been entwined with discomfort stemming from embarrassment at the close-up of the act projected on a large screen and shown on a loop.[19] "Magnified to Gargantuan proportions and repeated three times over it is absolutely disgusting," the reviewer John Sloan told readers of the Chicago literary magazine *The Chap-Book* at the time of its release.[20] The size of the projected image and the repetition of the kissing (when it was shown on a loop) were seen by Sloan as "indecent in its emphasized vulgarity."[21] There was a specific inflection to Sloan's discomfort, with ethnic and class overtones in his description of the Irwin and Rice film as "not more than a lyric of the Stock Yards."[22] The area around Chicago's Union Stock Yards was replete with saloons and hotels catering to the multiethnic, working-class community that populated the southwest side of the city: initially Irish, German, and later Czech immigrants, though by the turn of the twentieth century the area also included Poles, Lithuanians, and Slovaks. To call the film "a lyric of the Stock Yards" was to associate it with lowbrow taste, tawdry entertainment, and ethnically determined, unbridled sensuality. (It also invoked olfactory pungency of animals, butchery, stockyard laborers, and the cacophony of violence. These offenses were beyond the capacities of the moving image but certainly associated with its working-class venues and environments.)[23] Sloan's vitriolic response was an outlier, though the interplay of attraction and revulsion of the magnified act of kissing generated much interest, constituting an attraction in its own right.[24] A scandal for a few, perhaps, the film was a sensation for a great many more.

Its acclaim lasted for years. As an exhibitor catalog advertised in 1898, "This subject has met with unequaled success, and is the most popular ever shown on the kinetoscope or projecting machine."[25] Success begat success. Concurrent with the ubiquity of its circulation, the film spawned a decade-long cycle of imitators produced by other film manufacturers in the United States and the United Kingdom.[26] These included a more immediate cycle of variations, including Edison's own remake with younger, more slender performers, released as *The New Kiss* in 1900, and a year later, his *Bowery Kiss*, which featured performers Kid Foley and Sailor Lil, "two typical Bowery characters, [who] give an exhibition of the manner of kissing on the East Side that defies description."[27] With black eyes and missing teeth, the lovers known for their "tough dance"—a dance that reenacts combative passion—spectacularized a caricature of working-class Irish rough romance.[28] The attraction, then, would presume voyeuristic pleasure of transgressing both ethnic and class lines through the medium of motion pictures, accessing a close-up on intimacy among highly segregated groups within private spheres increasingly mingling in public arenas. The movies made virtual "slumming" possible.[29]

Blackness provided one of the premises for variations on *The May Irwin Kiss*. Between 1898 and the first few years of the twentieth century, a set of films was produced featuring Black performers kissing and marketed as "burlesques" on the Rice–Irwin kiss. These included films made or sold by Selig, Siegmund Lubin, F. M. Prescott, and Eberhard Schneider's American Miror-Vitae with titles such as *Darkies' Kiss*; *Those Affectionate Darkies*; *Whose Baby is You?*; *Colored Kissing Scene*; *New Colored Kiss No. 2*; and *Something Good—Negro Kiss*. Until recently, none of these films were thought to have survived. Given that the titles were found in exhibitor catalogs, though, scholars have pointed to them as evidence of early cinema's egregious representational racism, and *Something Good—Negro Kiss* was duly treated as an exemplary bad object. For example, film historian Charles Musser notes that Selig's comedies of this period "portrayed African Americans as childlike beings—unsocialized, opportunistic, and easily frightened—and ultimately, as comic counterparts to the white world," and he points to descriptions of *Something Good* in particular as an example of this kind of parroting.[30] When the film was considered lost, these kinds of assumptions made sense, especially given the rampant racist representation on display in contemporaneous films. And yet, access to the film underscores the utter incongruity between producer descriptions, exhibitor framing, and the film itself; we can no longer make such blanket assumptions. Film finds can change film history.

If incomplete, film marketing does provide vital information on the intentions of producers and presumptions of audiences. The marketing of *Something Good—Negro Kiss* as an "osculatory burlesque," for example, could have signaled not just minstrel humor in general, but the more sexual lasciviousness implied in the notion of the burlesque. The imbrication of minstrelsy and burlesque was by design, as cultural historian Robert C. Allen has traced; minstrelsy was waning in appeal even by the 1870s, and the "white fantasy of blackness" at the heart of the minstrel show was giving way to the inclusion of white women burlesque performers. Both burlesque and minstrelsy were organized along "principles of transgression and inversion," in Allen's formulation, whereby "ironic, low-other characters" were designed in such a way as to navigate the "ideological problematics" of race and gender.[31] So, while the term *burlesque* broadly referenced a humorous caricature or a grotesque imitation of a referent presumed to be dignified, it nonetheless carried performative legacies of racial and sexual inversion. In other words, *Something Good* was marketed as crossing borders of race, class, and gender.

At one level, then, the actors in *Something Good* function as "comic counterparts to the white world."[32] Yet this description posits Edison's film as a simple and stable object of reference. It is not. In fact, May Irwin's apparent whiteness unravels when we consider the ethnic subtexts informing the play's notorious kiss scene and Irwin's own negotiations of blackness. Sloan's invective was less a fever dream than it may have seemed.

The May Irwin Kiss most directly references a scene from *The Widow Jones*. As Musser has shown, that stage kiss was itself a burlesque on English actress Olga Nethersole's infamous "salacious" kiss from *Carmen* (1895).[33] Nethersole created quite a sensation, and her sultry kissing in the play drew attention from theater critics who commented on, for example, the "good deal of talk in town" concerning this feature of *Carmen*. As a *New York Herald* critic noted, "The recollection of these few moments of too passionate osculation hangs rather heavily over the balance of the performance."[34] Nethersole's kisses were notable not just for their repetition but also for their ardor, leading to "a certain amount of discomfort" for theatergoers and critics.[35] In contrast, Irwin's highly stylized kiss with John C. Rice, taken from the play in which they perform a similarly performative kiss, was met with laughter—a reaction, Musser asserts, that was predicated on a recognition of the "burlesque" on the Nethersole kiss. The adaptation of the kiss from *The Widow Jones* to the Vitascope added another level to the burlesque. As Musser reminds us, the Vitascope showed films on a loop, so the Irwin–Rice kiss was in effect relentlessly repetitive. He argues, "Its repetitive kissing structure parallels the constant kissing done by Nethersole in *Carmen*. The film spoofs her excessive kissing through its mechanical means. Again, this is an American kiss with American technology."[36] What led to Sloan's objections—magnification and repetition—were aspects that underscored the humor of the film for spectators who recognized its satire of *Carmen*.

The Americanness of Irwin's kiss on the Vitascope brings into focus another aspect of *The May Irwin Kiss*'s allusion to Nethersole. Audiences tolerated Nethersole's passionate displays because they were understood to derive from her well-known, and well-publicized, Mediterranean ancestry.[37] Assumptions of ethnically determined character gave an intonation to Nethersole's performance that informed that of May Irwin. As such, the kiss as attraction was marked as ethnic at its foundation.[38] With this context, Sloan's apparent insult that *The May Irwin Kiss* is nothing more than "a lyric of the Stock Yards" becomes doubly inflected with xenophobic charge.

The May Irwin Kiss and its imitators can be understood as cinematic efforts to grapple with the heterosexual mixing that came with modernity, especially the position of women in the urban public sphere and the concomitant rise of "mashing" culture. Kissing films negotiated "several intertwined desires and anxieties," as film historian Amanda Ann Klein argues, "the desire to see sex acts filmed in close-up, the changing nature of public, heterosocial socializing, the high stakes of objectification, and the (symbolic) policing of white male sexuality."[39] The comedy of "ludicrous" performative kissing functioned to mitigate the various anxieties surrounding modern life on the cusp of a new century.

In *The May Irwin Kiss*, however, race is more than subtext and more than general context. It is also not just about (white) ethnicity. What film history has overlooked in the assessment of *The May Irwin Kiss* is the fact that Irwin was not just any middle-aged white actress, and hers was not a straightforward white body. May Irwin was a minstrel performer, and a very popular one at that.[40] As such, her appearance onstage as well as on-screen was inextricably associated with blackness.

MAY IRWIN: THE "ONE BOSS BULLY"

In John J. McNally's *The Widow Jones*, the play from which Edison's kiss film was based, Irwin played a "'fat-fair-and-forty' widow."[41] In this farce, Irwin's character masquerades as a widow of a man presumed dead in order to escape the unwelcome attentions of gold-digging suitors.[42] The songs she performed, however, were not written for the play but instead were taken from her standard repertoire as a "coon shouter," an interpreter of Black-themed songs on the vaudeville and musical comedy stage. Having nothing to do with the plot, these songs were nonetheless a key feature of the play. In its review of *The Widow Jones*, *The New York Times* critic noted the actress was "as pink and white and as blue-eyed as ever"; however, "when she sang her new darky songs ['I Want Yer, Ma Honey,' and 'The New Bully'] one forgot her blonde hair, her peaches-and-cream complexion, and her blue eyes; every tone of her voice, every expression of her countenance, every gesture and motion combined to create an illusion now of a lovelorn Virginia darky, now a dangerous Tennessee 'coon.'"[43] This last character—"a dangerous Tennessee 'coon'"—directly references the musical's biggest hit, "The Bully" (also known as "The New Bully"), which became a phenomenon and Irwin's signature number.[44]

That Irwin, as a stage performer of her time, would be involved with minstrelsy is not surprising. With the emergence of ragtime in the late nineteenth century came singers, mostly white women, who were "negro specialists" in what were called "coon songs" and "coon shouting." For white comediennes, "blacking up one's voice" was the main performance method (a practice that extends to the present day).[45] Indeed, coon songs were practically synonymous with ragtime. Drawn initially from white caricatures of blackness, the genre also included Black performers who benefited from its popularity (even as they were stymied by systemic racism), ultimately evolving into the blues and other musical forms derived from African American culture and its imitations. The popularity of coon songs can't be overstated. At their heyday in the 1890s, successful coon songs sold millions of copies.[46] To be sure, as music historians Lynn Abbott and Doug Seroff remind us, the racist epithet "coon" is at the root of the generic designation "coon song" and "coon shouter," but the term as employed in the musical genre did not carry the same racist charge. As they resignedly note, "it is impossible to investigate black popular entertainment of the ragtime era without directly confronting coon songs."[47]

Irwin was a key figure in the rise of coon shouting and one of the genre's most popular performers. In contrast to the "refined" style of Clarice Vance, another popular white coon shouter, Irwin was known for her uncouth stage presence and a singing style with no pretense toward refinement. She preferred to assert an "authentic" interpretation of the genre with a voice that, as *The New York Times* put it, was "untrained."[48] Irwin was an interpreter of "modern" coon songs rather than antebellum plantation throwbacks, and she was known for her portrayal of urbane and threatening African American men. A *New York Times* review of her performance in the 1896 musical comedy *Courted into Court* offers this evocative description of her interpretation of the play's musical numbers:

> The Southern negro she impersonates in "Crappy Dan" and "The New Bully" is not the old plantation darky, happy in his bondage, primitive in his simplicity, but a product of the new civilization, the bad town darky of the present age of transition. That he is susceptible to humorous treatment Miss Irwin proves, and the manner in which she thus puts him before us in all his badness and audacity, without the aid of make-up or scenic effect, is, in its small way, a triumph of art. But this same crappy Dan, with his dice loaded for "sebens" and his "'quaintance wid a gun," represents a grave social problem.[49]

In Irwin, as in other turn-of-the-century minstrel dandies, the antebellum figure of Zip Coon—an urban sort mocked for his pretenses of sophistication and class—is reimagined as a threatening character whose very efforts toward sophistication belie his ruffian roots. What she represents, in other words, is the perception of the threat of Black men in the increasingly multiracial urban environment and the efforts of popular culture to mitigate that threat.

The "grave social problem" Irwin embodied in performing coon songs, albeit with an attempt at neutralizing humor, was at the core of a growing movement of "scientific" accounts for racial difference and arguments for white supremacy. Under the banner of social science research, the promotion of notions of white manliness, ideals of Victorian womanhood, and the belief in the animalistic and predatory nature of Black men increasingly present in northern urban areas instigated a "new image of the murderous urban Negro."[50] As historian Khalil Gibran Muhammad has detailed, "For white Americans of every ideological stripe—from radical southern racists to northern progressives—African American criminality became one of the most widely accepted bases for justifying prejudicial thinking, discriminatory treatment, and/or acceptance of racial violence as an instrument of public safety."[51] Popular culture became the stage for these beliefs. They were broadly promoted in work such as Charles Carroll's pseudoscientific, theological study *The Negro a Beast* (1900) and Thomas Dixon Jr.'s novels and plays, including *The Leopard's Spots: A Romance of the White Man's Burden 1865–1900* (1902) and *The Clansman: A Historical Romance of the Ku Klux Klan* (1905), which would be adapted for film by D. W. Griffith as *The Birth of a Nation* (1915). It may have been pseudoscience, but it served as the premise for the nation's first blockbuster, as well as the justification for lynch mobs, disproportionate incarceration of Black people, and a century of rampant disenfranchisement and social and economic inequity.

Black music, too, became imbricated with criminality in the white imagination. Offering Irwin a tip on where to find possible artistic inspiration, the *Kansas City Journal* suggested that she visit the "nigger floor" of the county jail if she were "ever on the watch for new and catchy" so-called Negro songs: "The forty negro prisoners on that floor of the jail have little to do but eat and sing. In that crowd of darkies from everywhere, new songs evolve as naturally as mushrooms spring up on a muck heap."[52] For Irwin to appropriate the music of incarcerated Black men entailed a theft that reinforced the insidious twinning of blackness and criminality.

May Irwin's body, then, served as a site of projection of a range of anxieties and desires around race, class, gender, urbanism, and modernity—that is, "the present age of transition." What this also means is that when Irwin kisses John Rice for Edison, the "bad town darky" is also in the embrace, carrying all of the transgressive allusions of her presence into a film otherwise seemingly unconcerned with such tawdry context. The scandalousness of Edison's *Kiss* has, I believe, been overstated. But if it was shocking to some, it might have been because of these associations and not simply because of the magnified exhibition of the intimacy of a kiss. To later twentieth- and twenty-first-century eyes, *The John C. Rice–May Irwin Kiss* doesn't seem to have anything to do with race. Not only is this wrong, I would describe *The May Irwin Kiss* as the first commercially shown minstrel film.[53]

THE BULLY: IN SONG, IN PRINT, AND ONSTAGE

To understand how thoroughly Irwin's stage persona was imbued with racialized performance, we need only turn to the hit song of *The Widow Jones*: "The Bully."[54] In the song, Irwin sings as "a Tennessee nigger" hunting a "bully dat's just come to town." The song traces the singer's search and eventual finding—and slaying—of the titular bully, concluding with "When I got through with bully, a doctor and a nurse / Wan't no good to dat nigger, so they put him in a hearse; / A cyclone couldn't have tore him up much worse. / You don't hear 'bout dat nigger dat treated folks so free; / Go down upon the levee, and his face you'll never see; / Dere's only one boss bully, and dat one is me."[55] Not only does Irwin sing as "a dangerous Tennessee 'coon,'" she chronicles a righteous quest to find a tyrant who has been wreaking havoc among the Black population, "a layin' their bodies down." Irwin's new "boss bully" is a community protector who violently removes, then replaces, the upstart.

May Irwin's "Bully," however racist, is not a straightforward example of racialized cultural appropriation, class masquerade, or cross-gender performance (if any of those things could be straightforward). The song and her performance of it are complex sites of interracial exchange, appropriation, and claims over authenticity. The song "The Bully" has a trajectory that is as circuitous and confused as minstrelsy itself, as various versions circulated in the nineteenth century. The version made famous by Irwin was composed by a sportswriter and judge of horse races named Charles E. Trevathan. Irwin reportedly met Trevathan on a train from Chicago to San Francisco. During the journey Trevathan entertained his fellow passengers with songs, including a tune he claimed he learned from Black singers in Tennessee. Irwin supposedly was hooked by the catchy tune and encouraged Trevathan to set words to the melody.[56] It is his version that Irwin sang in *The Widow Jones* and that was published as the authoritative version.

Irwin quickly became inexorably associated with "The Bully." An arts writer noted in 1897:

> Nobody on the stage sings negro songs like May Irwin. In the first place, her mellow voice adjusts itself admirably to the requirements of this class of music, and then the expression she puts into the songs and, indeed, into everything that she does—that is the despair of all who try to imitate her. The popular mind has associated Miss Irwin so closely with the singing of these negro dialect songs, and her rendering of these melodies has come to be so generally regarded as the nearest possible approach to the real thing, that one is prepared to believe she has made a life long study of the negro. Certainly one is quite unprepared for the statement which she made in the course of conversation. "I was born in Canada," she said, "and I never saw a colored man or woman till I came to 'the states,' and I have not seen a great many since. I have never studied the negro. I think any success that I may have with these songs comes from intuition rather than anything else."[57]

While Trevathan claimed authenticity by his proximity to actual Black people—a trope going back to the white composer of minstrel songs Stephen Foster and white minstrel T. D. Rice before him—Irwin's disavowal of authority-by-intimacy is telling. Despite reviews that lauded her "fidelity to the African dialect," the "negro" she impersonates is itself a phantasm.[58] The "intuition" she claims as key to her success has no grounding in reality or experience. In Irwin we find a direct and honest expression of minstrelsy's racialized operations. Rather than an imitation of blackness, it is—quite explicitly—an impersonation of an imagination of blackness.

The ambiguity that surrounds Irwin's raced body (and voice) is reflected in the visual iconography presented on the sheet music covers for Trevathan's song that marketed the hit as "May Irwin's 'Bully' Song." The version published by the White–Smith Music Publishing Company shows a drawing of a characteristic Zip Coon figure holding an enlarged frame with Irwin's autographed professional cabinet card in his left hand. Peering at her image from behind the photo, he looks pointedly—even menacingly—at Irwin and, importantly, holds a razor blade in his right hand, open and poised at the hip. Yet the lyrics of "The Bully" place the "trusty blade" in the singer's hand. Is the Zip Coon the community protector coming after the Bully, figured here as Irwin herself? Is he Irwin's double? The relationship between the figures is ambiguous, as the photo of Irwin shows her right arm leaning on a backdrop positioned exactly at the level of the Zip Coon figure's blade. Is this a reach for the razor? It almost suggests a pantomime of

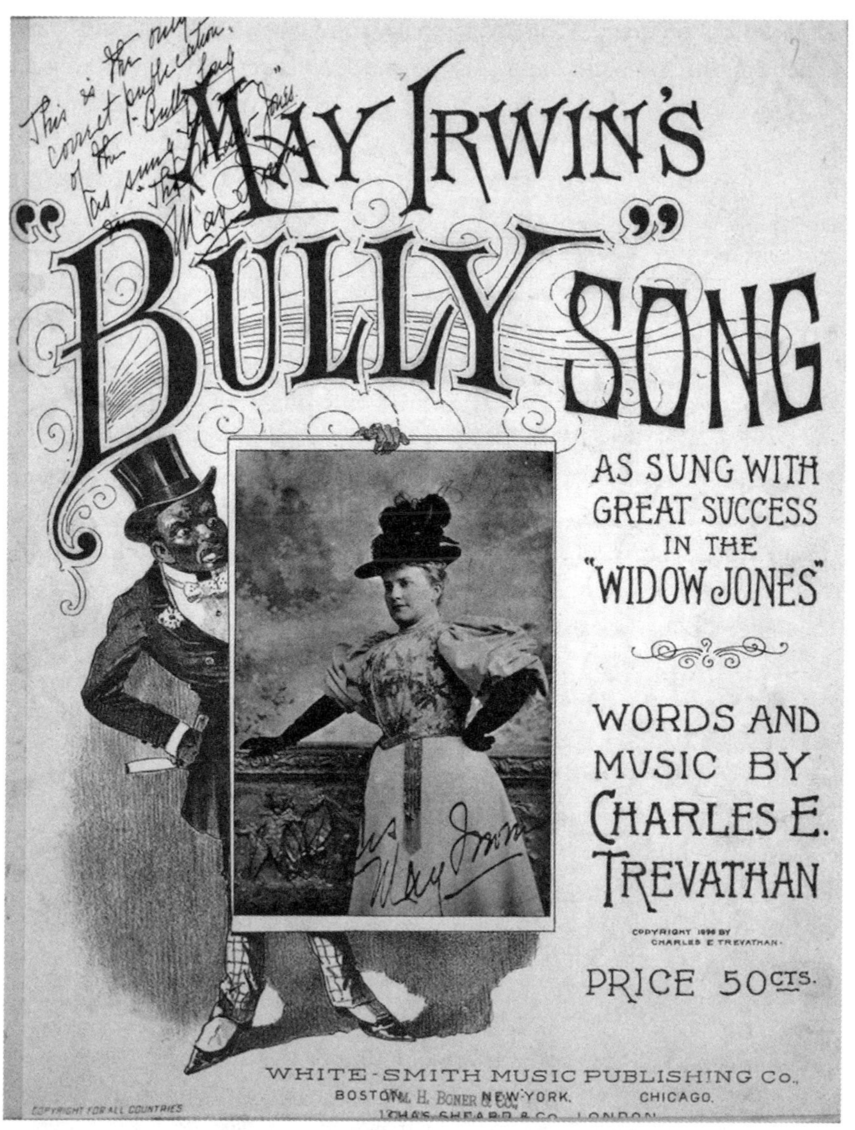

FIGURE 15. Sheet music cover for Charles E. Trevathan, “The Bully,” the White-Smith Music Publishing Co., 1896. Courtesy of the Lester S. Levy Sheet Music Collection, the Sheridan Libraries, Johns Hopkins University.

the actions of the song, in which the singer searches for the "new Bully" only to become the "one boss bully" in the end. The cover invites still another reading, one in which the threatening expression on the drawn figure's face incongruously meets the inscrutable stare of Irwin in her theatrical portrait pose. Who wields the power when a white woman faces a Black man holding a razor? The position of her right hand, albeit gloved in black, suggests castration or the threat of lynching—a real danger that attended the "grave social problem" decried by the *Times*. In the hegemony of the late nineteenth-century criminalization of blackness, the "one boss bully" was the white woman.

Another printing of the sheet music features a cover that does not include Irwin's photo but centers the caricature—this time with an apelike visage and hands—which is clearly marked as a minstrel figure in costume and stance: not the Zip Coon of the other cover but rather the ruffian "bad town darky" of the song.[59] Here, the premise of Carroll's *The Negro a Beast* is in full effect. More beast than man, the barely upright figure's animalism is not concealed by his clothes, and there's no contrasting figure to structure a gag. The figure also carries a blade. This is Irwin portrayed as her stage persona, the "peaches-and-cream complexion" unmasked to reveal the grotesque, ugly caricature beneath. This may be a little joke on Irwin, perhaps made for the benefit of her fans, but the face is haunting in its wide-eyed stare, exaggerated mouth, and apish figure. As *The New York Times* reviewer makes clear, Irwin signified "the bad town darky of the present age of transition," even if she was not attired in minstrel costume. Her voice and physicality alone transformed her into the bully.

This connection is even more directly asserted in the staging of Irwin's concerts of this period. For example, according to an 1896 review, when she sang "The New Bully," after the first verse the curtains behind her would part,

> and a genuine negro, in the most impossible conventional negro minstrel clothes is disclosed holding a large razor in his hand. The effect is dreadful. It dampens the enthusiasm of the audience immediately. The song is a bit of fantastic, exaggerated burlesque, founded in no respect on fact, and quite without reality. So the apparition of the living negro introduces into the scene an element entirely at variance with the effect of Miss Irwin's song, which is what the audience has been enjoying. But this tableaux is really the least disillusioning of the series. As the song progresses more real negroes, more painted backgrounds, and more complicated attitudes do all in their power to destroy the attractiveness of the song. But they don't succeed, and this result is a great tribute to Miss Irwin's sense of fun and her power of transmitting it to others.[60]

FIGURE 16. Sheet music cover for Charles E. Trevathan, "The Bully," Supplement to *The Journal*, April 12, 1896. Courtesy of the Frances G. Spencer Collection of American Sheet Music, Baylor University.

This scene is jaw-dropping, but the critic's description is informative in its language, especially in its repeated assertions of the song as fantasy, divorced from any real-world referent, an insistence that reads as overdetermined given Irwin's reception as "authentic" in her portrayal of Black men. The "living negro" belies Irwin's masquerade, breaking any illusion or pretense to the act (though the reviewer insists on it being "without reality"). But in revealing the razor-wielding Black man as existing only in the context of performance, the act not only neutralizes the threat but also asserts the image of threat as itself a representation.

At times Irwin even brought small Black children onstage as she performed "The Bully," a practice that Irwin's biographer Sharon Ammen notes was regular enough that on closing night of *The Widow Jones*, the ushers presented her with a parting "gift" of what appeared to be a barrel containing food out of which two Black children jumped to surprise her.[61] This anecdote might explain the motivation for a set of studio portraits from 1897 of Irwin and a Black baby (likely between ten- and eighteen-months old and impossible to gender), one made as a cabinet card and signed by Irwin with "May Irwin + The Newest Bully 1897."

On one level, these images are part of Irwin's long-standing association with children. Despite the persona of "The Bully," Irwin cultivated a self-presentation of childlike innocence in demeanor and attire, even dressing as a baby herself in promotional photographs. There is a set of clear representational allusions activated in these images. It is, on the one hand, an inversion of the maternal imagery of Black women as caregivers for white children—Irwin, then, plays the role of "mammy" here. On another level, however, there is the way in which Irwin, neither caregiver nor mother, displays the child for the camera, which is consistent with the presentation of Black children in contemporary moving pictures. Irwin's relationship to the figure of the child echoes that of her relationship to the Black children who appear in her stage act: as actor and scenery, prop master and prop. In these images Irwin presents the baby to be photographed as if posing with a curiosity or with a presentational appeal that beckons, "Behold this interesting object!"[62] Blackness, youth, and the incongruity between Irwin's figure and the child are all mobilized and structured in a stance of display. In this reading, Irwin is like a carnival barker displaying the Black child as an attraction for a presumed white spectator.

Positing blackness as infantile was characteristic of white-authored and -performed coon songs. But the strange posture of protection/abuse on

FIGURE 17. "May Irwin and The Newest Bully," 1897, Billy Rose Theatre Division, the New York Public Library.

display in these cabinet cards also visually echoes early filmic subjects such as *A Hard Wash* (American Mutoscope Co., 1896) and *A Morning Bath* (Edison, 1896), in which the presumed joke is that the mother cannot "clean" the skin color off her (clearly distressed) baby. Given Irwin's use of Black children onstage, the early film attractions *Dancing Darkies* (American Mutoscope Co., 1896) and *Dancing Darkey Boy* (Edison, 1897)—in which Black performance is presented as spectacle, essentializing dancing as something innate to Black people, especially children—become intermedial intertexts to Irwin's star persona and what her image signified. A raced body trading on race, racialized imagery, and presumptions of comedy, and in the process doing much to construct that very racialized image ironically underpinning the claims to authenticity of coon shouting as a genre, May Irwin kept blackness close at hand.

The doubling of the "bully" in these photos—Irwin and "the newest bully"—should also be seen against the doubling presented by the sheet music covers. In each of these images, the question of who represents the original bully and who is the new "boss bully" is ambiguous and contradictory. The theme of the two bullies that the song presents turns back on itself in the encore that Irwin would often perform: "When you see me comin', hist your windows high; / When you see me goin', hang your heads and cry; / I'm lookin' for dat bully, and he must die. / My madness keeps a risin', and I'se not gwine to get left, / I'm gettin' so bad dat I'm askeer'd of myself. / I was lookin' for dat bully, now he's on the shelf." This final verse, as Ammen notes, presents an "obvious paradox of a bully who is more vicious than he himself can handle." Coupled with "Irwin's childlike demeanor," the victorious new "boss bully" is by the end of the song facing deposition from an upstart—even if the newest bully resides in the singer's (childlike) self.[63]

Of course, in the cabinet card, the humor presumed by this photo derives from the absurd assignation of "bully" to the unwitting baby. There's an insidiousness at work whereby the Black child is figured as a threat despite his or her age, as if the child's innocence itself is a ruse for the razor-wielding bully. Indeed, as Ammen shows, Irwin mobilized—even, I would argue, weaponized—her childishness in her rendition of the song.[64] However, by marking the child as the "newest bully," Irwin incorporates the child into the fictive world of the song and, implicitly, passes the torch of being the "new" bully to the Black baby. This makes things significantly more complex. Remembering the aspect of the song that posits the singer-narrator as the new "boss bully" and as community protector who defeats the "red-eyed river roustabout" for the sake of public peace, we might then see the child in a different light. Irwin is now the deposed bully "who treated folks so free" and whom the child has dispatched. On the cusp of the new century, the child represents the ambivalence of the song's figuration of the "Bully" but also, and importantly so, the overthrowing of Irwin's racial masquerade. The "newest bully," then, is a generational rejection of the oppressive but clinging-on-to-power representational regime of white minstrelsy embodied by Irwin. There is, as so often with matters of race in America, nothing simple or straightforward in these representational practices.

SOMETHING GOOD—NEGRO KISS: A JOKE ON WHITE MINSTRELSY

Restoring minstrelsy to Irwin's performance persona allows us to revisit the historiography on *The Widow Jones* and *The John C. Rice–May Irwin Kiss*. At a basic level, Irwin's racial masquerade further underscored her "Americanness" (even if she was, in fact, Canadian by birth) in contrast to Nethersole's sensual Europeanness. As theater critic Alan Dale wrote in 1897, comparing her with the French comic actress Anna Judic, "May Irwin is the American Judic, but she is wholly, absolutely and unrestrainedly American. There is no foreign clime about her art. It is a home product, and in these days when home products are relegated to the background for the sake of those marked with the foreign inks, it is a good thing to shriek a little and do the patriotic."[65] American? Yes. White? No. Irwin might have registered as a more "'wholesome' American response" to Nethersole, yet the intertwining of the public display of affection and racialization was still there.[66] Irwin's warbles as a minstrel performer perhaps more than anything proclaimed her as American: a white minstrel performing an imagined notion of blackness.

My claim, then, is that May Irwin's screen kiss—even if not performed in blackface or by Black actors—is a racialized performance *and* that it would have been recognized by audiences of the day as such. As a result, an important feature of *Something Good—Negro Kiss* suddenly becomes visible. Suttle and Brown's kiss references not just *any* white-performed embrace but one that is itself *already* racially coded as "negro" via Irwin's status as a minstrel. *Something Good* and its imitators thus make visible what was implicit all along in the Irwin–Rice kiss. These films, in effect, restore racialized performativity to the screen and in so doing call out the racist dynamics that undergird Irwin's presence.

The "joke" of *Something Good*'s burlesque unfolds into another level of reference, one that destabilizes an already indefinite set of allusions carried by and through minstrelsy. What does it mean, we might ask, to do a racial burlesque of a film that was already racialized? While it certainly draws attention to the elision of race at the surface of *The May Irwin Kiss*, it also adds a layer of humor, placing the humor not on the bodies of African American performers (whose work was presumed to be that of comedy) but instead redirecting it, in a gesture of irony, back to Irwin herself. *Something Good* makes overt the implicit "joke" of the Rice–Irwin kiss.

There's every reason to suspect that everyone involved with the staging and filming of *Something Good*, including William Selig and his camera operator Thomas S. Nash, as well as Saint Suttle and Gertie Brown, would have known that May Irwin was a minstrel. Edison, Heise, and John C. Rice certainly knew it as well. Such was Irwin's popularity that it would be hard to imagine that filmmakers and fellow performers, especially in the minstrel circuit, would have been unaware of this fact. Earlier, when I described *Something Good*, I highlighted the apparent naturalness and affection that Suttle and Brown display toward each other, an image of Black love outside the constraints of racialized representation. But what if we think of it differently? What if we see *Something Good* not just as an improvised performance or as an alternative to mainstream racist representations but rather as a media savvy form of engagement with the still-popular Edison film? What if *Something Good* is a response not to Irwin's kiss but instead to her minstrelsy?

If we follow this logic, then *Something Good*'s burlesque posits Suttle as the corollary to Irwin. Suttle was certainly less famous than Irwin, and as a consequence far less documented, but he was nonetheless a professional minstrel and vaudeville performer who consistently, if probably unsteadily, worked in the profession into the early 1920s. In 1898, when Suttle and Brown kissed for Selig's Polyscope, they were part of a vaudeville act with John and Maud Brewer called the Rag-Time Four, which appeared across Chicago stages and in other midwestern cities for about a year before disbanding. Understanding their act, especially Suttle's dandyism, helps explain the joke at play in *Something Good* as a commentary on Irwin's minstrelsy. Through the figure of Suttle, I see *Something Good* as working to depict the "present century" dandy to Irwin's "bad town darky."

In the film, Suttle is costumed as a "swell," an elegantly attired dandy, and Brown wears a dress whose wide shoulder ruffles match the exaggerated lapels of Suttle's overcoat. They both wear bows: a dark bow tie for him, and for her, a light bowed ribbon on her neckline and another around her waist, tied in the back. These are their primary stage costumes but with significant alterations to Suttle's attire: in the film, his minstrel top hat is absent, and his collar and bow tie are not the comically enlarged versions he wore as part of the Rag-Time Four's vaudeville act. Precisely because he sets aside these trappings of performative minstrelsy, Suttle appears alongside Brown not as a caricature but as a man. Indeed, the impression of naturalness and ease conveyed by their rapport with each other might be rooted in their act for Selig's

Polyscope machine being performed, in effect, offstage from the standpoint of theatrical minstrelsy. Off the stage—but on camera—Suttle and Brown can shed minstrelsy's comic exaggeration and turn the humor on Irwin and Rice's staid embrace.

Suttle's public presentation targeted the kind of grotesque minstrelsy Irwin embodied. As the *Police Gazette* noted, "Mr. Suttle is the composer of a great many up to date songs."[67] The term "up to date" signaled African American coon shouters—as opposed to white minstrels in blackface—and would come to be associated with the rising generation of Black women blues singers such as Gertrude "Ma" Rainey and Bessie Smith.[68] "Up to date" also reflected Suttle's performance persona, the dandy minstrel, or, as one of his original compositions put it, "The Present Century Coon." Neither the old minstrel trope of Zip Coon nor its threatening reimagining embodied by Irwin, Suttle's persona aspired to refinement: a self-made man who is able to woo wealthier women and move in cultivated circles but has more working-class roots. He was, as the Selig description of *Something Good—Negro Kiss* notes, a "swell 'coon.'"[69]

Suttle's songs reflected the dandy persona on display in *Something Good*. On first glance, Suttle's compositions appear to be standard coon-song fare with lyrics peppered with racialized caricature and slang, completely commensurate with contemporary popular music. Titles such as "Old Jasper's Cake Walk" and "Blackville After Dark" support this reading. However, there are notable instances in which Suttle's compositions take on additional valences when put up against the popularity—and ubiquity—of "The Bully" and similar popular minstrel tunes. Suttle's composition "That Creole Gal of Mine" is a charming song about getting married.[70] In his lyrics, Suttle takes the figure of Parson Jones (a generic name for a clergyman, with good rhyming potential in "Jones") that "The Bully" degrades and instead elevates him. The Parson in "The Bully" hosts a "wingin'" (slang for dance or ball), where the song's narrator eventually finds and kills the bully.[71] "Creole Gal" features a party, but it's no wingin'; the wedding party has cake and wine, and friends and relations that "will favor us with quite a grand ovation." Suttle's clergyman who pronounces the couple married—"old Parson Jones has given his decision"—is notable for not being key to the rhyme scheme (*decision* is meant to rhyme with *the season*). Whether or not Suttle is explicitly subverting the terms of "The Bully," his lyrics reconfigure the dynamics at play in Irwin's hit. Suttle doesn't avoid the term *coon*, but he deploys it to highlight a class distinction between the bride, "a member of the Blue Vein Society," and the

FIGURE 18. Sheet music cover for Saint Suttle, "That Creole Gal of Mine," S. Brainard's Sons Co., 1899. Courtesy of the University of Illinois at Urbana-Champaign Music and Performing Arts Library.

"dudes," who are "daffy" over her "because she is divine." Suttle's refrain concludes, "I've got the best of all the coons with that creole gal of mine."

Class and sophistication are the themes of many of Suttle's songs. For example, in "The Present Century Coon" (copyrighted in 1898 and published in 1899 by the S. Brainard's Sons Co.), Suttle describes himself as "a coon that's always up to date." He sings of being "dressed in the latest style" and how he expects "to cut an awful dashin' prance / In nineteen hundred at the Fair, / And the Frenchmen gay will go into a trance / For to see that I'm a coon that's natur'ly there, / I'm goin' to represent the colored swells / That you see round our cities ev'ry day, / For I'm a corker and they'll surely yell / 'Mister, Parley Vous Francaise.'" Just as "up to date" signified Black performers, the future-minded lyrics of "The Present Century Coon" announce the singer as fashionable—not just current but on the vanguard. Indeed, in 1898 when the song first appeared, the "present century" was the nineteenth, but the song imagines the singer's self-display—a dandy on showcase—at the 1900 Paris Exposition (itself a celebration of the previous century's accomplishments and an exhibition of technological feats driving innovation into the twentieth century).

Importantly, Suttle presents himself as representative of "the colored swells" that populate "our cities." If May Irwin's bully represented the "grave social problem" presumed to attend Black male bodies in urban spheres, Suttle cuts a different figure, as evinced by the cover of the published song by S. Brainard's Sons Co. The sheet music features a sketch of a dandy figure with Suttle's photograph for the face, complete with a monocle and a top hat drawn over the photo. While there are visual markers of a minstrel costume—white gloves, a diamond stud, an enlarged flower-like boutonniere, and mismatched patterns on his shirt and vest—there is nonetheless refinement to the costume. The jacket lines are sharp, the pleats on the pants are crisp, and the gloved hands are gracefully poised, one by the boutonniere and one holding a ribboned cane. The figure also wears a single die as an embellishment to his pants, an allusion to illicit crap shooting that is presented here almost discreetly and with elegance. Unlike the Zip Coon figure portrayed on the covers of "The Bully," there's no ostentation with "The Present Century Coon." Here, Suttle takes the figure of Zip Coon, one that he invokes across his compositions, and its characteristics—vanity, dandyism, bon vivantism, dancing, and mashing—and tempers them to present a figure that is dignified and refined.

Watching him move with Gertie Brown in *Something Good*, we see his elegance on display and the grace of his movement, a dancer's ease with his coy partner. His gentle hand holding, confident grasp of her body, and ebullient smile all evoke professional skill combined with personal amusement. For a figure working within a genre predicated on a white fever-dream fantasy of blackness, these gestures of dignity, humor, and affection are deeply powerful. This is not to lose sight of Brown and Suttle's presentation as a performance or to confuse performance with reality. Rather, it is to understand the performance as working to directly refute the terms of the era's racialized attractions onstage and on-screen. It is a performance of naturalness yet taking shape against a wider media context known to filmmakers and performers alike.

FIGURE 19. Sheet music cover for Saint Suttle, "The Present Century Coon," S. Brainard's Sons Co., 1899. Courtesy of the British Library.

I emphasize Suttle and Brown's performance for the Polyscope as agentive not just because Suttle functions as the corollary to Irwin, with representational resonances between his self-fashioning and her racial masquerade. It has to do with production methods. While producers might select the subjects, camera operators were largely concerned with the technical aspects of filming. In the era of single-shot, static camera setups, the profilmic space allowed for a degree of performative control over the subject that would become increasingly forfeited to directors, cinematographers, and editors as the industry developed. In terms of how the films functioned discursively, the performances of the actors, as framed by the camera and projected to audiences, determined signification to a greater extent in these early years than we might ascribe to later stages in the development of the film industry. In this way, the era of filmic attractions afforded performers agency over their act closer to that which they enjoyed on stage than to later filmic recordings.

Of course, how the films were displayed and how audiences received them were entirely contingent on exhibition contexts and broader social valences. In *Something Good—Negro Kiss*, the presumed comedy attendant to Black performers joined the presumed comedy of the projected display of intimacy, all while the film negotiated the anxieties around Black (male) visibility in the public sphere. The cinematic attraction of Black affection offered a retort to the racial masquerade of May Irwin and in so doing established a powerful image of Black humanity that unmasked minstrelsy's grotesque fantasies of blackness.

. . .

Six miles south of the Hopkins Theater, in Hyde Park, where I currently live, a church once stood at the end of my block. The Hyde Park Mission, an African Zion church in a segregated white neighborhood, mainly served the neighboring Black communities of South Side Chicago. On a January evening in 1902, the church held a Polyscope spectacle. Perhaps the screening was a fundraiser for the church, or perhaps an itinerant exhibitor rented the church as a venue for his moving-image entertainment. A Black journalist in attendance declared the event a "great success," telling readers of the Indianapolis *Freeman*, "A large number of white people attended."[72] This brief notice constitutes the sum of the historical record on the event. The specific film subjects screened and the response of those in the interracial audience are lost to history.

There are many questions that arise from this brief newspaper mention. Presuming, quite plausibly given Selig's catalog, the Polyscope entertainment included *Something Good*, how might the responses to the spectacle of a Black couple kissing have differed between the white visitors and Black parishioners? Would there have been racial, gender, or generational gaps among spectators who were amused by the display of affection versus those who found it unrespectable? Certainly, some audience members would find kissing to be a subject unbefitting a church, an embarrassment compounded in an interracial audience perhaps. However, some spectators may have welcomed the film's clear departure from commonplace racist ridicule in early film attractions. Perhaps some in the audience recognized Suttle and Brown from the vaudeville stage as local celebrities captured on film and projected for an appreciative audience.

We can know very little about how individual spectators received early films. We do know that audiences, then as now, are not monoliths. Indeed, there were likely as many reactions as there were people in the church that night. What is clear, though, is that many, if not most, of those in attendance at the Hyde Park Mission and other venues would have seen *Something Good* as a parody of *The May Irwin Kiss* and would have understood the joke as one turning on Irwin's racial masquerade. It is harder to know how that joke would have played among an interracial audience in a South Side Chicago church, of course. At the very least *Something Good* would have evoked a complex set of references, racial terms, performative traditions, and forms of parody *in addition to* the attraction of affection on display.

From 1898 through the early 1900s, exhibitors included *Something Good* at a wide range of screening venues: a boardwalk theater in Atlantic City, a state fair in Dallas, and a department store in Wichita, Kansas, among countless theaters and exhibition venues.[73] Each of these sites (along with the other titles in a given program) would have inflected the audience's experience of *Something Good*. Whether as comedy, parody, tender actuality, or record of a vaudeville performance, twenty seconds of film evoked generations of complex negotiations around race, racial masquerade, and performative dynamics for diverse audiences at the turn of the twentieth century.

FERRELL
INNES'
DRY GOODS CARPETS & MILLINERY

☞

George Innes & Co. Department Store

WICHITA, KANSAS, 1899

DURING THE THIRD WEEK of December 1899, the George Innes & Co. department store in Wichita, Kansas, mounted a "Christmas Treat to Christmas Customers" in the form of a Vitascope exhibition. The show was free, with purchase, for its patrons.[1]

Innes's Main Street location had recently suffered a major fire and was undergoing a complete three-story remodel. The renovations were not ready in time for the Christmas season, so the store had moved into a temporary home two blocks away, on South Market Street, and transformed part of the second floor into a four hundred-seat moving-picture theater, surrounded by consumer goods, to lure patrons off the Main Street thoroughfare.[2] *Shoppers perused pretty handkerchiefs and kid gloves, ruffled curtains and polka-dot French flannels, velours and tapestries, dolls and sterling silver novelties. Eventually, they made their way upstairs and were encouraged to rest at the Vitascope spectacle.*[3] *Innes employees ran continuous shows from 2 to 6 p.m. early in the week and then until 10 p.m. as Christmas neared. Two days before Christmas, the store offered a special show free for school children. Management invited clerks from rival stores, policemen, and firemen to attend without a purchase.*[4]

The principal attraction of the Vitascope entertainment was a set of Edison films featuring the return of Admiral Dewey from the Philippines and related celebrations and parades recorded in September and October. The Dewey Parade *was advertised as offering an identical experience to that had by the millions of spectators on the streets of New York City.*[5] *To complement the program of Dewey films, the Innes store also projected a variety of short subjects—"much more diversified in character"—including* Something Good—Negro Kiss *(advertised under the title* Colored Kissing Scene*),* Pillow Fight, Boxing Scene, Bull Fight, Horse Market, Interrupted Lovers, Tickling the Old Man, *and* Fire Department on the Run.[6] *For the first half of the week, these supplementary films became the main event as the Dewey pictures didn't arrive until Thursday.*[7]

The gimmick paid off. Even before the Dewey films arrived, shoppers crowded the exhibition, with nearly 1,800 spectators attending the moving-picture show on Wednesday.[8] *And Innes continued to draw large crowds, more than making up for the cost of the Vitascope entertainment. As one local paper put it, "There is more than one way to skin a cat, and the business man who is up to date will never allow himself to be discouraged by reason of misfortunes or disasters."*[9]

It's notable that the press understood the Vitascope show in financial terms: these displays were treated as consumables within the department store's holiday scheme. The image of Black affection thus became another good on offer to shoppers. Alongside and in contrast to Interrupted Lovers *(Edison, 1896), a brief comedy in which the "wrathful father" interrupts "a pair of bucolic lovers,"* Something Good *offered uninterrupted affection for the amusement of holiday shoppers.*[10] *And not just shoppers. Innes had a number of Black employees, and it's tempting to imagine them taking pleasure in seeing Suttle and Brown's act of courtship. How did these two groups watch the film in the same space? Was the response of Black employees complicated by the fact that Innes's patrons were largely if not entirely white? How would these white audiences receive the sight of Suttle and Brown's repeated kisses? Would they be shocked at the Black couple's intimacy? Amused by the mere spectacle of blackness, so associated with comedy? Disgusted by the presentation of Black affection without comedic inflection to make it palatable to whites? Surely different viewers would have different responses, but I like imagining that the Vitascope exhibit smuggled in an image of Black joy and affection that perhaps confronted shoppers with an image of blackness distinct from the pernicious stereotypes circulating in consumer culture.*

THREE

To Take the Cake

THE RAG-TIME FOUR FROM STAGE TO SCREEN

ON THE AFTERNOON OF NEW Year's Day, 1897, Black musicians Saint Suttle and H. C. Winn had professional photographs taken at Hough & Son's photography studio in the basement of 308 State Street, Chicago. According to a story that ran the next day in *The Chicago Chronicle*, Suttle and Winn came in from the cold street, placed their instruments on a table, and proceeded to pose for a set of photographs under the studio's newly installed electric lights. The bright lights may have been a bit glaring for the musicians, possibly still a little fatigued from the previous night's gig, their New Year's Eve revelry, or both. The tabloid reported that after a short sitting, and having spent only twenty minutes on the affair, they left the studio with six tintypes in hand. They appeared satisfied with Hough's work.

According to the *Chronicle*, Suttle and Winn proceeded to show the portraits off to friends around town. This did not go well. Something in their friends' reaction—mockery instead of admiration, perhaps—led the musicians to return to Hough's studio at 10 o'clock at night to demand a refund. Finding Hough still in the gallery, they pressed the photographer: "Do you think that looks like me?" Suttle interrogated, throwing the tintypes on the counter. Hough replied, "Certainly I do!" Suttle retorted, "Well I don't! And if I don't get my money back there's going to be trouble in this place." Hough refused to acquiesce, and Suttle drew a revolver. Shocked at the sudden escalation, Hough shouted "Murder!" and the police came running. Chicago police officer Lane arrested Suttle and Winn after a struggle.[1]

We don't know how the episode was resolved, but given that Hough depended on Chicago's entertainers for business, it is quite probable that he dropped the charges quickly. As with many "official" stories, the tabloid notice reflected and fed the culture of presumptive criminality that shadowed the Black male figure in the urban sphere: Suttle and Winn are painted as irascible swells and weapon-wielding bullies. The story gives us no reliable insight into their actions or motivation, and the paper never followed up, satisfied with the pithy assessment of the article header: "Objected to the Tintypes. Colored Men in Trouble."[2] The objectionable tintypes have been lost.

The following year, while performing as a member of his vaudeville quartet the Rag-Time Four, Suttle looked again at a camera—this time, a motion-picture camera. He performed several short subjects before Selig's Polyscope, including two kiss films and two cakewalks. And this time, if he ever saw the resulting images, I like to think he would have been pleased.

These two episodes in Saint Suttle's career as an entertainer come to us in different ways: through text and image. With no picture against which to read the story in *The Chicago Chronicle*, and no other records that I have been able to glean, the only conclusion I feel confident making is that Suttle understood the importance of the photographic record and valued self-presentation, not least as a form of self-promotion. The other episode—Suttle's performances with Gertie Brown and members of the Rag-Time Four before Selig's Polyscope—comes to us as moving pictures, with no further account of the circumstances of their production. These images offer a glimpse into the care with which Black performers worked to navigate, and sometimes flout, public expectations and assumptions. As ragtime-era Black performers, the four actors recorded in Selig's studio in spring 1898 built their careers around a careful negotiation of popular racialized tropes and defiant artistic resistance. At the center of their balancing act was the cakewalk.

THE CAKEWALK: "A REMARKABLE KIND OF IRONY"

The cakewalk originated as a dance performed by enslaved people as early as 1840.[3] A form of double address, akin to spirituals' "double-voiced" subversion, the cakewalk served as a form of covert mockery of unsuspecting whites and their aspirational airs.[4] These self-styled American aristocrats imitated the European dances—waltzes, grand marches, and minuets—that carried both class and old-world sophistication. In a brilliant gesture of parody, the enslaved onlookers responded with their own iteration of these moves, "mocking the snobberies and smugisms of nineteenth-century white elites," as one writer put it.[5] Not getting that the joke was on them, the whites saw the slave dances as an amusement, at once pathetic and entertaining. As befitting the ethos of capitalist- and white supremacist-driven enterprises, they turned it into a competition. As Estella Jones, formerly enslaved in Georgia, recalled to a Works Progress Administration researcher, "De couple dat danced best got a prize. Sometimes de slave owners came to dese parties 'cause dey enjoyed watchin' de dance, and dey 'cided who danced de best."[6] During celebrations on plantations, Black dancers would compete for "cakes" made of ground cornmeal baked in ashes, hence the name "cakewalk."[7]

Accounts of formerly enslaved people attest to the subversive origins of the cakewalk. Musician and composer Shepard N. Edmonds, born in Tennessee in about 1870 to formerly enslaved parents, told jazz critic Rudi Blesh, "The slaves both young and old would dress up in hand-me-down finery to do a high-kicking, prancing walk-around. They did a take-off on the high manners of the white folks in the 'big house,' but their masters, who gathered around to watch the fun, missed the point. It's supposed to be that the custom of a prize started with the master giving a cake to the couple that did the proudest movement."[8] Similarly, actor Leigh Whipper, talking to jazz scholar Marshall Stearns in 1960, remembered a story told to him in 1901 by his former nurse when she was more than seventy. She attributed her good health, he recalled, to her skills as a dancer in her youth in the 1840s; this skill spared her hard work in the field, because she was frequently entered in dance contests by the white owners. Whipple recounted what the nurse told him: "Us slaves watched white folks' parties where the guests danced a minuet and then paraded in a grand march, with the ladies and gentlemen going different ways and then meeting again, arm in arm, and marching down the center together. Then we'd do it, too, *but we used to mock 'em*, every step. Sometimes the white folks noticed it, but they seemed to like it; I guess they thought we couldn't dance any better."[9] As Stearns notes of this use of satire, "The Negro was frequently embroidering upon the mask of what was expected—making oblique fun of white folks. It was both satisfying and stimulating, since it was risky, and at the same time, called for subtle improvisations."[10]

After Emancipation, as dance historian Megan Pugh has traced, the cakewalk traveled north to urban areas, where the performative acrobatics of the dance's stunts found a stage, first in restaurants and ersatz venues like streets, barns, and recreational halls, and eventually in the popular theater.[11] Along with the trajectory of minstrelsy, the cakewalk was reconfigured as a form of blackface entertainment performed by white musicians and dancers. It later developed into a crowd-pleasing component of minstrel shows and as a trendy stand-alone spectacle, featuring in popular entertainments for nearly a quarter century before it became a ubiquitous national and international fad in the 1890s.[12] This fad—or "epidemic," as it was described in *The Los Angeles Times* in 1898—defined popular culture's qualified embrace of perceived Black expressivity at the turn of the century.[13] The cakewalk's subversive riskiness carried through Black performances of the dance, while white performers played with a politically neutered form of racist simulacrum.

While never completely segregated in terms of influence, the dance's significations initially developed in tandem among white and Black dancers. Soon, however, the lines of satire, masquerade, imitation, and mockery moved in a multidirectional muddle. As the dance entered broader popular culture, it could claim no racial authenticity other than the very interracial imbrication of antebellum cultural exchange under the overarching condition of antiblackness. In his 1963 *Blues People: Negro Music in White America*, Amiri Baraka commented parenthetically on minstrelsy's introduction of new dances to a mass audience and the cakewalk's popularity: "If the cakewalk is a Negro dance caricaturing certain white customs, what is that dance when, say, a white theater company attempts to satirize it as a Negro dance? I find the idea of white minstrels in blackface satirizing a dance satirizing themselves a remarkable kind of irony—which, I suppose, is the whole point of minstrel shows."[14]

When Black cakewalkers performed, they carried onto the stage the interracially entwined history of the dance's genealogy as backdrop to its contemporary craze. They also negotiated claims to authenticity (in contrast to white performers) and studied expertise (in their role as professionals). The dance's structure, with solos punctuating the group dance, allowed them to showcase their individual talents and personae while combining forces in synchronized movements. For white audiences watching Black cakewalkers, however, insidious presumptions of innate racial expression tended to eclipse their awareness of practice, talent, and professionalism. As performance scholar Daphne Brooks has traced with Bert Williams and George Walker in Britain, critics saw the cakewalk as "the natural expression of a racial instinct" rather than the result of the professional labor of training and practice, never mind the dance's subversive associations.[15] This seemingly incommensurate concurrence of "essentialist racial categories and the constructedness of such roles," in Brooks's terms, forms the unstable foundation on which minstrelsy was erected.[16] The cakewalk, then, staged the negotiation of racial performativity and the performance of minstrelized blackness by both white and Black performers. In blackface makeup or not, the blackness associated with the cakewalk was an act. With the cakewalk, race and class trotted down the promenade lines, swapped partners, and vied for audience approval.

The vogue for the cakewalk in the 1890s coincided with its reinvention by Black performers. The success of Black superstars Williams and Walker made the cakewalk a sensation in white upper-class American society and in Europe. The famed duo even challenged amateur society cakewalk champion William K. Vanderbilt to a contest.[17] The cakewalk was in such demand that Williams and Walker were compelled to add it to performances of *In Dahomey* in their 1903 British tour at the behest of the royal audience.[18]

The cakewalk was, confusingly, simultaneously a nostalgic throwback *and* a display of Black theatrical modernity. As Pugh notes, "Its syncopated music, strutting steps, and improvised solos made it distinctly modern."[19] Yet cakewalk performances in the years of its popularity often were presented as competitions that echoed the dance's origins on plantations. The terms of performance had shifted, however, and these competitions were now serious business. Performing for crowds of thousands, winners received not only a cake—three-feet tall and "iced like the Chilkoot Pass"—but also pricier items, including, in some cases, a gold watch and an upright piano.[20]

The Chicago Tribune offered a rich description of a typical 1892 competition. Like others, the competition began with a display of "plain and ornamental walking," followed by character walks known as "gallus," which included "everything in the gamut of steps, from the 'spirit slide' to the 'buzzard lope,'" in which the antics and the "individuality of the walker" were on display.[21] Each performer strived for originality: the more outrageous, the more memorable for the audiences (and the judges). One dancer's moves were likened to "that of a turkey running from a Thanksgiving executioner."[22] Competitors adorned themselves with elaborate costumes and preposterous accessories, such as exaggerated boutonnieres and corsages, enlarged hats, and canes. Costumes transformed into props as the dancers twirled their canes and raised their comically large top hats. For the finale, after marching in pairs, the women and men did solo turns before reuniting with their partners to march down in a single line in one last appeal to the judges.

Saint Suttle and John Brewer crossed paths at cakewalk competitions, with Suttle besting his soon-to-be partner on several occasions.[23] Before some competitions, the crowd would be entertained with a vaudeville show, acrobats, buck dancing (a form of percussive clogging), and popular songs. At one event, a competition at Bailey's Opera house in Evanston, Illinois, Suttle warmed up the crowd with "comical singing," demonstrating his versatility in advance of the competition and setting the tone for the irreverent display of the cakewalk.[24]

The audiences for these competitions consisted primarily of members of white "society," though attending such events meant skirting the limits of respectability. As one newspaper reported, "It was a curious sight to see some of the well-known society folks trying to leave the opera-house so their friends would not see them." The crowd was especially surprised at the attendance of three prominent white pastors, who "left their serious desks and watched the colored folks do their best at walking and bowing. Some people were a bit surprised at the sight of the three ministers, and expressed their horror by much whispering and nodding of heads."[25]

While Evanston's white society folks sheepishly—yet eagerly—sought out Black entertainment, a movement was afoot in the Black community to protest the dance. The Rev. S. A. Hardison, prominent pastor of Evanston's African Methodist Episcopal church, strongly—and publicly—objected to the cakewalk competition, dissuading parishioners and respectable Black folks from attending.[26] The very irreverence and insouciance that champion cakewalkers were known for was, to Black elites, degrading. And, when performed in front of white spectators and so-called judges, the cakewalk was denounced as humiliatingly damaging to the uplift of the race.

Cakewalks may have been amusing, but according to many race leaders, the ridicule was dangerous. An editorial in a Black newspaper excoriated churches who held cakewalks as fundraisers:

> And what is a "cake walk"? Yes, what is it? The "cake walk" of our time is not a "cake walk" at all, but a "cake dance," and one of a very low grade at that. In these parts it is not even a respectable dance. It is a performance, dignified by the name of "cake walk," filled with vulgar motions and evil suggestions, which cannot be otherwise than demoralizing. If there are actors who will not permit their children to attend the theatre, because of its evil influences, how should Christian parents feel about their children attending a church or other entertainment, where they are to witness the modern "cake walk?"[27]

Detractors tried to unmask what they saw as the profane character of the cakewalk under its seemingly benign name. Its popularity was confirmation of its menace. The cakewalk's association with ragtime also raised concerns over the perceived infectiousness of syncopated jazz, fueling concern over the uncontrollable spread of the craze.

The risk of ridicule was most acute in front of interracial—or predominantly white—audiences. Speaking about a 1897 cakewalk competition in New York's Madison Square Garden attended by an interracial audience, celebrated African American poet Paul Laurence Dunbar lamented that the crowd did not comprise "the best colored people" and "the audience and performers looked like a human crazy quilt, the audience not more than the performers," suggesting attendees were as garishly attired as the dancers.[28] In addition to the class of spectators, Dunbar critiqued the "barrenness of vulgar inanity that characterized most of the so-called negro exhibition."[29] Recognizing the antebellum origins of the cakewalk, Dunbar posits the current version as degraded, "exaggerated and magnified by the glasses of the present."[30] Despite these objections, some Black leaders viewed the immense popularity of the cakewalk and Black theatrical comedy as an opportunity for the advancement of the race. Both Booker T. Washington and W.E.B. Du Bois, for example, publicly expressed admiration for the performances of Bert Williams and George Walker.

For working performers, critiques of race leaders, tinged with class-based scorn for popular audiences, were of little concern. Given the popularity of the cakewalk, it's unlikely that many Black performers were too preoccupied with these debates. Their bread was buttered on the popular stage, and their performance personae hinged on class-based lampoons. Besides, controversies over the cakewalk were good publicity, and the Rag-Time Four—like many contemporaneous performers—milked its notoriety while developing their own version of the dance.

Suttle's songs capitalized on this notoriety. Performed before the competition began, his songs would have been drawn from the standard "coon song" repertoire popular at the time, to which he, as a composer, contributed. His own creations play with the tensions surrounding respectability, perception, and self-representation. For example, Suttle's "That Creole Gal of Mine" recounts an anticipated wedding between the singer and "an angel just from heaven." With verses tenderly celebrating the impending nuptials with pride, the refrain veers to comedy:

> For her name is El-u-e-za Lu-za-e-za Hen-ri-et-ta Cyn-thi-an-a Brown,
> She's a mem-ber of the Blue Vein So-ci-e-ty, And one of the most re-nown.
> The dudes o-ver her are daf-fy Be-cause she is di-vine,
> But I've got the best of all the coons
> With that creole gal of mine.

The joke rests entirely on the ridiculous name of the "Blue Veined" bride and might also be made at the expense of Gertie Brown, also known as the "Creole gal," but whose given Louisiana name was Gilberta Gertrude Chevalier. Keeping "Brown"—a name with excellent rhyming potential—Suttle connects Gertie's stage name to her birthname, gently teasing his partner. Brown's face appears to be collaged onto the sheet music (see Figure 18).

Suttle's songs about the cakewalk also stage tensions surrounding respectability. For example, in "Old Jasper's Cakewalk" (copyright 1899), Suttle sings of a "swell affair" held by "Jasper Johnson," where "coons of all descriptions at this demonstration, / They had to look the part of millionaires." The song is replete with Suttle's familiar repertoire of fashionable swells but also includes the epithet "nigger" and tropes of chicken and liquor. The refrain, though, posits the degrading term as a counterpoint to the stated elegance of the affair: "Oh swing around, my lady, an' look me in the face, / For we are here this evening to represent the colored race; / You are a red hot member, an' that's no nigger talk, / We are sure to be the winners at Old Jasper's cake walk." As in "The Present Century Coon," Suttle presents himself as representative of his fellow dandies, in contradistinction to the lowbrow figures against which the dandy is posited ("that's no nigger talk"). If Suttle represented Black men in the urban North, per "The Present Century Coon," and the "colored race," in general, per "Old Jasper's Cakewalk," these associations were ones in which he embodied the contradictory representational tendencies of turn-of-the-century Black minstrelsy.

When Suttle, Brewer, Gertie Brown, and Maud Brown began working together in spring 1898, it made sense for them to capitalize on the cakewalk fad. Indeed, partnering as dancers, the four seasoned performers built their act around an original interpretation of the cakewalk. All could sing and dance, but they came from varied backgrounds, and each brought distinct skills to the quartet: Suttle was also a composer, John Brewer a leading comedian, Maud Brown a "Samoan" belle, and the young Gertie Brown a "creole" ingenue. Theaters promoted them as a "Southern" quartet, a common euphemism for Black performers, yet they were actually urbane Chicagoans with southern—and in the case of Maud, Hawaiian—roots.

In May 1898, the four performers visited Milwaukee to participate in a celebration of the thirty-second anniversary of the Emancipation Proclamation, held at the Lyceum Theatre as a benefit for a local Black church, Salem Baptist, that had fallen into debt. For that performance,

Brewer served as stage manager and Suttle as assistant stage manager, with Maud Brown as costumer. The large spectacle "took the shape of a real 'before-the-war' Southern plantation scene and cake-walk" and featured more than a hundred performers managed and directed by Black Chicago impresario Louis Young.[31]

Presumably a celebration of the end of the war and the abolition of the institution of slavery, the program was characterized by nostalgia for an imagined antebellum pastoral combined with contemporary popular music and dance. In the first part of the program, current "up to date" coon songs were intermingled with Stephen Foster minstrel standards like "Old Folks at Home" (1851)—better known as "Swanee River"—sung by Gertie Brown, and spirituals like "Poor Mourner." The second part of the program included "levee scenes," buck dancing, sketches, songs, and other "specialty work."[32] In addition to performing in the first two acts, the foursome almost certainly participated in the cakewalk dance in the program's third part, described, variously, as an exhibition of "the fashionable colored man's society" in which eight couples delivered an "excellently rendered" performance of a "genuine darkey cake-walk."[33] A loose historical thread may have driven the program, but the event's assertions of Black progress, as presumed by the celebration's premise, relied on tropes of performative blackness. Suttle, Brewer, Gertie Brown, and Maud Brown specialized in race as spectacle as they adeptly toggled antebellum minstrel songs and popular ragtime.

Sometime shortly after the Emancipation Proclamation celebration, the quartet formed a new act they called the Rag-Time Four. Before long, in spring 1898, they visited Selig's Peck Court studio and shook their dusters for the Polyscope.

CAKE WALK (WILLIAM SELIG, 1898)

Likely on the same occasion as their recording of *Something Good—Negro Kiss*, Suttle and Brown were accompanied by John Brewer and Maud Brown. Selig (or his agents) probably encountered the troupe at a vaudeville theater or an ephemeral outdoor show—or, as Suttle lived in the same neighborhood as Selig's studio, the men may have been acquaintances from the Levee District. Whatever instigated the studio visit, it was undoubtedly motivated by the popularity of Black performance and Selig's wager that it would translate into marketable motion pictures.

Probably unaccompanied by music, given the pace of motion-picture production, the Rag-Time Four danced a modified version of the cakewalk at Selig's studio, resulting in two fifty-foot films, each about thirty seconds long. The first version survives as a fragment of eight seconds discovered on a mixed reel of nitrate films deposited at the Library of Congress. The second version was deposited at the George Eastman Museum in Rochester, New York, in 2023, also on a mixed reel of films, and quickly identified thanks to the publicity around *Something Good*'s naming to the National Film Registry.

The fragment discovered at the Library of Congress begins with John and Maud Brewer on the sides of the frame, and Suttle and Brown at the center. The Brewers dance toward each other, John raising his hat to Maud; they then shuffle back and forth, mirroring each other in unison, before bowing to the camera. A splice marks missing footage, and the print picks up with Brown and Suttle in the foreground, Suttle facing the camera and Brown facing the Brewers in the background, dancing back to their starting positions.

The fragment provides some clues to the production process and the set. The wainscoting and detailed wall paneling suggest an interior space, but this is likely Selig's outdoor set given that the film is shot in natural light, with relatively short shadows indicating late morning or early afternoon. This is a different background than Selig used for *Something Good*; rather than a casually hung canvas backdrop, there is a Victorian curtain with knotted fringed tassels across the lambrequin and bottom edge, barely dusting the floor. The rug over the wood floor is also different than the striped rug visible in the Leksvik version of *Something Good*. The Rag-Time Four perform their dance across an oriental rug, laid against the rear curtain, allowing for a significant amount of exposed wood floor space on the stage. Indeed, two distinct chalk lines are visible on the wood floor in the foreground, serving as blocking marks for the performers, demarcating the space within the camera's viewfinder. With this mise-en-scène, Selig gestures to vaudeville staging while emphasizing the intimacy of a private, salon-like presentation.

Unlike the dancers in other surviving cakewalk films, the Rag-Time Four performers seem distinctly "off duty" when they aren't dancing, almost as if they were offstage. Brown holds her hands at her hips while Suttle fidgets with his comically oversized prop cane, and neither smile nor even seem aware of the camera. Similarly, in the few frames that show Suttle and Brown in the foreground, the Brewers don't smile. This may stem from an unfamiliarity with motion pictures, and specifically with the depth of action that the

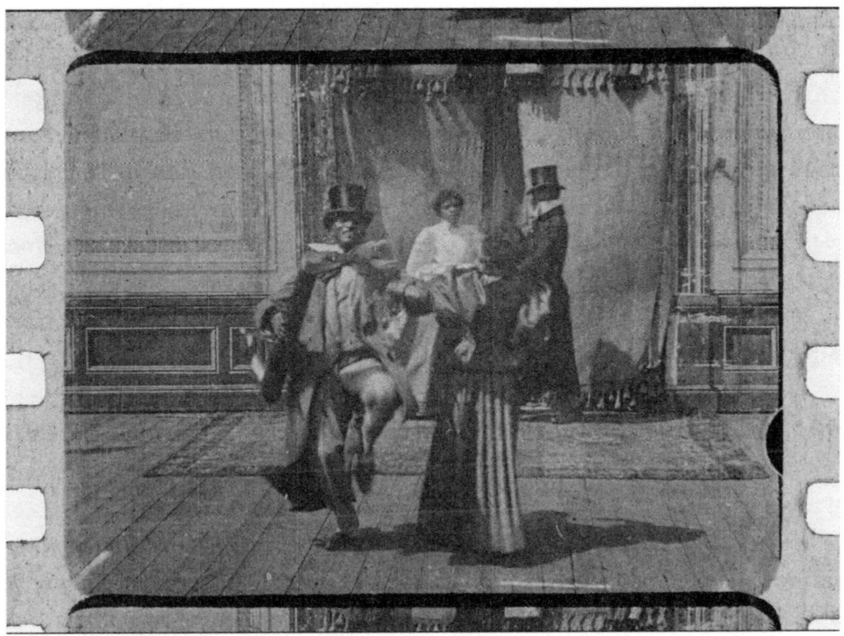

FIGURE 20. *Cake Walk* (Selig, 1898). Saint Suttle and Gertie Brown in the foreground, Maud Brown and John Brewer in the background. Frame enlargement courtesy of the Library of Congress.

camera could capture: the dancers might have considered their upstage actions as practically offstage. Or perhaps the film captured their act as it appeared in vaudeville, where the performers' casualness might evoke a social dance atmosphere, killing time before it was their turn to be showmen, suggesting easy authenticity along with professional bravura.

While in the background, however, each pair does move in a curious way. They seem to adjust their positions, moving more to the right, perhaps to the center of where the foreground dancers are. This could be in response to direction from the camera operator to keep them visible or to ensure that the foreground figures are most effectively highlighted against the staged background. Whatever the case, there is strong evidence to suggest the Rag-Time Four's filmic appearance echoed their theatrical presence. And while the audience for movies largely overlapped with those of the popular stage and seasonal fairs where the Rag-Time Four performed, a single film could travel much more widely than its performers, helping spread the "epidemic" of the dance.

Selig's catalogs advertised *Cake Walk* as being "well executed by people who have a reputation in this line," referring to their status as professional minstrels and vaudeville performers.[34] But his description also reinscribed the presumption of innate Black dancing ability: "This film is one of the finest of its kind, portraying a number of swell darkies engaged in the popular past time of walking for the cake." The relative shortness of the film, compared to the stage performance, may have made it easier for audiences to believe in this conflation of performance and authenticity, to have their own biases strengthened. In other words, *Cake Walk* enacts the tension between minstrelsy as presumed authentic cultural expression and as entirely constructed by the white imaginary and then reimagined—ironically and subversively—by Black performers.

THE RAG-TIME FOUR IN VAUDEVILLE: THE "BLACKVILLE TWINS" AND "THEIR BEST GIRLS"

The Rag-Time Four debuted in vaudeville at the Alhambra Theater in Milwaukee the week of October 23, 1898, and were proclaimed "a tremendous hit" by the local Black newspaper.[35] From October to December of that year the quartet performed at various popular vaudeville houses in Chicago, Milwaukee, and Duluth, and likely smaller venues in between.[36] Suttle and John Brewer were billed as "The 'Blackville' Twins" and their partners as "Their 'Best Girls'" in an act that consisted of coon songs, dancing, and a cakewalk.[37] They shared billing with jugglers, acrobats, illusionists, ventriloquists, pantomimists, juvenile comedians, and dogs and cats, as well as musicians, dancers, singers, storytellers, impersonators, comics, and equilibrists (including a combination wire performer and expert rifle shot). On the vaudeville variety stage, race became a novelty akin to circus stunts at the same time it was a celebrated talent like practiced skills. Like wire acrobats, Black vaudevillians walked a tenuous line between curiosity and ability.

The Rag-Time Four were seasoned performers and knew how to appeal to vaudeville audiences. Suttle's compositions, sung by the quartet, display a keen awareness of performance expectations. For example, on this tour Suttle introduced his song "The Present Century Coon," which I discussed in the previous chapter as a counterpoint to May Irwin's "Bully" song. Likely led by Suttle as the "Black Millionaire," "The Present Century Coon" is a song about shaping public perceptions through self-fashioning. "Dressed in the latest style," the singer presents himself as "the fashion plate of the day."

Songs like "The Present Century Coon" amplified intra-racial, classist, colorist views onto the popular stage with the "little octoroon" portrayed as the epitome of desire for the "lord of all the coons." Performed by Black singers, however, such songs risked purporting to offer insight into Black sociality. Whereas white interpreters of coon songs traded on the humor of the racial masquerade, Black performers were seen, in the words Williams and Walker used to market themselves, as "real coons."

This dynamic played out in the Rag-Time Four's first week at the Olympic, a theater in Chicago's Loop offering continuous vaudeville, as they shared a bill with Flo Irwin, sister of May and likewise a well-known white coon shouter. The previous year she had appeared in Chicago in *The Widow Jones*, playing the role made famous by her sister.[38] The quartet must have felt that their star was on the rise sharing a bill with an Irwin sister, and the connection to *The Kiss* (would they have confessed their parody to Flo?) may have seemed a sign of good fortune. It may have also underscored to them the peculiar phenomenon of Black performativity in vaudeville, whether enacted by white or Black performers.

But it was also a familiar position. On the vaudeville stage, the Rag-Time Four were frequently the only Black performers on a bill, though they were not the only interpreters of coon songs. At Chicago's Haymarket Theatre in December, they performed immediately after Belle Wilton, a white singer of "character songs and coon ditties."[39] As with their recorded acts projected in the context of a variety program of short films, their act on stage was in unavoidable dialogue with what it followed and preceded. When Irwin and Wilton and other white clowns of racialized humor enacted their schtick on the same stage as the Rag-Time Four's more refined coon songs, the Rag-Time Four could be viewed within the same frame. But they also had the potential to subvert—and redirect—the humor presumed by the white minstrel's imagined notion of blackness.

Even during their time on stage, the Rag-Time Four's songs seem to have subverted minstrel tropes, albeit subtly. At the Olympic, they introduced another Suttle composition, "The Black American Girl."[40] I have yet to find the sheet music, but it was reportedly published by Rohlfing & Sons of Milwaukee.[41] German immigrants, the Rohlfings were a major publisher of European classical sheet music and served as the Milwaukee agent for the famed piano company Steinway & Sons.[42] They signified the big time in music publishing, though they focused less on coon songs than on sentimental ballads and classical music. For Suttle to be published by the Rohlfings indicates, perhaps, their desire to expand their "saloon" music list to include popular ragtime. But what about Suttle? Was it just about pay and publicity? Did he aspire to expand his composition repertoire from coon songs to other forms? Certainly, the title—"The Black American Girl"—makes a stark departure from coon songs in which the term "Black" rarely features. The title lays claim to the nation, suggesting a far wider scope than his locally focused coon songs. Rohlfing announced the song, which was sung onstage by Gertie and Maud, as "the first song of its kind that has ever been presented to the public." Then again, Rohlfing also called it "the first coon soubrette song ever written," so perhaps the song was not such a break in the ragtime repertoire.[43] With the sheet music lost, the nature of the composition remains a mystery. In any case, sung from a female perspective, it marks an intriguing departure in Suttle's known repertoire.

Only one song survives that is directly attributed to Brewer and Suttle's Rag-Time Four: "Shake Yo' Dusters, or Piccaninny Rag," written by white Chicago bandleader William Henry Krell—one of the first ragtime composers—and copyrighted June 1, 1898.[44] Typical of contemporary coon songs, the lyrics are in dialect, replete with familiar minstrel tropes, though sung from the perspective of a mother, praising the dancing skills of her little boy. Despite the abundance of racist language and likely infantilization of Brewer and Suttle, the song depicts the singer's affection and pride, as in the refrain's conclusion, "I feels mighty proud, en' ma heart does beat, When dat pic-ca-nin-ny shake his feet!" We can imagine how the Rag-Time Four staged this song: perhaps Maud Brewer and Gertie Brown sang while Saint Suttle and John Brewer danced; perhaps the group burlesqued the song and the men sang as the mammy and the women danced as mammy's boy; or perhaps they performed the two-step all together, all sang, or danced with no lyrics. One Duluth newspaper reported, "the famous Southern quartet" delivered their act "in talking manner all the latest negro medleys and coon songs," though just what that means is hard to parse.[45] More ephemeral than 120-year-old nitrate, these aspects of their performance routine are probably irrecoverable.

What is clear, however, is that the cakewalk figured prominently in their act. We get a sense of the significance of the cakewalk from Suttle's own compositions. For example, "Old Jasper's Cake Walk," mentioned above, is about a cakewalk competition—"a swell affair"—thrown by Jasper Johnson in "Darktown." Like most coon songs of the period, it too leans on stereotypes and familiar tropes ("Chicken, gin and wine was flyin'") and does not eschew offensive epithets (Suttle rhymes "mister Nigger" with "cut the figger"). But like "Present Century Coon," the song centers on a concern for representation and expertise. The competition recounted in the song relies on originality and impersonation:

> Each individual thought that he would win it,
> But Bill Taylor, with his forty movement way,
> Said, "I'm the originator an' you all are imitators!"

When the Rag-Time Four sings "we are here this evening to represent the colored race" in the context of the cakewalk, they are asserting mastery over white cakewalkers. Authenticity over imitation.

The timing was ideal for the Rag-Time Four. The year 1898, when the quartet was most active, was an auspicious one for Black musical theater and dance, as it saw the inauguration of Black-authored and -performed Broadway spectacles with the premiere of *Clorindy, or the Origin of the Cake Walk* in New York City on July 5. Composed by Will Marion Cook and written by poet Paul Laurence Dunbar, *Clorindy* brought the cakewalk fad to Broadway and reclaimed it as part of the Black popular performance repertoire.[46] *Clorindy* starred famed minstrel performer Ernest Hogan, considered one of the fathers of ragtime, whose 1896 epoch-defining hit with a pernicious title—"All Coons Look Alike to Me"—helped ignite ragtime's popularity. The cakewalk was the feature of the finale, "Der'll be Wahm Coons a Prancin'." As Cook recalled, "The Darktown finale was of complicated rhythm and bold harmonies, and very taxing on the voice. My chorus sang like Russians, dancing meanwhile like Negroes, and cakewalking like angels, black angels!"[47] Syncopated rhythms performed by Black musicians were a novelty on Broadway, if they were no longer a novelty on the vaudeville stage. The success of *Clorindy* in New York nonetheless lent it an aura of importance when it came to Chicago, in November 1898.

Advertised as the "stellar event of the season," *Clorindy* was billed in Chicago as "The original rag time operatic novelty, introduced by 35 graceful and musical artists, with new songs, darkyisms, and dances."[48] As the *Chicago Daily Tribune* reported, "One of the most attractive features of the production is its negro melodies, while the 'coon' dancing and cake walking surpass anything done in Chicago for some time."[49] Also in Chicago at the time were the Black Patti Troubadours, led by Madame Sissieretta Jones.[50] The success of *Clorindy* and Black Patti fueled the fad for the cakewalk and Black musical theater, surely benefiting the Rag-Time Four as they developed their talking "cake dance."

The quartet rode the cakewalk wave at its crest, even as Chicago's theaters were crowded with the Black Patti Troubadours and the *Clorindy* troupe competing for audiences. While the Rag-Time Four held its own in a competitive market, as winter approached, John Brewer and Maud Brown calculated that their fortunes—personal and professional—lay elsewhere.

Performing the part of sweethearts every night was hardly acting for John and Maud. The Browns' courtship blossomed that autumn, perhaps propelled by the nightly repetition of intimacy, humor, and the grace of dance. Their magnetism onstage must have strengthened as they fell in love. On November 26, 1898, while performing in the Rag-Time Four's final week at Chicago's Haymarket Theatre, John and Maud received their marriage license from the Cook County Clerk. Just after their last show, on December 15, they were married.[51]

In the new year, the two halves of the quartet parted ways. The members of the Rag-Time Four would perform together on occasion, but as an act they went on indefinite hiatus. Yet while their act might have been short-lived, lasting under a year, their nitrate doppelgängers continued to cakewalk across screens for the following decade before lying dormant until their rediscovery more than a century later.

JOHN AND MAUD BREWER DOWN UNDER

John and Maud Brewer probably felt quite fortunate. Vaudeville afforded them relatively steady employment and the opportunity to hone their craft. The stage could be a brutal workplace, but there were certainly worse ways to make a living, as the disapproval of the occasional unappreciative audience beat laboring at backbreaking jobs or scrubbing floors. John and Maud persevered through weak casts, uneven programs, and fickle audiences. If not exactly stars, they were bona fide professionals. In an unstable career at a tumultuous time, they had paychecks they could more or less count on. And in a business teeming with hustlers and charlatans, John and Maud had found each other. Less than a month into their marriage, the Brewers embarked on the opportunity of a lifetime: an overseas tour.

Touring Australia, New Zealand, and the South Pacific must have been like a working honeymoon. Despite the hardships of nineteenth-century travel, the promise of other shores—and stages—beckoned, especially when

Jim Crow segregation, low wages, unscrupulous theater managers, and deplorable stage conditions—when they were lucky enough to have a stage, not dirt, beneath their feet—marred the comforts of working on the domestic vaudeville circuit. Overseas, Black performers could be stars, or at least wear the costume of stardom for a little while.

The newlywed Brewers joined Orpheus M. McAdoo's Georgia Minstrels and Alabama Cake Walkers on their tour of Australia. Celebrated Black impresario McAdoo had managed a troupe of Jubilee Singers for several seasons in Australasia and returned in 1898 with the addition of a vaudeville company. The Brewers were part of this second group, joining the show in the new year. McAdoo combined the acts into a program opening with jubilee songs and choruses with solos, followed by secular songs constituting the second half of the show.[52] The Brewers appeared in the second half, and their portion of the act included comedy sketches "introducing some clever dancing."[53] The motivation for the sketches seems to have been to establish a premise "to delight the audience with buck and wing dancing."[54] John also played alto saxophone in the orchestra.[55] The tour allowed the Brewers to expand their repertoire, show off their skills, and experiment with new acts.

McAdoo made several additions to the company after trips back to the US to recruit talent and opened as McAdoo's Georgia Minstrels and Alabama Cake Walkers in June 1899 in Sydney.[56] The addition of "cakewalkers" in the tour name was, as Bill Egan suggests, a marketing strategy to exploit the current American craze for the cakewalk promoted most notably by Aida Overton Walker, George Walker, and Bert Williams.[57]

The marketing paid off. As a member of the troupe wrote to the African American theater community via the Black press from Sydney, "Our show, O. M. McAdoo's Georgia minstrels, has been going a week at this writing. We arrived Saturday, June 10, and opened Saturday, June 17. . . . The theater was jammed when we opened and I suspect it will be that way at least two months. Mr. McAdoo has a great reputation in this country; he is talked about among all classes, the people over here talk of him just as we do of Fred. Douglass in the States. So, you see our popularity and success are assured."[58] One Australian newspaper reported that the cakewalk was the most "novel" part of the show as a "relic of the days of negro slavery."[59]

Most of the performers enjoyed working Down Under: even when confronted with degrees of prejudice and ignorance, it was nothing compared to the systemic and relentless racism they endured at home.[60] They also encountered less professional competition and could capitalize on the novelty of their foreignness.

Beyond the pay and acclaim, a tour abroad lent shine to aspiring stars. Upon returning stateside, actors could point to a high-profile tour to boost their profile as *international* phenomena. They could also reinvent themselves more broadly. When the Brewers returned from six months in Australasia, they seem to have tactically emphasized some aspects of their backgrounds over others. Maud began to promote herself as "the Samoan Girl."[61] It's possible her parents were Samoan, or she may have adopted the heritage for performance reasons, evoking the allure of Polynesian exotic sex appeal for a white audience. It's not clear if John did the same, and we have no idea how such allusions may have inflected their performance. But vague exoticism functioned like a costume, and insofar as it distinguished them from Black Americans, it could also serve as armor against Jim Crow.

John and Maud had booked their next tour through the Western US while they were still in Australia, so theater proprietors sometimes presumed the troupe to be Australian. Arriving in St. Paul, Minnesota, the Olympia Theater's Italian manager and German proprietor confronted the pair. "I thought you all were foreigners!" They were expecting Australians, but John and Maud looked Black to them. John spoke "plainly," according to his own account, and replied that they were from Australia.[62] His American English belied his ruse. The management eyed the troupe suspiciously. "Nah, you're regular American Negroes!" Despite John's insistence that they had indeed come from Australia, the Olympia refused to honor their contract and they lost two weeks. Minnesota laws allowed the performers to collect one week's salary, but beyond that, they had little recourse.[63] Blackness had been a celebrated novelty in Australian theaters, but back in America, it licensed white disrespect.

To be sure, the hostile reception the Brewers encountered at the Olympia was not typical of all white-owned theaters, many of which eagerly solicited Black acts. And the story may have been inflected by John's own humor: he reported it to the *Freeman*, an African American newspaper with a large theatrical following. For audiences already attuned to the racial imitation and subversion in the cakewalk's history, John's claim to be coming from Australia—a fact of itinerary if not birth—would have landed as another joke. Either way, the Brewers, like other Black performers, were authentically enacting racial masquerade.

Touring as a woman was risky business. If you weren't careful, you might be left behind at a far-flung port or rail station, unable to get home or move along with the troupe. The stage columns of newspapers were peppered with notes about "lady members" of various companies remaining in towns along the circuit.[64] Everyone knew what that meant: a performer was pregnant, and it likely had been unplanned and unexpected. Costumes wouldn't fasten, dance steps were too slow, downcast eyes were evasive. Whispers preceded open acknowledgment, and it was probably better for pregnant women to wait it out far from work or home and hope the episode would be forgotten before next season.

John and Maud Brewer had been touring the South Pacific successfully for six months, with stops in Honolulu, Samoa, New Zealand, and Australia, when John wrote back to the Stage column of the Indianapolis *Freeman* with the news that two women on the tour, including Maud, had "lost their health, so I am to see them home."[65] At least Maud wasn't alone; she had a traveling companion and her husband alongside her. They returned to the US in November 1899, and Maud and John parted ways with their unnamed and presumably unpartnered female colleague. Four months later, in March 1900, just a few months before John presented himself as Australian in Minnesota, the couple welcomed a baby girl.[66]

The Brewers settled in Pueblo, Colorado, in early 1900. They had done well on the tour, even if it was cut short, and despite being occasionally stiffed for pay by unscrupulous theater managers, they could afford to rent a sizable house and sublet several rooms. The mountains weren't like Chicago; here the Brewers could be heads of a household in a nice neighborhood with white lodgers—respectable folks even—a carpenter from New York and a German baker and his family.[67] Together, the strangers made up what I like to imagine as a motley but friendly home.

It's not clear why the Brewers remained in Pueblo. It's likely that they were performing with a minstrel troupe at a local theater for that season, or perhaps Maud needed to convalesce before returning to the stage. Pueblo would have felt like a frontier town, like John's native Texas, and the familiarity might have been comforting. It would be a nice place to raise a family. But by June 1900 when the census man came to the Brewers' home, he only counted the pair and their lodgers. The baby that had been born in March was gone.

Perhaps the baby was adopted or given to a family member for care, but it's likely that the baby did not survive infancy.[68] If the child died, I'd like to think the carpenter crafted a small but tasteful coffin and the baker supplied them with free loaves while his wife hushed her children playing in the yard. But such compassionate gestures are a fantasy that disavows the harsh realities the Brewers certainly faced. This imagined domestic scene says more about my desire to comfort Maud—mother to mother, even across more than a century—than it does about her actual experience or about the culture of boardinghouses in frontier towns. This image of interracial domestic harmony is a projection of my own wishes for the dynamics of the Brewer household. As the child's disappearance from the archive suggests, the Brewers enjoyed a fragile domesticity at best.

Life and livelihood in a traveling minstrel troupe were precarious, especially for Black performers who were cheered on-stage and shunned—or worse—offstage. The work and the stress of travel would have been taxing on Maud's pregnancy. And yet she survived, even if her daughter did not.

Maud's ordeal has weighed on me. Even knowing that infant mortality in 1900 was all too common, I have continued to search for any sign of the Brewers' baby, for a life lived out of childhood. The census tells me nothing about her. What I know—but what the Brewers couldn't know—is that this baby would be their last. I also know how little has changed, for as I was searching for evidence of the infant Brewer's survival, the scandal of vastly disparate maternal health outcomes for Black women in our time, two decades into the twenty-first century, came to broad public attention. In the United States, Black women are three times more likely to die from a pregnancy-related cause than white women.[69] Cuts to public health programs, especially targeting nonwhites, and attacks on reproductive justice efforts threaten to return us to a precarious era for physical health. At the turn of the twentieth century, infant mortality was high, especially for the working poor, immigrants, and Black citizens: twice that of white babies. Today, the ratio is nearly the same.[70] The legacy of infant mortality and poor maternal health outcomes among Black women today trace a direct line from nineteenth-century attitudes about childbirth. History is never relegated to the past and, in the case of white supremacy, continues to threaten Black lives.

. . .

Historical inheritances come to us in many ways. Systemic racism bequeaths a heavy legacy of ongoing harms, from attacks on public health to historical elision and erasure. We access the artistry of the Rag-Time Four through a vexed web of fragments of word and image. Disparate pieces aggregate to form a composite picture of lives lived on and off the stage, and of the unseen forces that defined their world and circumscribed their ambitions.

Recall the episode that opened this chapter, with Suttle's rejection of the tintypes and his subsequent arrest for allegedly threatening the photographer with a weapon. The fight over the tintypes unfolded in an environment in which performance and representation—especially for African Americans—had high stakes. The tabloid column describing the incident portrays Suttle, in effect, as the phantom May Irwin conjures in "The Bully": the armed and dangerous Black man whom she deposes in her song. In these contexts, Suttle (as person and performer) embodies the "grave social problem" *The New York Times* warned of when describing the Black men Irwin depicted on stage. In the tabloid account and Irwin's comical rendering, the projections of menacing criminality are rendered humorous, neutering the perceived threat of the Black man.

In an environment that pegs the Black male figure to criminality, Suttle's self-presentation as a refined dandy swell assumes a sense of urgency. Though they shouldn't be taken entirely as self-representations, much less transparent ones, his screen performances with Brown and the Rag-Time Four, along with his published compositions, provide a lens into Suttle's self-fashioning and the quartet's efforts to navigate fraught racial hierarchies. The cakewalk offered them a vehicle for advancing their careers, and it was elastic enough a form to accommodate their assertion of individuality against a backdrop of racist perceptions. For the Rag-Time Four and the Brewers, in particular, we might also see dance and performance as ways of asserting life, liveliness, motion, and self-definition amid the omnipresence of death, loss, criminalization, and circumscribed movement.

HUEY & PHILP H
TEXAS STATE FAIR
THE
DATE.
OPENS OCT. 1st
PICTORIAL
SIGNS
WE COVER TEXAS
& DALLAS EXPOSITION.
AS YOU
WILL
SEE US
AT THE
BENCH
SHOW.
CLOSES OCT. 16th

☞

Dallas State Fair Advertising Car

TEXAS, 1900

IN JULY 1900, THE DALLAS State Fair Association sent a train car on a tour of Texas to advertise the upcoming autumn fair, spreading news of the wonders in store for visitors. Described by a small-town reporter as "an exposition hall and music hall combined and placed on wheels," the advertising car aimed to entice Texans to the fair by way of an itinerant moving-picture show and gramophone concert.[1]

The train car crossed the state carrying a four-horsepower gasoline engine to provide electricity to fifty incandescent lights strung along the eaves and the motion-picture projector. For shows, the operator hung a thirty-by-thirty-foot canvas from an iron frame set up fifty feet from the projector.[2] *Thousands of viewers turned up for the free spectacle. For many Texans, the annual excursion to Dallas for the fair would be their only trip away from home, and the advertising train whetted their appetite for the event of the year. For those unable to travel to Dallas, the train offered a glimpse of the fair's many attractions, along with the spectacle of the up-to-date technology of electricity and recorded sound and image.*

Throughout the summer, town to town, as the sun went down the outdoor entertainment would begin. Slides and stereopticon views of the fairgrounds were interspersed with films to hold audience attention and showcase the exhibits. Amplified phonographs playing band music, solos, songs, and comical speeches drawn from a repertoire of twenty records accompanied the projected images. Together, the show lasted nearly two hours.[3] *The operator could tailor the program to each town's interests.*

The films spanned a range of genres. Some provided thrilling views of events related to the recent Spanish-American War: Fighting in the Trenches in the Philippine Islands, Scaling the Walls at Manila, Red Cross at Work on the

Battlefield, Execution of Prisoners of War in Cuba by Spanish Soldiers, *and* The Young Republic of Cuba Under Protection of the Stars and Stripes. *Others were comedies:* Scene in a Sausage Grinder's Factory, The Bewitched Barber Shop, *and* Two Quarreling Fishermen. *Romance, or titillation, was represented with* Love Scene in a Park*; suggested—at least in the title—in* Midnight Scene in a Female Seminary*; and on view in* Something Good—Negro Kiss, *listed in a local paper as* Celebrated Colored Kiss.[4]

Without a doubt, the train reached more people, and a far more diverse audience, than actual attendees of the state fair. About twenty percent of the population of Texas in 1900 was Black, and to call the Dallas State Fair segregated would be a gross understatement. Only one of its fifteen days was open to Black visitors—the so-called Colored People's Day—who were otherwise not welcome.[5]

Associated with such an expressly exclusionary fair, what impression did Something Good *leave on spectators as the advertising train car traveled the state and projected its films to rural Texans? What did they make of the spectacle of an uncaricatured Black couple kissing and laughing? As it happens, we have some evidence. That same year, a San Antonio paper reported on the "interesting scene" at the train depot as "the colored soldiers pulled out for the Philippines" and their wives and sweethearts gathered on the platform "crowding around the dusky heroes to kiss them good-bye."*[6] *The paper presented the sight of Black love as an amusement for its white readers, likening it to an attraction for gawking spectators. The motion-picture projection of a Black couple kissing functioned as a similar novelty, presenting the display of Black love as fitting for a fairground attraction.*

FOUR

"The Black Millionaire" and "The Creole Gal"

AFTER THEIR 1898 TOUR AS half of the Rag-Time Four, Suttle and Brown followed a different path than their erstwhile partners. With the now-married Brewers abroad with the McAdoo Minstrels, Suttle and Brown restaged their act as a duo. Central to their reinvention was their creative interpretation of the cakewalk, turning the promenade spectacle and its competitive connotations into a dance performed as a pair. They billed their version of the cakewalk with a straightforward and marketable name: "the Cake Dance."

We can't be sure how Suttle and Brown's Cake Dance differed from the Rag-Time Four's cakewalk, but it likely retooled familiar elements of the group promenade for a solo pair. That probably included some comedic elements, such as the "gallus" clowning of cakewalkers, some interactivity between the couple, and footwork suggestive of a march or promenade. It's possible that their solo act had little connection to cakewalking apart from their association with Black minstrelsy and former partnership in the Rag-Time Four. But the surviving record suggests the "Cake Dance" was a major component of their act.

By autumn 1899, Suttle and Brown had achieved enough of a reputation as a duo that they were featured in *The National Police Gazette*, a popular tabloid-like men's lifestyle magazine with an emphasis on sensational stories and popular culture (and only a tenuous relation to policing). Many entertainers—Black and white—appeared in its pages. The *Gazette* lauded the duo as the "originators of the latest craze in cake walking known as the 'Cake Dance' which is rapidly becoming popular" (see Figure 12).[1] The *Gazette* noted, "They were formerly connected with the famous Rag Time Four," and that "Mr. Suttle is the composer of a great many up to date songs."[2] The magazine included a photo taken at the Chicago studio of J. B. Wilson, showing Suttle and Brown in their stage costumes with added embellishments: Brown with flowers in her hair, a waist sash, and feathered fan, and Suttle with a top hat and ribbon-decorated cane, though not the exaggerated one he brandished in Selig's filmed *Cake Walk* (see Figure 20).

This rare studio photo of Suttle and Brown reveals their self-presentation as refined, elegant entertainers. Perhaps the pose was taken from their act, a moment frozen for the flash of the camera. Though they are costumed in the garb of minstrel performers, their poise, confidence, and posture work to counteract minstrelsy's stereotypes. Consider the stock figure of Zip Coon, the vulgar urban dandy counterpart to the country (enslaved) figure of Jim Crow: by contrast, Suttle and Brown look truly debonair. Facing the camera, Suttle gestures to his partner as her head is turned to him, her face framed by the feathered fan in her right hand and the elaborate weave of flowers adorning her hair. She stands with her left arm akimbo, slightly lifting her dress to reveal her pointed-out foot.

Over three seasons as a duo, Suttle and Brown redesigned and expanded their act to include sketches or playlets like "Just from Sunny Tennessee," advertised as "a New & Original Darky Sketch" and a "a typical plantation sketch," which they performed at the Olympic, Haymarket, and Chicago Opera Houses.[3] Such comedy sketches provided a structure to string together a set of popular songs and allowed performers to expand their repertoire to meet audience demands.

In the summer, as midwestern weather turned more hospitable, Suttle and Brown performed outdoors. They were part of sideshow entertainments at venues like Ferris Wheel Park in Chicago, and they played at local fairs and festivals, such as the Kewaunee County Agricultural Fair in Algoma, Wisconsin.[4] Sideshow minstrelsy lacked the prestige of the legitimate vaudeville stage, but work meant pay, and it helped tide the performers over until the regular theatrical season recommenced in the autumn. In the meantime, they honed their act.

Their ease with one another must have grown with each season they shared a stage. Billed as the "Popular Darky Comedy Duo" who brought "the very latest from Blackville" to Chicago stages, Suttle and Brown in autumn 1901 performed on the vaudeville circuit in Chicago and St. Louis with "coon songs" and "their original Creole cake dance."[5] What made their Cake Dance "creole" is unclear, though for audiences the term likely evoked the culture of mixed-raced, free New Orleanians. They may have performed songs that at least superficially highlighted Creole culture, and potentially Gertie Brown's

New Orleans roots, such as Suttle's "That Creole Gal of Mine," discussed in the previous chapter, and "My Gal from New Orleans (as she does the Creole Dance)."

"My Gal from New Orleans (as she does the Creole Dance)" describes "the very latest craze" from the city, "Where the coons are always gay," and gives directions for the steps, "done with grace and ease," that the pair may have demonstrated while Suttle sang:

> Gents, politely look your lady in the eye,
> Wheel around and do the Alabama sunrise.
> Now to the Buffalo fair, with the Louisiana prance,
> That's my gal from New Orleans, as she does the Creole Dance.

Suttle's lyrics invoke a broad geography and eclectic moves, but they also work to differentiate the Creole Dance from familiar steps, explaining, "Now they don't care for buck and wing, for that's done ev'rywhere," referring to the long-established minstrel form that was a precursor to tap dance. "Buck" referred to tap dancing and "wing" involved a lateral move that extended the dance in a horizontal direction through side-brushing or the inclusion of a scraping step.[6] As Constance Valis Hill has traced, buck-and-wing developed from percussive precursors such as jigging, a combination of African and Irish stepping traditions, and Appalachian clog dancing derived from antebellum African American plantation square dances.[7] Buck-and-wing added syncopation, marking it as a ragtime-era Black vernacular form (also appropriated by white minstrels) akin to the cakewalk, which shared a genealogy with buck-and-wing but formed a more palpable dance for crossover onto popular stages. As Hill describes, "The cakewalk was the graceful fraternal twin of buck-and-wing."[8] If the "Creole dance" was indeed Suttle and Brown's "Creole cake dance," they may also have been promoting it as an up-to-date alternative to typical cakewalks or buck dancing—perhaps while also cashing in on the fad.

The sketch on the cover of the sheet music for "My Gal from New Orleans" shows four identical sets of elegantly attired men and women framing a single woman dressed in red, hand posed on hip, and feathered fan raised high. Her pose echoes that of Gertie Brown in the *Gazette*. The image evokes the hybrid of promenade partner dancing and solo flourish that marked the cakewalk, though with the individual turn performed by the "gal from New Orleans" rather than a couple. The song's emphasis on "swell coons" "dressed up in silk and laces" who dance "with grace and ease" underscores Suttle's "Black

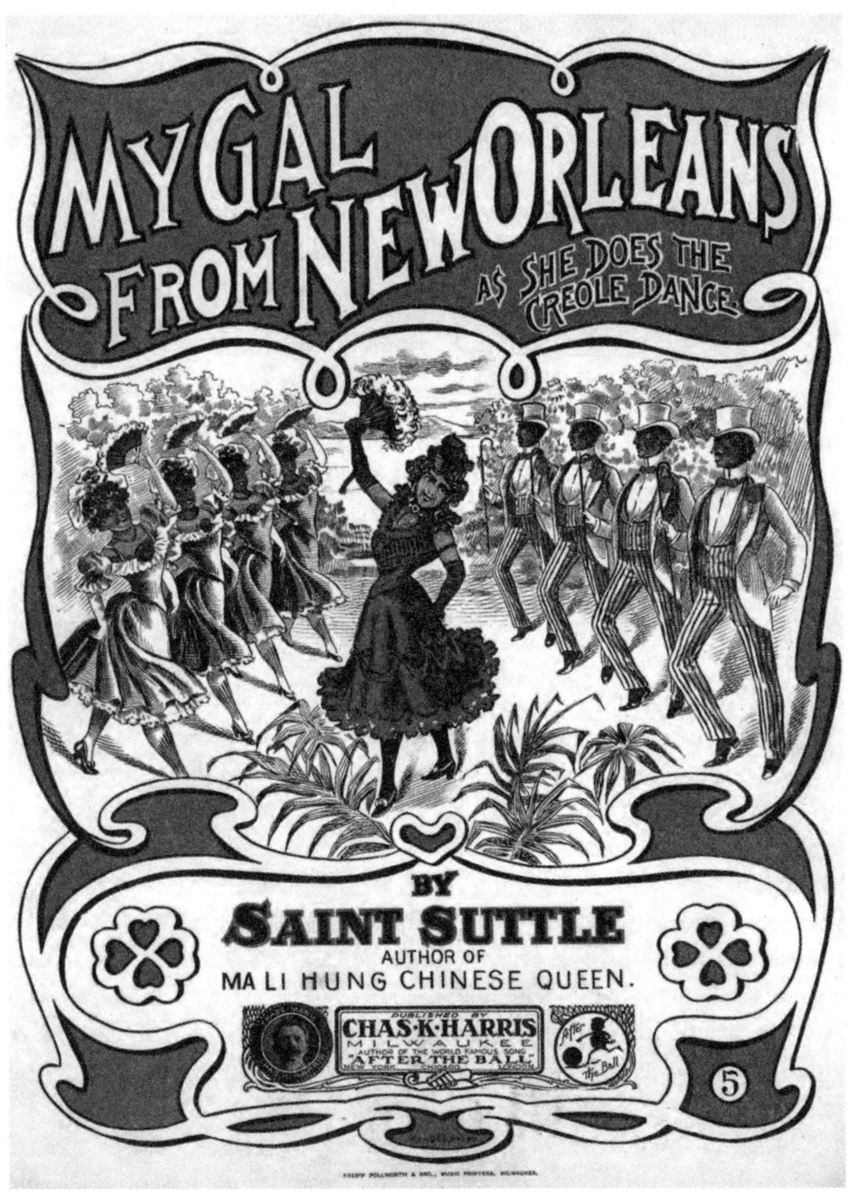

FIGURE 21. Sheet music cover for Saint Suttle, "My Gal from New Orleans (As she does the Creole Dance)," Charles K. Harris, 1901.

Millionaire" persona and his and Brown's efforts at presenting themselves as refined up-to-date performers. The "Creole Dance," perhaps not formally distinct from other Black popular dances on stage at the time, offered a mechanism for Suttle and Brown to distinguish themselves from other performers by emphasizing their own class and refinement. At the same time, their efforts at dignified self-presentation on stage were met with constant challenge by the racist presumptions of lowbrow entertainment that dogged Black traveling performers in this period.

THE LEKSVIK KISS

We are fortunate that visual records of these performances survive. As we've seen, *Cake Walk* shows the Rag-Time Four in action, while *Something Good—Negro Kiss* gives us a sense of Suttle and Brown's duo act. But there is another film as well. In 2019, a print was discovered in the National Library of Norway's vault in the municipality of Leksvik, near the Arctic Circle. Longer than the USC print, this version records what was likely a capsule of a skit or enacted song, constituting an early film "attraction." A departure from the parody of *The May Irwin Kiss*, the Leksvik version embeds kissing in a complete act in which Suttle attempts to woo an unconvinced Brown but in the end succeeds in his advances. It reveals, in other words, a better sense of what audiences experienced in their comedy sketches.

Without the direct allusion to *The May Irwin Kiss*, where Suttle and Brown's kiss would be understood predominantly in a parodic frame, the Leksvik version of *Something Good* risks spectacularizing Black courtship as a titillating attraction for predominantly white gawkers. Fantasies around Black sexuality informed racial performance, and actors and troupes had to negotiate audience expectations—and desires. But actors also defied racist mockery, and we can see, in the Leksvik kiss, how Suttle and Brown simultaneously engaged tropes of Black romance and desire and refuted their more insidious insinuations.

In a long shot capturing the full figures of both performers, the film begins with Suttle approaching Brown from her side, his arms outstretched imploringly. She stands facing the camera, looking toward him with skepticism bordering on disdain. Her hands shake him away. He kneels before her, yet she still rejects him. Unimpressed, she shoos him away again, now turning her back on her persistent suitor. He rises, leans toward her, and pulls her in

FIGURE 22. *Something Good—Negro Kiss* [Leksvik version] (Selig, 1898). Frame enlargement courtesy of the National Library of Norway.

for a surprise kiss. They part and she raises her arms up again, but this time her gesture of refusal turns to surrender, and they kiss a second time. Now seduced, she matches his enthusiasm for their third embrace, and they engage in a much longer kiss. He claps his hands together happily and she returns the gesture, mirroring his delight. They then join in a fourth kiss, which he celebrates with a gleeful shake. They kiss yet again before he spins her to kneel beside him, pausing a moment before she spins again to rise in his arms, kissing once more before the film ends, in media res, with a final twirl.

Assuming that Selig's extended film reveals an excerpt from Suttle and Brown's theatrical performance—whether as a duo or as part of the Rag-Time Four—it's fitting that these few moments were selected for the film. Motion pictures could not record the words or tunes that would have been central to the pair's vaudeville act, but film could assert the primacy of bold action, and with Suttle's forceful embrace, it did.

Where Suttle's and Brown's movements in *Something Good* suggest impromptu affection, the Leksvik version appears both rehearsed and rushed. Perhaps that's because, even with the greater running time afforded to this extended version, the pair was limited by technology and convention. Filmic attractions at this time were brief, without much time for narrative. Here, it's as though Brown and Suttle are trying to cram in a story that onstage would doubtless have lasted longer than the minute allotted for the film, especially if the sketch followed a song. Perhaps it's because they abridged and sped up their act that Brown accedes so suddenly to Suttle's kiss and seems unprepared for the somewhat clumsy twirl at the end, where Suttle seems to catch her slightly off guard.

The motion pictures might offer a poor substitute for Suttle and Brown's vaudeville act, but it's notable that nothing in it suggests "the very latest from Blackville" or a "typical plantation sketch." Their rapport—and perhaps their act, too—seems entirely focused on each other, their costumes the only concessions to the broader tradition of minstrelsy. Marketing and other sketches aside, courtship and affection, not racial mockery, form the arc of this filmic attraction. And while the Leksvik kiss forefronts a fantasy of masculinist bravado and sexual conquest, Brown seems neither lascivious nor ridiculous. Rather, the film presents her as worthy of wooing and depicts Black romance via sincere expressions of affection.

While Suttle and Brown's theatrical performances remain ephemeral, the Leksvik kiss brings alive the theatrical rapport between the duo. Their gestures, glances, footwork, and rhythm can help us imagine how they might have appeared onstage, both as a pair and in their solo pursuits.

TRAVELING MUSICAL THEATER

While Suttle and Brown were appearing as a duo, they also pursued other ventures as time allowed. For example, Suttle partnered with Will Lewis and James Worlds as the "Ragtime Trio," likely capitalizing on the success of the Rag-Time Four. In spring 1900, they performed for the Democratic Committee in Milwaukee and were welcomed as guests of the editor of the local Black paper, *The Wisconsin Weekly Advocate*.[9] This may have been a typical social call, but it suggests a level of dignity and good repute. (Suttle's connections in the city also included music publisher Charles K. Harris, who put out "My Gal from New Orleans.") Still, at the turn of the century, Suttle's partnership with Brown continued to bear fruit.

The year before, in late 1899, Suttle and Brown had incorporated their duo into a traveling show under the auspices of Edwin Moore's *Coontown 400*. John Brewer joined them while Maud convalesced after their recent return from Australasia.[10] Moore's *Coontown 400* was a minstrel variety act, one of a number traveling under that name. As Tom the Tattler told his readers in the pages of the *Freeman*: "The theatrical woods are certainly full of Coontown 400's [*sic*]. It seems to be as easy to organize a company of that kind as it is to get together a band of jubilee singers."[11] The name evoked white illustrator Edward Winsor Kemble's racist "Coontown's 400" sketches, grotesquely drawn caricatures mocking an imagined elite of Black society. (A city's elite citizens, the slang term went, were its "400.") Kemble's Black caricatures first appeared in *Life* magazine from its founding in 1883 and the "Coontown's 400" sketches were collected in an 1899 publication by the same name. Kemble's drawings both picked up and reinforced the racist framework of turn-of-the-century popular culture, in which both page and stage conspired to mock the idea that there could be such a thing as a dignified, deserving Black elite. The message of Kemble's sketches, of course, was that polite society was exclusively white and that Black class aspirations should be met with laughter.

Traveling shows like *Coontown 400* aggregated existing acts under the loose auspices of seeming Black aristocracy, with musical numbers, dances, and sketches the entire company could perform. They might follow the structure of traditional minstrel shows or take minstrelsy as inspiration for the presentation of specialty acts. This structure allowed for changes in both actors and acts, as necessary, with minimal interruption to the company as a whole. Moore's spectacle seemed to have been typical of other "colored attractions," presented to audiences as a kind of voyeuristic spectacle of watching "the 'coons'" having "a jubilee."[12]

The show toured Indiana and Illinois, advertising its four-week run at Chicago's Great Northern Theatre in its appeals to small-town audiences.[13] Yet once outside the city, the management had difficulty maintaining a consistent roster of performers. Moore apparently stooped to "subterfuge," allegedly stealing the trunk of star cakewalker Carrie Washington to "force her to join his company."[14] Undeterred, the dancer "swore out a warrant for the arrest of the manager on the charge of obtaining goods under false pretenses."[15] Likely securing favorable pay in return for dropping the charges, Washington reconciled with the show's management and officially joined the company.[16]

A veteran of the Black Patti Troubadours, Washington had toured with an earlier *Coontown 400* that had dissolved due to the management not paying out owed salaries.[17] Reunited with her trunk and banking on the promise of remuneration, she was billed as the show's main star, leading the company across Midwest stages. Suttle and Brown received positive notices, too. Local reviews referred to Suttle as "the big-mouthed comedian," a description that—like the one used to advertise *Something Good* by singling out "the size of the colored man's mouth"—connects Suttle to a legacy of Black minstrel performers known for broad, toothy grins.[18] Suttle and Brown were also identified as a distinct pair, described as "the charming comedy duo."[19]

Press coverage gives fascinating information about audiences at the time. In one case, we learn about the Black wife of a Chinese laundryman from Michigan who was so "carried away by the glamour of stage life" that she packed her trunk—and half the town's laundry—to follow *Coontown 400*.[20] According to the local paper, the laundryman, identified as Charles Whow, had married the "sombre colored lady" the year before. While unidentified in the scandal column, the wife, Mary Smith, a native of Virginia, worked as a servant in the Upper Peninsula town of Bessemer, a white mining town of fewer than four thousand residents. She had married the laundryman in December 1898.[21] Perhaps the arrival of the all-Black troupe put her isolation in relief and represented a community she longed to join.[22] Or perhaps someone in the company enticed her to join them—and to bring plenty of clean laundry with her. Whow followed the route of the show, trying to recover his wife and livelihood, but the press quit following him after his arrival in Escanaba, where he was said to have just missed the troupe. He went north on their trail, the search continuing but no longer of interest to the press.[23]

The drama that *Coontown 400* seemed to attract extended to its production woes. The tour continued in the northern Midwest through the season with frequent cancellations, no-shows, and rocky performances. The management seems to have given up on the company in February. After performing in L'Anse, Michigan, the actors were reportedly abandoned by the show's managers and had to raise train fare to their next destination.[24] With one of the company members assuming the role of manager, the show plodded along for the rest of the season. It's not clear if Suttle and Brown stayed on or jumped ship as the company struggled.

The next year, though, the pair returned to a new iteration of *Coontown 400*, now under the management of Guy Watson. A white man, Watson seems to have been an enthusiast of Black popular music, or at the very least aspired to gain a foothold in a crowded industry. After a series of rehearsals, the company opened its "ragtime comic opera" in Kokomo, Indiana—Watson's hometown—on January 31, 1901.[25] Though Watson lacked the luster of impresarios like Orpheus M. McAdoo, who had enlisted Maud and John Brewers on their Australasian tour, he had hired real talent. Both

Brewers joined Suttle and Brown for Watson's *Coontown 400*—Maud was back from her convalescence—and the Rag-Time Four were reunited.[26] Other acts on the bill—at least some of which had appeared in Moore's version of the show—included the renowned comedy trio Howard McCarver, Harry Reed, and William McCarver; duo acts, including Goodman and Spencer and "musical monarchs" Scotte and Deleo; and performers D.E. Johnson, Sadie Citizen, Georgia Dobbs, Lilly Garey, Emma Thompson, Bertha Stone, and Lizzie Taylor, all of whom were frequently mentioned in the entertainment pages of the Indianapolis *Freeman*.[27]

Like other traveling shows, Watson's *Coontown 400* was organized with a modular structure so performers could come and go, if needed, through the show's run.[28] Suttle's dandy "Black millionaire" persona and songs caricaturing Black blue bloods would have fit right in with the spectacle's presumed showcase of the "negro in the East today."[29] Advertisements promised "New songs, catchy dances, up-to-date specialties" and elicited spectators to "Hear the Coontown Quartette. See the latest fad, The Great Cake Walk!"[30]

The show was also advertised as "A Second Uncle Tom's Cabin"—that is, a sequel to Harriet Beecher Stowe's antebellum antislavery novel—which put *Coontown 400* in the tradition of Tom Shows.[31] Such shows emerged alongside the novel's serialization in the early 1850s and took various forms over the following half-century, becoming ubiquitous by 1900.[32] While some shows retained the abolitionist politics of Stowe's novel, many mined the scenario for tableaux of its key plot moments. Some spectacles merely used the Tom concept as loose pretext for showcasing song and dance from minstrelsy, as was surely the case here. "Little Eva is dead, what became of Uncle Tom?" read one advertisement. "This question has been repeated many and many times, until G. Watson, the Eastern King of theatrical enterprises has decided to produce a continuation of the old immortal play, 'Uncle Tom's Cabin,' called 'Coontown 400.' This play, though more on the style of a comic opera, with lots of ragtime music, is the correct portrayal of the negro of today—where 'Uncle Tom's Cabin' is the negro of the days of slavery."[33] Ultimately, though, the plot probably mattered little, if at all. The show consisted, as various papers put it, of "high class singing," including plantation songs and contemporary ragtime music, giving a "realistic picture of the negro of today" via "somewhat of a medly [*sic*] of concert, minstrelsy and farce comedy."[34] Another announcement cut to the chase, describing the show simply as "Minstrels in a tent."[35] And subsequent advertisements dropped the references to *Uncle Tom's Cabin* altogether.

Traveling with their own scenery, the company of forty-five performers—including a band and full orchestra—reportedly played to crowded houses nightly across Indiana and Michigan, before starting city engagements in Grand Rapids then returning to Chicago.[36] In early April, Suttle reported to the *Freeman*: "Our company is doing a big business in the State of Michigan." And, writing of himself, "Saint Suttle as the 'Black Millionaire' in his original songs, never fails to get all that is coming to him, no matter where he is placed."[37] On the eclectic program, the Brewers performed as a duo, billed in Indiana as "the Black Brewers, comedy artists and real ragtime singers," as well as Georgia Dobbs in buck-and-wing dancing and the now-reunited "famous" Rag-Time Four "in popular selections, to conclude with a genuine Southern colored creole cake walk, introducing Suttle and Brown in their original creole cake dance."[38] In this way, the performers revived the Rag-Time Four act and augmented it with their solo and duo turns.

Customary for traveling minstrel companies, in each new location along the itinerary the troupe paraded through the center of town at noon to advertise its evening show. The big city *Coontown 400* company was a novelty for small-town audiences, and some members of the community may have lacked sufficient experience to assess whether or not the company's portrayal of Black people was "realistic." Without naming the novelty of Black performers directly, one local Michigan paper noted, "It was something out of the ordinary for Alma theatergoers as it was a strictly city vaudeville show." The paper noted that Suttle "was as good a colored artist we have ever seen."[39] Suttle wore many hats on the tour; in addition to dancing and performing in comedy sketches, he served as stage manager.[40] He also composed and performed original songs.

SAINT SUTTLE'S RAGTIME COMPOSITIONS

In *Coontown 400*, Suttle likely drew from his ragtime repertoire, singing original compositions like "Present Century Coon" that showcased his persona as a fashionable dandy. He also likely introduced new songs written at this time, such as "She's Ready Money," "Ma Li Hung, Chinese queen," and "My Gal from New Orleans (as she does the creole dance)."

Like his 1898 song "That Creole Gal of Mine," Suttle's "She's Ready Money" celebrates a well-resourced, light-skinned "yellow gal" who is liberal with her wealth: "she's a gal that burns the coin and all she needs is the

FIGURE 23. Sheet music cover for Saint Suttle, "She's Ready Money," Joseph Flanner, 1901.

match." The second verse stages the cakewalk as a scene for the display of the couple's finery. In the spectacle, dancers, then, could promenade along with the lyrics, enacting the story as it was sung.

Both songs posit Suttle's "Black Millionaire" status as one achieved through the largesse of a woman. It's unclear if Suttle's role in *Coontown 400* was as the up-to-date Uncle Tom, but the music suggested that the Black aristocracy was dependent on women for status. Reflecting the era's broader economic realities—limited job prospects for Black men, lack of opportunities despite the hopes of migrants to the North—Suttle's self-presentation glosses financial insecurity with a veneer of agentic control. If Suttle's "Black Millionaire" counters the Zip Coon figure, it nonetheless retains its neutering premise and does not pose an economic threat to white masculinity.

Suttle's compositions were successful beyond *Coontown 400*. "She's Ready Money" seems to have gained some traction and traveled among musicians as far as New Orleans.[41] More prominently, "Ma Li Hung, Chinese queen," sold as "A Chinese Rag Time Oddity," found a place as a popular contribution to the subgenre of ragtime invested in orientalist tropes. The song was likely inspired by Bob Cole and Billy Johnson's "The Wedding of the Chinee and the Coon" (1897) from their celebrated musical revue *A Trip to Coontown* (on whose tailwind *Coontown 400* was certainly propelling its tour) and other popular songs drawing on prevalent stereotypes of Chinese people.[42] Might Suttle also have been inspired by the imbroglio between the "Bessemer Chinaman" and his runaway spouse?[43] Only a few years after the renewal of the 1882 Chinese Exclusion Act (made permanent in 1902), both the song "Ma Li Hung" and the press coverage of Charles Whow's search for his wife trafficked in anti-Asian stereotypes and capitalized on the national anti-Chinese fervor—even while, at least in the case of Suttle's composition, exoticizing Asian women.

Typical of Suttle's songwriting, the female subject is an aristocrat—in this case the daughter of "the king of the Ching Chinamen"—and the singer praises "her standing and her station" while staving off rival "Mongolians" with a razor blade. With such tropes, Suttle combines the novelty of a stereotyped Chinese subject with the hackneyed motif of the razor-wielding Black man. If Suttle's "Black Millionaire" appeared unthreatening, his invocation of the razor blade conjured the image of menacing criminality that his stage persona aimed to counter but that white audiences would readily associate with Black masculinity.

TRAVAILS OF THE TRAVELING SHOW

Traveling through small towns and performing for unsophisticated audiences may have worn on the members of the company. When the show came to Chicago in late February 1901, the Brewers ended their run and stayed in the city to pursue other opportunities.[44] Business had been rough. In Logansport, Indiana, the audience was "principally in the gallery" at the local opera house, suggesting a predominantly African American audience relegated to segregated balcony seating, with only a few white spectators in the orchestra seats below.[45] With lower ticket sales due to the cheaper gallery seats and the stigma of an empty (white) orchestra section, the show suffered financially and reputationally.

In early March, *Coontown 400* had a three-night engagement in Greencastle, Indiana. Met with poor crowds, the company supplemented its income by arranging an underground performance featuring four women of the company in a "houchy couchy" [*sic*] show at the Delta Tau Delta fraternity of DePauw University.[46] Watson had been a recent student and member of the fraternity; he may also have wanted to show off to his "brothers." As the local paper reported, "This performance was to be rich, rare and racy, in 'the altogether,' so report has it, and the ditties and dances were to harmonize with the occasion and the surroundings."[47] The performers, accompanied by a few of the men from the company, were setting up for the show when a local marshal appeared and broke it up. The performers hastened away; the fraternity was shut down for three months; and the students who attended the "assemblage" were suspended for the rest of the term.[48] Whether Suttle and Brown were involved in the Delta Tau Delta fiasco or not, the entire company was implicated in the local scandal by association. Incidents such as these that brought the company under the scrutiny of local authorities could turn a town's frosty tolerance into outright hostility and even aggression toward the outsiders.

The association of the Black traveling performers with hoochie-coochie acts also reinforced racist perceptions of wanton Black sexuality. Sexually charged performances and actual sex shows, as Cynthia M. Blair has demonstrated, combined Black popular music and dance with white fantasies of depraved Black sexuality.[49] Extending from the social functions of the minstrel stage, hoochie-coochie shows served to reinforce racist hierarchies for white male patrons by eliciting the enactment of abject behavior.[50] While the moonlighting of members of the *Coontown 400* company was outside of the brothel structures discussed by Blair, theater folks and sex workers walked similar cobblestone streets, as we saw from Suttle and Brown's entrée to Selig's Levee District studio. Further, given the paltry pay for company performers and inconsistent bookings of even the most anticipated shows, this kind of extracurricular activity may have been relatively common but off the books—and therefore off the record—unless, as in the DePauw incident, it came to the attention of local authorities. *Coontown 400*'s only distinction in the unseemlier side of show business was in getting caught.

With his name in the paper associated with the Delta Tau Delta scandal and the reputation of *Coontown 400* in free fall, Watson struggled to sustain the tour. Beyond leading his company into disrepute, Watson proved to be an ineffective manager. The situation quickly deteriorated for the cast of *Coontown 400*. While the company played small theaters to tide over open dates, revenue was never sufficient to meet payroll or basic needs. The ephemeral paper trail reveals the desperation of the situation. I found reports of court cases showing that Watson stiffed local businesses for laundry service, causing the authorities to seize the company's trunks until he settled his bills.[51] Their livelihoods tied up with those trunks, the performers reportedly "attempted forcible resistance" when the constable attached the goods, requiring several large deputies to intervene. Far from a glamorous occupation, working Black troupers—the hoofers and grinders, the journeymen and the chorines—took the stage in every town they visited with a heavy curtain of precarity poised to drop on them at any instant.

Threats also took more sinister shape. Exacerbating the strain dogging Black companies on the road, common theatrical vicissitudes were often compounded by acute racial terror. Watson was bleeding cash and unscrupulous in his business dealings, but his whiteness shielded him from imminent harm. For itinerant Black performers, however, traveling through inhospitable towns carried serious risk. Here, too, the archive's fragments hint at the harrowing climate the performers weathered. The print record dispassionately announces the racial order of white supremacy that surrounded the stage and often infiltrated its fantasy of social remove. Next to advertisements for coming shows, local papers would carry stories—often celebratory—of extrajudicial lynchings of Black men and women. Another form of racialized spectacle, the public lynching of Black men, women, and children formed the long shadow of racial terror under the same ground as Black performers.

To make matters more perilous, the Midwest had a terrifyingly high concentration of sunset towns, also known as sundown towns, where Black people were in danger of extrajudicial violence if they were caught out after dark. Illinois, Indiana, and Wisconsin led the nation in the number of towns and counties inhospitable to Black travelers.[52] For Black performers, no matter how celebrated, sunset towns were dangerous places to visit or even pass through. One local paper reported that in Grandview, Indiana, a notorious sunset town on the Kentucky border, Mason's *Coontown 400* company, one of the many troupes touring under that name at the time, gave a performance to "warm reception" only to be violently accosted later that evening. A paper from a nearby community reported, "The rowdy element of the town surrounded the hall in which the coontowners were quartered for the night and smashed in the windows of the building with rocks and brickbats. Several shots were also fired. The 'coons' felt themselves equal to the occasion and appeared on the street with guns to meet their foe, but they had flown. The names of the rioters are known and they will pay dearly for their fun."[53] Dismissing the terror inflicted on the besieged performers as "fun" enacted by a "rowdy" crowd, the paper downplays the horror of the incident. The last line, while ostensibly equating the "rioters" with the "rowdy element," is ambiguous enough to allow readers to consider it a veiled threat to "coon-towners" who fought back against the violent onslaught.

Even when welcomed by local theaters and the public, Black troupes were constantly under suspicion. In April 1901, Watson's company cancelled a date in Lawrence, Kansas, for unspecified reasons.[54] The following day a man claiming to be part of the company was arrested for alleged murder.[55] Was the cancellation related to the alleged crime? Was the troupe harboring the suspected assailant? Or was cancellation an unfortunate coincidence that served as a pretext for finding the man suspicious? Traveling troupes risked becoming targets of racial hatred no matter how cautiously they moved or how "respectably" they conducted themselves.

Touring actors were accustomed to the risks of the Jim Crow road, especially with the perils of traveling through the Midwest's sunset towns, but with no financial upside and constant troubles, it might have been too much for some of the company. In the wake of these setbacks, Suttle took a break from *Coontown 400* at the end of April, supposedly "tiring" of the show.[56] Along with Suttle, James E. Hood, who served as chorus director, and Georgia Dobbs remained in Chicago while the rest of the company traveled East to close out the season.[57] It's unclear if Brown remained with the company or if she also abandoned it for more promising opportunities.

SUTTLE'S MUSICAL THEATER AMBITIONS

While taking a break from *Coontown 400*, Suttle started planning his own play "away from the average colored shows" and sought "the best colored talent" for his production.[58] Suttle envisioned running his own company and producing his own show in Chicago. He had long aspired to elevate Black popular theater, manage his own company, and write his own operetta. Now, the dream was close to realization. Suttle wrote and directed a thirty-five-minute one-act farce for the vaudeville stage and secured an opening date at the Victoria Theater on North Clark Street.[59]

This was terrible timing. Just as Suttle's plans were taking shape, the Victoria went out of business after a string of unfortunate events—attributed to "hoodoo" hanging over the players—starting with both a fire and a flood in the hotel that housed the fifty-member white stock company, an elopement between two actors, another actor fainting during a maypole dance, the theater lights habitually failing three times in each performance, and ending with the theater manager walking out, owing the remaining members of the company a week and a half in unpaid salary. The compounded catastrophes closed the Victoria. The theater eventually reopened as the New American but without Suttle's show.[60]

Suttle must have cursed his fate. The failure of the Victoria show marked a crossroads in his career. Had his show been staged and succeeded, perhaps it would have launched him into a higher echelon of popular entertainers. It might have given his original compositions a wider audience and possibly led to opportunities to compose songs for other performers. It might have been an inroad for his Black-cast musical theater company in a predominantly white venue.

Perhaps discouraged by the Victoria fiasco and in need of summer employment, Suttle, along with Hood and Dobbs, rejoined *Coontown 400*—now under new management—in May for the Southern and Western tour, spending the summer months on the road in the hottest parts of the country.[61] While the company seemed to do decent business on the tour, the show was met with lukewarm reviews and the occasional pan. *The Emporia Gazette*, for example, reported on a Kansas performance, summing it up as "the rottenest aggregation that has ever caught a gang of Emporia suckers."[62] The show also served as fodder for reviewers' punchlines, as in this sharp review: "The 'Coontown 400' was a swell affair. The afternoon parade made much fun and the tent was full at night. The best part of the performance was its brevity. The agony was all over at nine."[63] In New Mexico, one paper reported, "Those who did not attend were happier the next day than those who did."[64] The New Mexico reviewer used the show as an elaborate joke about rural infrastructure. Apparently, the town of Clifton had been eager to change the rails to broad gauge so that traveling shows could pass through and give entertainments. The paper reported, "Last week the first of the traveling shows made Clifton. The Coontown 400 went up there with their private car and gave the people of Clifton an example of their ability. The tent was crowded, and the people of Clifton presented a petition to President Colquhoun asking him to change the road back to a narrow gauge again. If this was a sample of the travelling shows they want no more of them."[65] In a briefer yet no less damning review, *The Albuquerque Citizen* went so far as to say the show was "not only absolutely without the slightest redeeming feature but was positively indecent and ought to have been stopped by the authorities."[66]

Not all reviews of *Coontown 400* were so negative. In Safford, Arizona, the "circus" reportedly "left behind a well pleased crowd." The local paper reported, "From the time the curtain raised until it dropped, the audience was kept in a continuous uproar of laughter."[67] And regardless of reviews, the "circus" maintained an allure. In Arizona, for example, the show attracted two teenage boys, sons of prominent white citizens, who became infatuated with the show and ran away with it, earning a dollar a day and board to assist in the erection of the tent until they were caught and brought home.[68]

Through the summer, the show seemed to do decent enough business. The tent was advertised as seating 3,000 and the nightly averages were reported between 1,500 and 2,000, respectable turnout for a traveling show.[69] *Coontown 400* stayed west through the summer, performing under canvas and in opera houses when the weather turned colder. At the start of the theatrical season, the company changed its name to *Darkest America*, invoking an earlier popular show led by white minstrel aficionado Frank Dumont, starring the Black theatrical celebrity Sam Lucas, and featuring many of the same performers as *Coontown 400*.[70] Many members of the company who had been traveling since April remained with the newly branded troupe.

Suttle seems to have left the show in July before the tour was complete, returning to the Midwest with Lord Denton's Famous Nightingale Comedy and Specialty Company, a variety show that included cakewalks, buck-and-wing dancing, marches, up-to-date songs, and a "watermelon feast."[71] Suttle performed his specialty, singing from his "Black Millionaire" repertoire, and drawing from his experience "showing off the Coontown 400."[72] While with Denton, Suttle again shared a bill with the Brewers, who were performing a comedy act, "scoring the biggest hit" with audiences.[73] Entertainments were multiple. The show included a "rag-time reception and prize cake walk."[74] More than just a professional demonstration, the company elicited amateurs to compete in the cakewalk, encouraging local "would-be cake walkers" to contend for the prize.[75]

The show's formula seemed reliable, but it didn't pay off. After a week of "very indifferent business," the troupe was stranded in Decatur, Illinois. Denton abandoned the troupers unpaid and in debt to the boardinghouse that lodged them.[76] Suttle was finally through with ersatz *Coontown 400*s.

Suttle and the Brewers then briefly rejoined a revival of *A Black Trilby*—the show that probably initially brought them together—produced by

McCabe and Young at the end of the summer.[77] In the autumn of 1901, Suttle rejoined Gertie Brown to sing coon songs and cakewalk on the vaudeville stage in Chicago.[78] After a tumultuous couple of seasons on the road, the predictability of Chicago's vaudeville stages—and the relative sophistication of the urban audiences—must have been a welcome return. Reuniting with Brown also allowed him to revive the most acclaimed partnership of his career, albeit not for a sustained period.

NEW COLORED KISS NO. 2

After his appearance in *A Black Trilby* and his brief vaudeville run with Gertie Brown, Suttle's immediate movements are a mystery. He continued cakewalking, but no evidence survives to indicate whether or not he occasionally partnered with Brown. Was she with him, for example, on July 4, 1902, when he performed with his "celebrated cakewalkers" for an Independence Day festival in Benton Harbor, Michigan?[79] If so, she probably regretted it. The company sweltered on an outdoor platform, cakewalking over two shows in the burning sun on an exceptionally hot day. Despite the heat, the cakewalkers drew large crowds in the coterie of contortionists, juggling dogs, wrestlers, and a balloonist engaged in providing entertainment for the holiday revelers.[80] In the evening, the performers may have enjoyed a dip in Lake Michigan under the Fourth of July fireworks.

Suttle continued to seek all avenues for his work, and not just with Brown. He even made another kiss film, likely inspired by *Something Good*, with a different partner. This version was probably produced sometime in the 1900 or 1901 season when Suttle encountered film producer Siegmund Lubin or one of his agents, either in their Philadelphia headquarters or while the filmmaker was on the road. For Lubin's company, Suttle and an unidentified female performer—possibly a companion from *Coontown 400* or *A Black Trilby*—apparently recreate the kiss scene that he and Gertie Brown performed for Selig's Polyscope. Lubin marketed the film as *New Colored Kiss No. 2*, "This is entirely different from the old colored kiss and shows a coon dude and his ladylove osculating in an interesting and improved style. The photography is perfect."[81] (See Figure 10.)

While a fragment far less complete than *Something Good*, *New Colored Kiss No. 2* replicates the charm of the original film. Suttle's partner wears an ornate costume while he dons the same suit he wore in *Something Good*, this time accessorized with a large floral boutonniere. They smile affectionately at each other while also seeming to be deeply amused by the affair.

The existence of *New Colored Kiss No. 2* and the identity of Suttle's screen partner are two of the intriguing mysteries remaining in the story of *Something Good*. While we might not be able to discern why Suttle appears in three kiss films with two different partners, the existence of this cycle of motion-picture subjects suggests Suttle and his partners were media savvy, seeing moving pictures as a new frontier to explore. Might they have been drawn to this new medium that promised to preserve actions and rebuff aging? Or, more likely, did they see film as a novelty, with only modest benefit to stage performers? Suttle's main ambitions lay in ragtime composing and musical theater, not yet within the reach of motion pictures' capabilities. As he hoofed and hustled into the twentieth century, he left cinema behind.

Fickle history, in all its precarity, likely would have overlooked Suttle had it not been for the chance rediscovery of *Something Good*. Perhaps it is a fitting irony that his theatrical legacy has been recorded because of the interest in his filmic performance.

☞

Grace Church

WILMINGTON, NORTH CAROLINA, 1901

IN 1859, A YOUNG MAN named Arthur L. Butt of Charlotte, North Carolina, began traveling the country with his hand-painted, fifteen-by-twenty-foot panorama, offering an illustrated lecture show to museums, opera houses, halls, and churches. Butt was a religious man, and his paintings vividly chronicled events of the New Testament, from the angels appearing to the shepherds on the plains of Bethlehem to the nativity scene to Herod's slaughter of infants to the crucifixion and resurrection of Christ.[1] *Part of a long tradition of biblical illustration, Butt's panorama joined other forms of nineteenth-century visual culture mobilized for religious messaging, from magic lantern slides to stereoscope cards to public lectures accompanied by various forms of illustration.*[2] *As the scrolled images rolled by, he explicated and interpreted the painted scenes. By all accounts, Butt's show was a success, and he was able to expand over the years. In the 1880s, he began including an illustrated lecture on the popular subject of temperance. By the 1890s his paintings had grown to 1,340 square feet of canvas rolled out on cylinders.*

In addition to being a man of faith, Butt was a showman, luring in spectators with pure sensationalism. In his temperance series, for example, he displayed twenty-eight paintings depicting what one paper called "the rollicking but sad life of the drunkard."[3] *The cause of temperance provided a pretext for dramatizing a range of sins to a decorous audience who otherwise might eschew popular entertainments. Butt earned a strong reputation for his painting skills and ability to sustain audience interest, whether in churches or outdoors at fairs or public parks.*

In spring 1901, after more than forty years on the road, Butt recognized the need to update his nineteenth-century entertainment and added moving pictures to his traveling show. He purchased an Edison Projectoscope and 2,100 feet of films—twenty-six subjects composing an approximately thirty-minute program—to complement his lectures.[4] Despite the range of religious subjects on the film market at the time (nearly every American and European manufacturer produced fiction and nonfiction films based on Judeo-Christian religious themes), Butt selected more profane moving-image topics. Perhaps this was to draw a broader audience, perhaps it was to offer cautionary tales—like the temperance images—of the wages of sin. Whatever his motivation, movies were a sure way to increase attendance for his religious panoramas.

In June 1901, Butt set up his temperance panorama and moving-image program outdoors behind Wilmington's Grace Methodist Episcopal Church, whose leaders had enlisted him to give an entertainment as a benefit for the church's organ fund.[5] For this occasion, Butt chose a lecture on St. John the Evangelist. He also showed a set of films. Two motion pictures selected for the benefit carried loose association with his religious themes. One was Mrs. Nation's Hatchet Brigade, a parody of the famous temperance crusader Carrie Nation demolishing a Kansas saloon. He also showed the trick film The Devil's Amusement, in which Satan transforms the head of a 300-pound woman into a lion, pig, frog, and bear, then a child magically appears and the woman and child perform a cakewalk.[6] The devil's frivolous trickery likely delighted young audience members more than imparting a sense of fear or caution.

Butt also showed more avowedly profane films. These included comedies like Butcher's Shop, in which dogs are ground into sausages for unsuspecting customers, and Interrupted Lovers, in which a disapproving father disrupts a smooching couple. Audiences also saw topical actualities like Queen Victoria's Funeral Procession (the monarch had died in January 1901). Among these assorted moving-image subjects, Butt screened Darkies' Kiss, the name the Lubin Manufacturing Company gave to its pirated copy of Something Good—Negro Kiss. That means audiences also saw Saint Suttle and Gertie Brown laughing and kissing with joy and irreverence.

While the range of filmic attractions was typical for early film programs, in the context of Butt's religious lecturing they surely carried difference valences. Did he extend his panorama lectures to provide voice-over commentary on the moving images? Or did he supply musical accompaniment? Lecturers were common in early film exhibition, and certainly less cumbersome for an itinerant showman like Butt. In this period, as film historian André Gaudreault has shown, film subjects were relatively easy for audiences to follow, so a lecturer might perform alongside the images "to embellish the apparatus' performance by compensating for its inherent 'mutism.'"[7] Yet how Butt framed the moving images remains a mystery.

In turn-of-the-century Wilmington, race as spectacle carried charged undercurrents. Butt was screening Something Good *only a few years after the 1898 Wilmington massacre, in which white supremacists terrorized Black citizens—killing as many as three hundred—and violently overthrew the elected local government. In this climate, Butt's selection of* Something Good *for his program might have been provocative, whether as a mockery of Black citizens or as a gesture of defiance that countered white supremacy with images of Black humanity. How could we tell?*

The previous December, before adding moving images to his panorama exhibitions, Butt had visited another Grace Church, this time in his hometown of Charlotte—Grace AME Zion Church, a Black congregation.[8] *A conservative group of Grace's parishioners were raising funds to erect a new church, and Butt's temperance panorama matched their passions. In highly segregated North Carolina, it would have been rare for Butt's public exhibitions to be integrated. Indeed, the Grace AME Zion event is the only occasion I have found where Butt entertained an African American audience. Yet the church's invitation to Butt suggests he may have been known as a friend to Charlotte's Black community, or at least not perceived as hostile. If he were a friend, was his selection of* Something Good *for his Wilmington program a means of projecting a positive image of Black love? Did Suttle and Brown's affection, joy, and humor splinter whatever form of reception Butt's white audiences might have tried to frame around their kisses?*

With the moving images representing the most up to date form of entertainment technology, Butt's inclusion of Something Good *in his religious program presents—whether intentional or not—an image of Black love as a modern presentation of blackness under the auspices of religious instruction. In Wilmington in 1901,* Something Good *confronted white North Carolinians with a powerful image of Black humanity for the new century.*

FIVE

Saint Suttle After the Rag-Time Four

IN SPRING 1898, WILLIAM SELIG filmed members of the Rag-Time Four multiple times: the two versions of *Something Good—Negro Kiss*, with Saint Suttle and Gertie Brown, and the *Cake Walk* films, which also included Maud Brown and John Brewer. It's possible that while the Rag-Time Four were in Selig's studio they also made a film that was called *A Night in Blackville*, a dance-action-comedy short subject with an all-Black cast. While the kiss films offered a refreshingly earnest portrayal of Black affection, and the *Cake Walk* films showcased their skills as dancers, *A Night in Blackville* trafficked in darker fantasies and tropes. The film is set in an all-Black music hall where a fight breaks out among the revelers, reflecting and reentrenching stereotypes of Black passions and violence that continue to haunt our mediascape. Despite its differences from the other films, *A Night in Blackville* gives us important context for Saint Suttle's career, not only because of the topic of the film but because of the way that Suttle's performance as a romantic, ragtime dandy was dogged by pernicious tropes of Black male criminality.

Over the next few decades after the Rag-Time Four disbanded, Suttle continued to perform in the Midwest, hustling in pursuit of theatrical success and working to stay afloat in a rapidly shifting entertainment scene. Like many Black performers of his day, he both deployed and pushed against stereotypes as he developed ambitious plans for Black musical theater. Once again, material artifacts provide an opaque map to trace his career, a kind of paper chase of clues that emanates from a single film print, encompasses the broader Selig catalog, and extends to the theatrical milieu Suttle was navigating.

A Night in Blackville appears on the same reel, archived at the Library of Congress, as the *Cake Walk* fragment and thirteen other shorts, including trick films, actualities, scenics, exotics, war films, and comedies, produced—or copied—by Selig between 1898 and 1902. The reel represents a varied program with broad appeal to an eclectic audience. Along with *Runaway Stagecoach*, filmed in Colorado, and *Ute Snake Dance*, shot in Wyoming, the reel includes Polyscope comedies like *Tramp and Dog* (Selig's most popular film of the period, in which a tramp attempts to steal a pie and is chased by a dog), *Murphy Has Trouble with His Wife* (the wife throws punches), and *Lover's Trouble* (a mother discovers her daughter's boyfriend hiding in the washtub).[1] *A Night in Blackville* was shot on the same set as *Lover's Trouble* and appears between the two other films featuring Black performers: *Cake Walk* and *Who Said Watermelon?*, a slapstick scene in which a group of children ambush a Black man carrying a watermelon. The melon smashes and pandemonium ensues; bodies dive to the ground, grabbing at pieces of melon as if scrambling for a fumbled football.

With this set of three subjects embedded in a reel of fourteen films, the exhibitor—or whoever last held the reel before it was deposited at the Library of Congress—created a cluster of performative blackness between the other actualities and comedies. Together, these films index a common set of stereotypes held by white culture about Black Americans, concerning outsized appetites, unbridled passions, frenzied movement, and criminality. Selig drew on these charged tropes in his 1903 catalog description for *A Night in Blackville*:

> Oh, my, but this is hot stuff. Shows a "coon" dance in full swing; all the boys have their best babies; the old fiddler and orchestra are shown seated upon a raised platform; the dance is on. Six coons are shown. A bad coon starts a fight. Razor drawn, girls faint, coon with razor starts to do some fearful execution, when little coon lets fly with a large 45 gun; finale, coon seen jumping through window; big bass viola broken and dance ends in general row. The picture is simply great; one continued round of laughter.[2]

Turn-of-the-century white exhibitors would have been drawn to this film for its promise of voyeuristic titillation, familiar racialized drama, and spectacular destruction.

The print is faded but appears to be largely complete. It is approximately forty seconds long and closely matches the catalog description of *A Night in*

Blackville with a few minor differences. (It's possible that two versions were made, as they were for *Cake Walk* and *Something Good—Negro Kiss*, and this print differs from the one in the catalog; it may also be that the description is written from memory and gets details wrong.) In fact, the scene consists of four women and four men dancing, along with the two male musicians, one playing a guitar and the other a trumpet. The trumpet player appears to be wearing white makeup, possibly meant to depict age or clownishness. Behind the musicians a handwritten banner announces "No Rasers Aloud," signaling both an illicit space, such as a levee, and the presumption that the weapon of choice in so many coon songs would pose risk. The misspelling invites audiences to laugh with a knowing sense of their own superiority, as is also the case with a crude sign above the door declaring "No Irish Admited to this Festival." Discrimination toward the Irish would also invoke laughter, both because of the anti-immigrant norms of the day and the sense that, low on the racial hierarchy, Black and Irish Americans grasped for an edge over one another. Of course, the joke ultimately landed at the expense of Black subjects, who faced much harsher forms of violence and discrimination, including from the Irish themselves. All this serves to reenforce the impression that (white) audiences were getting to peer in at an all-Black social space.

The film starts with a semblance of order: a paired dance. Two lines approach each other, part, and return. Partner moves lead to some ersatz solo buck-and-wing turns, and then the group circles hand in hand. Suddenly, one man pulls out a comically large razor and waves it menacingly at the revelers. A newcomer, smoking a cigarette and brandishing a gun, bursts through the rear door and breaks up the fight. After fumbling with the gun, he chases everyone out—they leap through the window and scramble through the door—before smashing a chair against the "No Rasers Aloud" sign. The scene ends with the armed assailant standing center frame, cigarette still dangling from his mouth. It's not clear why any of this has happened, but the "attractions" of movement and mayhem, not plot, are the point.[3] Like "The Bully" and other white-created representations of Black sociality, comedy and violence intertwined in a fever dream of unbridled Black passions.

On this reel, *A Night in Blackville*'s dance and destruction follow *Cake Walk*'s display of Black expertise. Within just a few frames, we see a progression from the cakewalkers "who have a reputation in this line" to performers depicting regular folk at leisure, to the slide of that leisure from dance to violence.[4] As we saw in Chapter Three, white audiences often presumed Black

FIGURE 24. *A Night in Blackville* (Selig, 1898). Frame enlargement courtesy of the Library of Congress.

cakewalkers to be innately gifted dancers. Here, we find the ongoing conflation of performance and actuality, as the revelers in *A Night in Blackville* are portrayed not as actors but as participants in the "'coon' dance." Put another way, the act of filming effaces performance as it purports to present direct representation of Black social space. The allure of spectacularized blackness—the promise of "hot stuff"—motivates the film's commercial appeal.

The ugliness of the film is hard to miss: *A Night in Blackville* represents a mocking portrayal of presumed Black sociality from a voyeuristic lens. I do not mean to dismiss that reality when I say that, as with *Something Good*, the film is also more complex—and possibly, if quietly, subversive. Other layers of meaning surface when we closely attend to the film, inspect it frame by frame, and consider the exhibition context in which it circulated.

In the early decades of motion-picture entertainment, performers were almost never credited, and *A Night in Blackville* is no exception. Parsing what's occurring on screen, let alone identifying who might be playing which figures, is not easy amid the maelstrom of movement. However, I believe there is a strong chance that the Rag-Time Four perform in this film as they

FIGURE 25. Details from *A Night in Blackville* (Selig, 1898). Clockwise from top left, possibly Gertie Brown, Maud Brewer, Saint Suttle, John Brewer. Frame enlargements courtesy of the Library of Congress.

do in Selig's other Black-themed films of this period. Given the films' proximity on Selig's inventory, they were likely made at about the same time, perhaps even on the same day. Gertie Brown may well be the woman in the white apron over a striped skirt. With the same hair style and blouse, is Maud the woman with the cigarette? John Brewer might be the man holding a cane, a prop very similar to the one he holds in *Cake Walk*. It is also possible that Saint Suttle is the razor-wielding man in the bowler hat. Plausible speculation lets us think beyond the verifiable.

There are deeper puzzles. The gunman—the "little coon" described in the catalog—appears to be a white actor in blackface, the only one in the film. The razor-wielding Black man, who may be Saint Suttle, appears in partial blackface. His makeup darkens the contours of his face in an oval, a theatrical convention employed here likely to make his character more fearsome or, on a practical level, more discernible to the camera in contrast to the others in the crowded scene. But he and the other actors, whoever they may be, are Black. In a film featuring an otherwise all-Black cast, what accounts for the intrusion of a white actor in blackface? And why in this role? The white gunman might be a Selig regular, perhaps the same figure who appears in drag in *Lover's Trouble*, pouring boiling water over an unsuspecting suitor as a scolding—and scalding—mother, and switching, here, from gendered to racial masquerade. But surely he was not just in the film because Selig had used him before, and in any case, his presence, and his mask, matter.

Perhaps a gun in a Black actor's hands would offend white sensitivities. The film's mise-en-scène naturalizes the razor's association with the figure of the Black ruffian and renders his weapon as comedically large. But access to firepower—more lethal, and more realistically deployed here—stays in the hands of a white man, albeit one masquerading in blackface. The casting also draws on extratextual associations. If I'm reading the figure of the gunman correctly, as a white actor in blackface, German American Selig could be making a little joke; with the blackface gunman entering the scene under the sign "No Irish Admited," he could be nodding to the history of blackface minstrelsy rooted in the popular culture of Irish immigrants. Irish immigrants assimilated into white American culture by putting Black people down; on the minstrel stage, blacking up was a way to affirm their own whiteness by enacting their difference from, and mastery over, Black Americans.[5] Selig's background as a manager of traveling minstrel shows led by Black performers certainly informed his sensibilities around racialized performance. Selig was also producing a series of comedies mocking Irish figures, one of which, *Murphy Has Trouble with His Wife*, appears on the Library of Congress reel and shows a couple fighting and then donning gloves and boxing until the wife vanquishes the husband. *Murphy* retains the stereotype of fiery Irish fighters—including hardy women who can knock out their husbands—and when we consider it next to the cluster of three Black-themed films, we should be reminded of how often early slapstick relied on the seeming unruliness of raced and ethnically marked bodies.

This would put the film into a broader context of minstrelsy. By the turn of the century, white blackface performance was becoming outmoded though not dead. With the rise in popularity of Black superstars like Ernest Hogan, Bert Williams, and George Walker—some of them in blackface themselves—white blackface performers were losing their long-held primacy in the field of minstrelsy and with it, their authority over performative blackness. *A Night in Blackville* seems to know this, or at least to subconsciously offer us an allegory for this moment of transition, in which the gun-wielding white man enacts a kind of revenge on a superseded performance tradition. At the same time, once he has banished Black bodies from the screen, he seems to have no further purpose; the film ends with him alone in the frame in a pose that could signify obstinance, dejection, or a bit of both. The film's conclusion suggests his work is necessarily predatory and therefore empty in the absence of blackness to appropriate. Yet it might also have given audiences a sense of threat put right: the Black revelers have been violently evicted from the stage (and thereby the screen), leaving only unthreatening racial masquerade before the camera.

Spectators may have accepted the co-presence of Black performers and white performers in blackface in the same film—even the same frame—with a willingness to suspend disbelief. This was not an unusual practice: it would occur again, in an amplified way, in D. W. Griffith's 1915 *The Birth of a Nation* and was already part of film and vaudeville programs that mixed performances by Black actors and white actors in blackface. But it's also possible to see the subversive energies unleashed by such configurations of performative blackness. In their adjacency, they shake the very fixity of the racial categories on which they trade. What dispels the illusion of racial masquerade more than its confrontation by actual Black bodies in the flesh or on screen? Seen this way, the blackface gunman's intrusion in *A Night in Blackville* disrupts the fantasy that audiences are seeing an authentically Black space. He also destabilizes the notion of race itself, allowing viewers to see it as costume, spectacle, and performance. From these representational upheavals, it's no

FIGURE 26. *A Night in Blackville* (Selig, 1898). Frame enlargement courtesy of the Library of Congress.

small leap from seeing race as spectacle to confronting the idea of race as performance, a fiction made real through the effects of its psychic strongholds and its legal creation as a meaningful category.

A NIGHT IN BLACKVILLE / BLACKVILLE AFTER DARK

Exhibitors in this era rarely advertised films by title. Sometimes showmen would promote films by subject, though typically programs were announced merely as an aggregated motion-picture spectacle. When titles do appear in exhibitor advertisements, we get a rare glimpse at where particular films screened and how they fit in a larger program—and, remarkably, *A Night in Blackville* was enough of a feature to be named in advertisements. Though it was marketed and sold under this title, it was exhibited under another: *Blackville After Dark*. Approximate titles were common, but the shift from *A Night in Blackville* to *Blackville After Dark*, likely enacted by a distributor or exhibitor, seems to have stuck. While similar, the new title emphasizes an immutable site of Black sociality—*Blackville*—not on a single night but as might happen whenever darkness falls. Further, the presence of both "Black" and "dark" suggests a kind of overdetermined, negative excess having to do with darkness of skin, time, and morality.

In the first decade of the twentieth century, audiences around the country—and as far abroad as Australia—saw *A Night in Blackville / Blackville After Dark*. We know that the film screened with *Cake Walk* and *Who Said Watermelon?*, as in the Library of Congress print, but also with *Something Good—Negro Kiss* and other varied subjects.[6] How audiences received these films remains an open question, but their context of promotion and exhibition reveals the vexed forms and meanings of Black representation in the first decade of the twentieth century. In Xenia, Ohio, for example, the film was on a variety program advertised as "so life-like, so true to nature, so perfect in detail are these pictures that you can scarcely realize that what you see is only a picture, and not reality. Better than a play on the stage. Wonder of the age."[7] Hyperbole aside, the Xenia exhibitor attests to the representational power of motion pictures to present audiences with a form of recorded reality and access to views otherwise inaccessible to most spectators.

Unsurprisingly, given the association of blackness with humor in white-authored popular culture, exhibitors often presented *Blackville After Dark* as a comedy. For example, the film screened as the highlight of a set of films shown "at the old furniture store" in Titonka, Iowa—which may have been particularly amusing given the destruction of furniture in the film—with the promise, "Laugh till your sides ache."[8] Advertisers also emphasized spectacle and imagined authenticity: at the G. A. R. Hall in Grand Rapids, Wisconsin, the Twin City Entertainers characterized the film as "showing a real plantation Hoe-down," misreading the scene's setting and thus demonstrating the presumption of Black dance necessarily coming from minstrel shows imagining an antebellum past. Often *Blackville After Dark* screened alongside actualities and comedies, including *Who Said Watermelon?*, and travelogues showing "many far off scenes of distant lands brought home to us, clear, large, and bright."[9] When the film traveled to Australia, it was marketed as part of a show with "all new and cute subjects from Yankeeland," including *Negro Kiss*, which "beats everything," and *Who Said Watermelon?*, described as a "fine picture, great hit." *Blackville After Dark* was advertised as "simply great, one continued round of laughter."[10] In each of these cases, film distributors perpetuated white fantasies of blackness, presenting African Americans as comical curiosities.

Like many early filmic depictions of blackness, *A Night in Blackville* asserted white hegemonic power through a negotiation of the twin spectacle of race as attraction and threat. The pages of American newspapers drove these associations home, as film announcements shared space with articles that—like the images of a razor-wielding Black reveler—reinforced fear of Black men in the public sphere. In Edgar, Nebraska, to take one example, the Rollan O. Ballard Moving Picture and Entertainment Company screened *Blackville After Dark* along with military films, a wrestling match, fire engine films, and "many others full of fun, interest, and excitement."[11] In the column next to the announcement for the spectacle, the local newspaper printed a story about a young woman, Miss Georgia Utz, who claimed she was "pursued by a negro who had a revolver in his hand" at midnight.[12] It's not hard to imagine that readers of that paper would go on to see the events in "Blackville After Dark" as confirmation of the idea that Black men were criminal, violent, and a threat to white women. It was, after all, a familiar rationale for antiblack terror—and this too showed up alongside advertisements for coming spectacles.

Combing through the newspaper archives recovers the juxtapositions. *The Paducah Sun* tells us that the film was screened along with military scenes and comedies, including *Tramp and Dog*, *Why Mrs. Nation Got a Divorce*, *Shaving with a Dull Razor*, and *Children's Pranks*, and—in a chilling notice running just below, "Lynching Approved"—that the "coroner's jury" in the case of a Black man lynched in Atlanta "approved the act of the lynchers."[13] As with most of these extrajudicial killings, "the names of the men are not known, or if known are not mentioned in the verdict."[14] Such announcements read as cautionary warnings for inhabitants of "Blackville," revealing the truth of what could occur, with impunity, after dark. They also remind us of the ways that lynchings were often forms of public spectacle, where people would gather, families would picnic, and local stores would display body parts in their windows. Lynching photographs circulated widely, even taking the form of celebratory souvenir postcards asserting a white supremacist racial order through their ubiquity.[15] Photographic representation directly participated in a horrifically casual regime of violent antiblack terror. When we consider early films alongside the era's lynchings, we see how even in the absence of direct representations of violence films participated in a broad campaign charging Black Americans as unworthy of freedom and in need of controlling by force.

The proximity of blackness as spectacle and antiblack violence structured film programs themselves, with terror and innocence often "balancing" a bill.

For example, in Osceola, Nebraska, an itinerant exhibitor named Baughan screened the film on the Fourth of July on a program that included comedies such as *Toodles and Her Strawberry Tart* and *Babies Quarrel*, along with the sensational twelve-part *Tracked by Bloodhounds; or, A Lynching in Cripple Creek* (Selig, 1904).[16] While the lynched figure in *Tracked by Bloodhounds* is a white "tramp," the film overlays its drama on contemporary events: the recent strike and riot in Colorado's Cripple Creek gold mine that formed part of the Colorado Labor Wars of 1903 and 1904. A decade after a major union victory following the Cripple Creek miners' strike of 1894, mine operators violently repressed strikers, who responded with insurgent resistance. Selig capitalized on the sensationalism of these events, advertising the film as showing "dozens of prominent miners and citizens" who were involved in the incidents. In this way, the film signals an intermedial set of associations among spectacle, actuality, and newsworthy events. The "tramp" becomes a stand-in for a union member, driven out of town (and, in the film, lynched) by vigilantes. *Blackville*'s adjacency with *Tracked by Bloodhounds* cements the association of dogs and lynching with terror on Black citizens, but also the more subtle slippage of cinematic fiction and its concurrent claims to factual representation. Put another way, if *Tracked by Bloodhounds* appealed to spectators on the basis of the cameraman being on site "when the exciting events occurred," even as the drama is clearly fictionalized, how might that have inflected audience's reception of *Blackville* as a view into "a 'coon' dance in full swing"?[17] Both films construct their appeals to audiences based on immediacy, the promise of witnessing, and a claim to veracity evinced by the motion-picture camera's recording capabilities. Under the banner of verisimilitude, sensationalism presents as visual evidence and fiction becomes actuality.

HUSTLING TO KEEP PACE WITH A CHANGING BEAT

When Suttle appeared in Selig's films—including, perhaps, *A Night in Blackville*—it probably never occurred to him that performing on film could sustain a career. And it probably couldn't. If he were paid for the handful of Polyscope films in which he appeared, his compensation would have been very little, or no more than what he earned in vaudeville. Short of fame, a working actor desired consistency. Fame eluded Saint Suttle and work was too erratic for comfort. Following his career allows us to see the possibilities and difficulties navigated by Black performers in these years.

Suttle's experience with the shuttered Victoria Theater and the tribulations of touring with musical theater companies underscored the need for some level of control in an industry plagued by vicissitudes. Black audiences too desired consistency—and parity—in treatment. Regardless of Black patrons' willingness to pay for orchestra or box seats, many theaters would only sell them balcony tickets. To address these needs, major Black theater figures, led by Dr. George C. Hall—a highly respected surgeon—and backed by both Black and white investors, developed a scheme to remedy unequal treatment of performers and audiences alike by "having a colored theater in Chicago, controlled by colored people and catering only to colored patronage," as reported by a local paper.[18]

Hall and his associates eyed a building owned by the Northwestern Mutual Life Insurance company at 1838 South Wabash. Previously known as the Adelphi, the theater had been standing vacant for several years. News traveled fast among Chicago's Black vaudeville performers that a dedicated theater for Black talent would soon open. As the *Inter Ocean* reported, the theater promised "a revival of the good times of old." The paper went on to note that the promoters of the new venture hired "the best known of the colored talent in the city" as consultants. The promoters conscripted Suttle, "well known as a cake-walk artist," to advise on the formation of an all-Black company to be based at the theater. The paper noted of Suttle, "he is a much sought man accordingly." Along with Suttle, vaudeville performer Billy Caldwell was brought in as a consultant, "and is the envy of the colored profession." Suttle and Caldwell envisioned a stock company that would perform in rotation with local talent. As the financial backers touted, "Chicago can furnish plenty of good colored talent as well as plenty of patronage for the theater."[19]

The theater did not come to fruition, likely for lack of capital. Shortly after Hall devised his scheme, however, the Black saloonkeeper and gambler Robert T. Motts converted his Pekin saloon and restaurant to a theater. At 2700 South State Street, the Pekin stood just a mile south of the Adelphi.[20] And while Suttle's centrality to Hall's initial planning for a stock company suggests he was a leader in the Chicago theatrical world at the time, he doesn't seem to have been involved with the Pekin. Reputation didn't always translate to opportunity. The Pekin Theatre became the first Black-owned theater in the country. It enjoyed a decade of prosperity, launched illustrious careers (including Gertie Brown's in stock theater), and became a fixture of Black Chicago's cultural scene—all without Suttle.

Two years later, Suttle shifted his base, albeit temporarily, to Wisconsin. Perhaps the move was because he had been left out of the Pekin venture, or because Chicago's entertainment scene was evolving and opportunities seemed brighter elsewhere. Certainly, the climate for minstrel performers was changing, and Suttle's "Present Century Coon" increasingly seemed to belong to the nineteenth century. Writing about Suttle's one-time co-consultant Billy Caldwell, *Freeman* theater editor Sylvester Russell quipped, "Billy Caldwell has written a new coon song with the word 'nigger' in it, in spite of disapproval. Even Saint Suttle has represented Chicago better than that."[21] Though Suttle's lyrics countered the worst stereotypes common in popular songs, they didn't eschew derogatory language to the degree expected by cultural gatekeepers like Russell. Such critiques of popular performers were gaining traction not just among known snobs like Russell but also among the Black middle classes, which saw minstrel tropes as undignified and damaging. As Henry Louis Gates, Jr., writes, "Black Americans sought to re-present their public selves in order to reconstruct their public, reproducible images."[22] Still, when Suttle moved to Wisconsin, the local Black newspaper, *The Wisconsin Weekly Advocate*, heralded the composer as "a welcome addition to the Negro society of the city. His talents as a musician and song writer are of no mean order."[23] Just two months after Russell's barb, that support must have brought relief to a beleaguered Suttle.

Suttle was already well-known to the *Advocate*, having served as the paper's Chicago advertising agent. It seemed to stick up for him again when, a few months later, in early autumn 1903, he had a run-in with the law. He had arrived in Milwaukee from Green Bay, the *Advocate* reported, "after experiencing there treatment from the authorities, which can only be attributed to a revengeful spirit, and of which more will be heard."[24] The paper does not seem to have gone on to print other details, but its coverage intimates unwarranted attention, and perhaps abuse, from police.

Stable employment in Milwaukee, however brief, enabled Suttle to continue writing and composing. In January 1904 he completed a two-act comedy, "A Georgia Camp Meeting," for L. E. Gideon, manager of Gideon's Minstrels. The theme "Georgia Camp Meeting" offered a pretext for singing, dancing, and humorous sketches, along with spirituals, popular with white audiences, and the physicality and fever of imagined Black religiosity. This was not an original concept: Kerry Mills had composed a wildly popular cakewalk piece on the subject in 1897, so it is difficult to trace this particular show and parse Suttle's comedy from the other traveling spectacles trading on

Black southern religion. The comedy included reportedly new songs, "Ma Mobele [*sic*] Queen," "She's Ready Money," "The Black American Girl," and "I Would Like to Correspond with You," though at least "She's Ready Money" was not entirely new, having been published in 1901, and "The Black American Girl" had been announced in 1898.[25] These songs belonged to a roster of compositions Suttle would introduce—and reintroduce—throughout his career.

Again, this too could have been a breakthrough for Suttle, but something clearly happened. The same month, January 1904, Gideon launched a musical comedy titled "The Georgia Campmeeting," written and staged by Dan Desdunes and Skinner Harris—and without Suttle's name.[26] Suttle's absence suggests that he either sold his work outright or otherwise separated from the company.[27]

In spring 1904, Suttle seems to have had a more serious encounter with the law than whatever occurred in Green Bay. The police arrested Suttle for allegedly brandishing a razor in a "saloon row" on Milwaukee's notorious Wells Street.[28] The local white paper identified the arrested Suttle as "colored" and "a composer of 'coon' songs" and noted, in an attempt at humor, "He is spending his time at the jail composing another which has for its burden the restrictions of a bachelor's courtship under conditions which Mr. Suttle is himself enjoying at present."[29] The simultaneous fear-mongering and mockery here are of a piece with the conflation of violence and entertainment in *A Night in Blackville*. They functioned to demean the work of Black men, cast them as presumptive criminals, and suggested that containment, or incarceration, was the most expedient policy for both local authorities and the press. While we can't know whether or not Suttle did brandish a razor blade, we do know that the assumptions that he was the sort of person who would engage in such violent display attended both his performative persona and his actual navigation of the world offstage.

By the end of 1905, Suttle was back in Chicago performing solo in vaudeville for a brief time.[30] For the next several years he lived on the road, managing traveling plantation shows and minstrel acts.[31] In this period of transient hustling, Suttle strung together itinerant work, often leading or contributing to sideshow acts embedded in carnivals and fairs, like Horwitz & Krause's Dixie Plantation Show, one of the Pike attractions at the 1907 Inter-State Fair held at the La Crosse, Wisconsin, fairgrounds.

While they lacked the glamour and autonomy of an all-Black stock company, fairs were major events and more welcoming to forms of entertainment subject to critique in urban centers. For the opening of the Inter-State Fair, area schools and businesses closed.[32] Special trains ran to La Crosse, bringing folks from all over to ogle exotic spectacles like the "Turkish Theater"; curiosities like Elma, "the largest girl ever born"; burlesque wrestlers and comedy acrobats like "Marzello & Millay"; horse races; and trained-animal acts.[33] In this context, blackness—specifically a white image of Black musical culture—formed a fairground attraction alongside other novelties.

Interestingly, the African American company and the moving pictures were under the same management. Ethel Robinson, a white woman who led the band and fair department of the Western Vaudeville Managers Association of Chicago, furnished moving pictures and the Plantation Show run by Suttle under the title "The Trip to Dixie."[34] While a savvy effort to diversify spectacles to ensure profit, Robinson's specialties also indicate how popular both moving pictures and Black performance were in this period. Robinson, a highly respected and successful manager, had her finger on popular culture's twin—and imbricated—passions: movies and blackness. In this context, it's likely that the fair's moving-picture show included Black-themed films, though the exact titles screened remain unknown.

The day-to-day operations of the fair are under-documented. Yet surviving records suggest that traveling under the auspices of the fair enabled performers to pursue creative side hustles. While in Louisville, Suttle also joined up with the circus, managing the Dixie Minstrels in the Gentry Brothers' shows, booked as part of the Greater United Carnival Shows through the United Fairs Booking Association.[35] Elsewhere, Suttle arranged matches between the fairground wrestler and local contestants. The Plantation Show's resident strongman, Jack Burns, claimed to be related to heavyweight fighter Tommy Burns, a lure for local aspirants to test their strength against the 140-pound wrestler.[36]

From show fights to fights at the shows, pugilism was an attraction. While on the road in 1910, Suttle translated his fairground show fight experience to a new venture, drawing from his theatrical prowess as an impresario to capitalize on the zeal for Black prizefighter Jack Johnson.[37] Johnson's victories in the ring were inspiring for Black citizens and terrifying for whites, for whom Johnson stood as a lightning rod for wider anxieties about Black masculinity. The racist discourse around the figure of Johnson wasn't mere subtext, it was explicit; when Johnson faced former undefeated heavyweight champion James J. Jeffries, the white boxer declared his motivation for challenging Johnson "for the sole purpose of proving that a white man is better than a Negro."[38] With Jeffries championed as the "Great White Hope," the July 4 event was billed as the "Fight of the Century." Stakes were high.

While performing in Louisville's amusement park known as the White City, "The Coney Island of the South," Suttle launched a venture around the Johnson–Jeffries prizefight.[39] For the event, Suttle rented the White City's skating rink—a 2,000-seat venue put to creative use in the offseason—and designed an entertainment around boxing returns. The show, *Jack Johnson in Town*, gave Black citizens of Louisville a venue to follow the prizefight taking place in Reno, Nevada, "by special wire from the ringside." Suttle was filling a need borne of white anxieties over Johnson's skill and popularity. The *Freeman* lamented that "indiscreet persons" who were concerned about "the possibility of a colored man whipping the only eligible white heavyweight" felt that segregating boxing fans would be "indispensable to the peace of society."[40] News traveled quickly in the modern mediascape. Johnson readily beat Jeffries, sparking white rioters to attack Black revelers across the country, including in Louisville. Whites took Jeffries's loss as a humiliation, while Black Americans celebrated Johnson as a hero. For Suttle, who had been jailed for allegedly fighting, it must have been somewhat vindicating to participate—and capitalize on—Johnson's very public victory.

Alongside the show fights, unsanctioned real fights occasionally erupted. In one instance, a violinist with the Dixie Plantation band claimed $16.50 in unpaid wages, leading the local constable to subpoena Horwitz & Krause. While they were in court settling the matter, a collector intervened and presented a bill for unpaid laundry service of the troupe's "bright red shirts, pink ties, and the usual bright hued linen of the 'real thing.'"[41] Unsatisfied with the promoter's response, the collector "bombarded Horwitz with the fists." Both were arrested and later, after the case was settled, released.[42]

Risks were always present, but working on the fair circuit allowed Suttle and others steady and gainful employment for the season. This security also allowed performers to experiment with new projects. In an environment in which familiar, denigrating stereotypes could stymie creativity, Suttle was also stretching his potential and pushing back.

BLACKVILLE AFTER DARK

More than a decade after Selig's *A Night in Blackville*, better known as *Blackville After Dark*, Suttle used the latter title for a new show and in it put forth a very different notion of Black intra-racial sociality. While "Blackville" was a common phrase at the time, "Blackville After Dark" was more pointed, suggesting that Suttle had Selig's film (or what it represented) front of mind. Details on the specific content of the show are scant, but it is clear that the stage offered Suttle a venue for presenting his original ragtime songs, comedic sketches, and the company's interpretations of popular dances, all under his leadership. I propose we read Suttle's *Blackville After Dark* as an ambitious reclaiming of the spectacle of Black sociality in Selig's film—and in American culture more broadly, where antiblack violence was so common as to constitute what Black Studies scholar Christina Sharpe calls "the weather."[43]

Suttle's goal, as ever, was to stage a musical comedy featuring his original ragtime compositions. With the fad for cakewalking having largely passed by the 1910s, *Blackville After Dark* allowed him to showcase his songwriting and comedy skills. Again, we learn about the show by picking up the traces it left as it played. In 1910, Suttle's *Blackville After Dark* company played one- and two-night engagements throughout Kentucky. They were a "big hit" at the Taft Theatre in Louisville and were reengaged for an extra week.[44] The company included newcomers Madame Creola Vaughn and Miss Minor Vaughn, "and several additional artists of note."[45] They played in parks and fairs in the offseason, including at Louisville's White City, where Suttle had promoted his Jack Johnson show.

While touring the South with the circus, Suttle returned to his hometown of Elkton, Kentucky, for the first time in more than twenty years to spend Christmas 1911 with his family.[46] Seven months earlier he had buried an infant in Louisville, so the return home may have been especially poignant.[47] For a while, his home state of Kentucky became his new base, perhaps so he could be closer to his family as he promoted "Suttle's Famous" *Blackville After Dark* company.[48] A December 1911 report notes that, while on hiatus, Suttle planned to return to vaudeville with *Blackville After Dark*.[49]

In April 1912, *Blackville After Dark* performed at a benefit for the Madisonville Band Boys, a local organization of Black youth musicians, at the Temple Theatre in Earlington, Kentucky. Advertisements announced: "Saint Suttle Chicago's Favorite Comedian, and 25 First Class Colored Performers, Male and Female in Suttle's Famous *Blackville After Dark Company*. Introducing Funny Comedians in Funny Songs and Sayings, Charming, Dainty Dancing Girls that will Set Your Brain Awhirl!"[50] Seats were reserved across the house for Black patrons, "from Pit to Dome," with a section reserved for any white people who wished to attend. After the regular noonday ballyhoo parade, the company performed two sketches, *School Days* and *Jack Johnson's Picture*: the first was about Rastus, the "Bad Boy," and the

"Country Teacher," and the second a "playlet" presumably centered around the appeal of the boxing star. Suttle's compositions punctuated the sketches.

At this time, the circus in which Suttle had been appearing combined with a touring horse spectacle to become the Mazeppa and Greater United Shows Combined.[51] The show employed more than two hundred people and included a dozen acts. As a Wisconsin newspaper told readers, "The Mazeppa-Greater United Shows comes with the proud distinction of being one of the largest and cleanest carnival organization[s] in the world."[52] Suttle appears to have rejoined the combined carnival when it opened in Kankakee, Illinois, in May, bringing the *Blackville After Dark* company with him.[53]

When the carnival came to Appleton, Wisconsin, in June 1912 it opened with a benefit for Mumm's Military Band. The carnival was a popular attraction; as the local paper announced, "The various shows drew large crowds to each performance and still larger crowds made their way from barker to barker to listen to their stories and to see the free exhibitions that were being staged."[54] Among those attractions hoofed Suttle and his company, vying for eyeballs and coins with their fellow showmen.

Once again, Suttle couldn't shake being associated with the razor blade. The night before the carnival opened in Appleton, Suttle got into a skirmish at a bar, allegedly drew a razor, and was "badly beaten up for his act." The local paper reported the incident, referring to Suttle as "the negro connected with the carnival." He had registered a complaint after the assault, but later withdrew the "John Doe warrant" and paid $3.50 to the court and settled with his assailants. The newspaper does not provide any context or background on the "fight" or what led Suttle to brandish his blade.[55] Regardless of the details of the incident, it's likely that he felt pressured to settle out of court so as not to risk his work in the carnival. Like the altercations from nearly a decade earlier, the reports imbricate race, performance, and criminality but offer little detail on the purportedly newsworthy events.

From Wisconsin, the carnival traveled to Michigan and then to Chicago, arriving in the city on twenty-two double-length railway cars.[56] The Colored Business Men's Association of Chicago engaged the Mazeppa—an "equine wonder," billed as "the horse with human brains"—and Greater United Shows for its annual August carnival.[57] The festivities involved a parade and large-scale street fair, as well as fireworks.[58] For Suttle, the return to Chicago with *Blackville After Dark* portended promise for larger and more discerning audiences than those found in the midwestern sticks. The auspices of the carnival provided some cover for potential criticism along the lines of respectability, as expectations would likely be low for its associated entertainments. Under the banner of a sideshow spectacle, perhaps Suttle aimed to smuggle in his vision of contemporary Black musical theater.

Once again, a promising venture was stymied. In this case, hinderance came in the form of controversy: the entire venture's respectability was questioned. Along with local African Methodist Episcopal and Baptist ministers, members and officers of the Local Business League expressed opposition to the very idea of the carnival for "bankers, merchants, lawyers, manufactures and all who are interested in the economic development of our people."[59] As they stated, "We believe that a street carnival with side shows and all the ordinary devices for separating people from their money such as usually accompany affairs of that kind, is not an appropriate way in which to entertain a gathering made up of the most distinguished and influential men and women of our race." They argued, "There is no more sense in arranging a street carnival to entertain men of that type than there would be to set up a merry-go-round to entertain the members of the Chicago Board of Trade." Leaning on uplift principles of public respectability and sobriety, the carnival opponents objected to the use of public streets for "demoralizing" purposes. Recognizing the popularity of such carnivals, however, the opponents focused their critique on the apparently dodgy way the license to hold the carnival was procured "in a way to make the Negro Business League and the Negro business men morally responsible in the eyes of the public for the whole enterprise."[60]

The objecting members wrote to Chicago Mayor Carter Henry Harrison, intimating that the carnival managers were engaged in coercive tactics that would "bring large numbers of objectionable characters to the neighborhood."[61] Scheduled to coincide with the annual convention of the National Negro Business League, which would bring 1,500 members to Chicago, the *Tribune* reported, "It is feared many of them will succumb to the wiles of the carnival concessionaires and will be swindled. It is said gambling games of various sorts are to be permitted on the streets."[62] In this case, however, the objections from upright civic leaders were not fatal, and the carnival was a tremendous success, drawing attendees from across the country.[63]

It's hard to know how progressive—or retrograde—*Blackville After Dark* was, as we don't have the libretto or any documentation of the show's contents from its two years of touring. But a decade and a half later, a song by the same title, by Suttle, was recorded, and whether it was in the show or not, it suggests a different take on Black sociality that may have been present in the stage production.

Only one of Suttle's compositions, as far as I can tell, was ever recorded. In 1926, the song "Blackville After Dark" was copyrighted as written by Suttle with music by Aletha Dickerson, a Black pianist and composer who owned a record store on the South Side of Chicago and worked as a booking agent for local theaters.[64] Dickerson's parents were both musicians—her father worked in a café and her mother was a music teacher—so she likely knew Suttle from the South Side cultural scene.[65] Black vaudevillian and blues singer Hazel Meyers would then record "Blackville After Dark" for the OKeh label in June 1926, a recording that stands as one of the few surviving traces of Saint Suttle's creative work.[66] Meyers recorded the song in Chicago, so it's possible that Dickerson and Suttle accompanied her to the studio for the recording. They certainly would have been aware of the occasion and likely were compensated for Meyers's use of the song.

The lyrics of "Blackville After Dark" share tropes and themes with Suttle's other songs, most notably "Old Jasper's Cakewalk," suggesting that it might have been an earlier composition only copyrighted upon Meyers's recording—possibly written as much as a decade before Suttle penned the eponymous show. In the 1926 recording, Meyers provides contralto vocals to the music of Starks' Hot Five, an instrumental quintet led by alto saxophonist Artie Starks.[67] After an extended musical introduction led by the alto sax, cornet, and trombone, and supported by the banjo and piano, Meyers's voice comes to the fore with her distinctive enunciation of Suttle's lyrics set to Dickerson's upbeat syncopated rhythm. The Baltimore *Afro-American* described her in vivid terms: "Miss Meyers is a 'blues' singer, but not one of those kind that you want to choke because she reverts to the hard-hearted mama role or renders her song in a gruff manner. She has a voice that is pleasant to hear."[68] She lent her light and graceful voice to Suttle's tribute to Black assembly.

Suttle—such as we can tell from Meyers's recording—reclaims the "Blackville" trope from its more pernicious misuses. With a jaunty tune, the song tells of a "grand festivity" of "up to date" swells "dressed to kill," an image that recalls the "Black Millionaire" persona Suttle cultivated earlier in his career: "In Blackville after dark the music played and never stopped / You could hear everybody singing and the banjo loudly ringing." Notably absent is the violence spectacularized in Selig's *A Night in Blackville*; instead, the song offers a celebration of Black community in which "the time they had in Blackville town was simply divine." In the recording, these words are tinged with a note of nostalgia, sung by Meyers a quarter century after Suttle's heyday, and in a very different historical and cultural moment. Whether at the moment or in retrospect, the song celebrates the intra-racial conviviality of the ragtime era in the representative "jubilee" it describes, eschewing racist tropes while paying homage to its communal splendors.

ILL FATE IN OHIO

At the end of the 1912 season, Suttle moved to Ohio. He embarked on a new venture, managing a theater for Black patrons named the Pekin Theatre, presumably—as with Black theaters across the country—after Robert T. Motts's famed Chicago theater. The Columbus Pekin was located at 488 West Goodale in Flytown, a lower- and working-class neighborhood with a sizable Black and immigrant population living among the area's industrial businesses. While there were certainly worse parts of town, Flytown attracted regular attention in the local press for instances of so-called vice among its poor, Black, and immigrant residents.

Originally populated by Irish immigrants and then by Italians and Eastern Europeans, Flytown saw its demographics shift in the 1910s with the increase of Black migrants from the South. To cater to this new potential audience, the Pekin opened on January 1, 1913, a few doors away from a settlement house and community center called the Godman Guild. (A Sunday school teacher had started it in 1898, after discovering one Sunday that all her students had been arrested that week and were in jail.) The theater was owned by Isaac Green, a Black Ohioan identified by the *Freeman* as "a well-known citizen of Columbus," and managed by Suttle, whom the paper deemed "a well-known old-time vaudeville artist."[69] With this new partnership, Green and Suttle's ambition for the Pekin included expanding their venture to a string of theaters across the state.[70] Green and Suttle might have had a chance at building a modest theater franchise, but shortly after opening the Pekin, two catastrophes struck, posing an existential threat to their livelihoods.

The first struck Green. As the *Freeman* noted, Green was "well-known" in Columbus, though perhaps more infamous than famous. In addition to working as a barber, Green owned a saloon at 99 West Maple Street in Flytown, a few blocks from the Ohio State Penitentiary. Green's saloon had frequent encounters with authorities. The run-ins accelerated following a change in Ohio law in 1913 that emboldened Liquor License Commissions to refuse licenses to saloons deemed undesirable.[71] Isaac Green was on the list of saloonkeepers "put out of business."[72] In anticipation of having his license revoked, Green and several other saloonkeepers resorted to bootlegging—as the police reported, "they were making hay while the sun shines"—and were arrested.[73]

Although arrests cited sanitary reasons or the desire to combat "notorious" establishments of all varieties, in practice the new license law targeted lower- and working-class establishments, those run by and catering to African Americans, and "unsavory places" run by "women saloonists" (apart from "old German women" whose businesses were, the *Columbus Dispatch* noted, "as common as corner groceries").[74] Fear of miscegenation fueled the moral outrage against these establishments. On one occasion, the police stopped twelve white women on their way out of a "colored saloon" and arrested the Black saloonkeeper.[75] The owner, Al Rogers, was also repeatedly raided "when white and colored men were found drinking together at hours when the saloon should have been closed."[76]

To stay in business, Green reclassified his West Maple Street saloon first as a "restaurant" and then as a "hotel," but the authorities again raided it in 1915, suspecting it of being a "blind tiger" establishment—that is, of selling liquor at all hours and without a license—and Green was fined and sent to the workhouse.[77] The presiding judge declared "Green's place should be closed up," asserting, "if his place was done away with we would have less of this illicit liquor business to contend with."[78]

Green's investment in the Pekin thus might have been an effort to diversify his business interests in anticipation of the clamp down on Black-owned saloons. And he might have been successful had it not been for the second catastrophe of that year: the Great Flood of 1913. In March, the Midwest was hit with massive rainfall that led to devastating flooding. In Columbus, the West Side and parts of downtown were severely impacted. Flytown stood along the Olentangy River, which was spared the worst of the Scioto River's flooding, though the area was nonetheless affected. The city's working-class Black citizens—those who also made up the clientele for the Pekin—were focused on survival and rebuilding, not entertainment. Liquor might have been seen as a necessity in a time of despair, but musical theater was not. The Pekin struggled.

Suttle and Green confronted this challenge with a timely pivot. Together, they partnered in a music-publishing venture and published "The Ill Fate of Ohio," a ballad composed by Suttle to commemorate the Great Flood.[79] Unlike Suttle's earlier "coon song" compositions, "The Ill Fate of Ohio" was a "memory song" meant to memorialize the event. The refrain laments:

FIGURE 27. Sheet music cover for Saint Suttle, "The Ill Fate of Ohio," Suttle-Green Publishing Co., 1913.

> The scene and ill fate of Ohio,
> Should live in our mem'ry for years,
> When we think of the poor souls awakened from dreams in to sorrow and tears
> Poor mothers with babes stood at windows, as angry waves swept them away;
> And rocked them to sleep on Death's billows,
> On Ohio's ill fated day.

Suttle's bad luck aligned with that of Columbus, and "The Ill Fate of Ohio" appears to be the only song published by the Suttle–Green publishing company.

Suttle's own life becomes harder to track. While working at the Pekin, Suttle lived in the tenements above the theater.[80] By November, the theater was under the management of Ollie Scott, a janitor by day, who by 1920 would become successful enough to live as a working musician.[81] Suttle moved out of the apartment above the theater, though he may have remained at the Pekin in some capacity. He seems to have stayed in Ohio for several years, and he continued to broaden his musical compositions away from his ragtime repertoire. For example, in 1916 he published a song co-written with William S. Parks, "The Gold Top for Mine," about Columbus brewery Hoster's signature Gold Top beer.[82] Hoster's commissioned the song and sold copies of the sheet music in the brewery.[83] The sheet music cover featured a portrait of Bill Old Top ("Old Top" being slang for friend), the brewery's advertising mascot, to whom the song was dedicated. In an up-tempo waltz, the carousing refrain revels:

> Old top take gold top
> I could drink and never stop,
> You may drink any old thing any time
> but nothing compares with this gold top of mine,
> Drink up and be of good cheer,
> fill your glasses with gold top beer
> For when I am out for a jolly good time
> a bottle of gold top for mine.

"Gold Top" referred to the beer—especially the foam top on a draft lager—but it had a double meaning with the adorned top of a cane, such as a minstrel dandy would hold. Suttle's "Black Millionaire" persona may have informed this double meaning, even as the song effaced blackness.

Nearly opposite in tone and tenor, "The Ill Fate of Ohio" and "The Gold Top for Mine" demonstrate Suttle's range and his musical acumen outside of ragtime. While certainly motivated by the need to earn a living, these songs were possibly strategic departures from his previous work—perhaps to showcase his breadth as a composer, or perhaps because his musical interests were evolving. Whatever the reason, Suttle's Ohio songs demonstrate his musical ambitions beyond the "coon songs" that marked his repertoire of a decade earlier.

RETURN TO CHICAGO

Suttle did not stand still and sought to parlay his popular compositions like "The Gold Top for Mine" as entrées to a "big time act" in Chicago.[84] The year after the Hoster's beer commission in Columbus, Suttle was back in Chicago, leading a group under the name Saint Suttle's Afro-American Female Band and Orchestra under the musical direction of Hattie Hargrow.[85] Ever the showman, Suttle likely recognized the novelty of an all-woman band as a gimmick to attract audiences, though he developed it into a serious enterprise of talented musicians. But Suttle's association with Hargrow and "lady" musicians, as well as his turn to band and orchestral music, also show him pivoting from minstrelsy toward more respectable, even uplifting, entertainment, befitting the era of the New Negro. What's more, his partnership with Hargrow allowed him to draw from his deep musical acumen, underutilized on the vaudeville stage. Hargrow was a celebrated alto-saxophonist who traveled with jubilee singers and was a member of the Federation of Musicians and the Chicago Musicians Association. Suttle seems to have managed the band of about thirty members, under Hargrow's direction, for several years.[86] In 1922, Hargrow reimagined the band as the Women's Band and Orchestra, aiming to create opportunities for women musicians, with monthly meetings at her home on Prairie Avenue.[87]

It was an exciting time to be in Chicago. The Great Migration was changing the dynamics—and demographics—of Chicago and the burgeoning "Black Metropolis" of the South Side. Thanks to the efforts of the largely middle-class professionals, many associated with the Business Men's Association, Black businesses thrived—though not without struggle. And with the ongoing demographic shift came backlash from the city's white population and immigrant newcomers. Increasingly, spaces in the Loop and other parts of the city became hostile to Black patrons. In Illinois, segregation may have been illegal by law but it persisted in practice.

In response to the needs of the growing Black professional class and the concurrent increase in de facto practices of segregation, the Idlewild Hotel opened in July 1917 at 33rd and Wabash as a "first-class" hotel for Black patrons, the first such lodging in the city.[88] The name "Idlewild"—after the Michigan resort town known as the "Black Eden"—signaled a haven from segregation and discrimination. Taking over the building from the Hotel Germania, the arrival of the Idlewild harkened the rapidly shifting demographics of the South Side.[89]

The Idlewild filled a need, but its success was not ensured. In support of the venture, the *Defender* encouraged its readers, "Every man, woman and child with a spark of Race pride is urged to become a booster of the hotel."[90] In turn, the hotel's reputation could lift the stature of those associated with it. The Idlewild became a hub for the Black middle class and aspiring newcomers to Chicago.

Not surprisingly, Suttle is around. We find that he was engaged to manage a "big patriotic carnival and celebration" over ten days in May 1918, located in a lot next to the hotel (and owned by hotel president Beauregard F. Moseley).[91] For the occasion Suttle sought concessions of all kinds, including rides, shows, and especially "colored Lady Musicians," combining his earlier carnival experience with his recent specialty in leading a female band.[92] In advertising for the carnival, Suttle gave the hotel as his address, both a practical consideration given the planned event and one that effectively elevated his stature higher than his regular Levee location.

But these opportunities were less and less common. Sometime in the 1920s, Suttle moved in with the Hargrows, the only lodger living with Hattie and her husband and two musician daughters and their young granddaughter.[93] Perhaps he had fallen on hard times yet desired to maintain a respectable front. Hattie Hargrow's parents were both from Kentucky, so it's possible she felt kinship with Suttle. He lived with the Hargrows until succumbing to carcinoma in 1932, a year prior to Hattie's own death.

Despite his ascent to a more refined entertainment milieu later in his career, when Suttle died his death certificate listed his occupation as "laborer." This was not a slur; it was probably because officials didn't bother to verify the assumptions of the medical examiner's office (an unfortunately common practice in official documentation of Black citizens).[94] No effort went in to filling out even the most basic details of his life. This death certificate—the last entry in the historical record of Saint Suttle—betrays the neglect that he and so many of his peers suffered at the hands of a society that applauded them as actors but denigrated them as citizens.

☞

The Empire Theater

ARDMORE, TERRITORY OF OKLAHOMA, 1906

IN MARCH 1906 IN DOWNTOWN Ardmore, Indian Territory, in what would become the state of Oklahoma the following year, local impresario Charles D. Brown opened a theater called the Empire Moving Picture Show. He carved out room for it inside the Turf Exchange, a horse-race betting venture that also featured a billiard and pool hall, all inside the Whittington Hotel building on Main Street.[1] *The addition of moving pictures allowed Brown to diversify his clientele, appealing to women and young children who would otherwise never take part in the Turf Exchange's rough and rowdy goings-on.*

Ardmore was a frontier town, some ninety miles from Dallas and surrounded by cotton fields. Railroad routes helped it flourish, and at the turn of the century it was one of the world's major cotton markets. The cotton industry was fueled by Black labor, and in 1906 about a quarter of the town's population was Black. They worked under racial and economic exploitation and lived under increasing threat of terror.[2] *The local paper frequently printed graphic stories of lynchings of Black men for alleged attacks on white women in predominantly southern states, though in 1906 it had been about a decade since a lynching was reported in Indian Territory. This changed with the June 29 extrajudicial execution of a Black man named John Fullbright, a mob act that was met with fear and outrage by the local Black population.*[3] *Later that year, when President Roosevelt spoke out against the national "epidemic of lynching" and appealed to "justice under the law and not the wild and crooked savagery of a mob," the* Daily Ardmoreite *provided a shocking response. Alluding to alleged assaults on white women, the paper wrote, "If negroes will stop that crime* The Ardmoreite *promises them that they will have no cause to complain of lynchings," but otherwise "human nature" "will rise above all else to avenge one woman and to protect all* women."[4] In this way, the paper condoned the terrorizing of Black citizens based on unsubstantiated, racially motivated allegations.

Ardmore was highly segregated, and the new Empire Theater was squarely in the white part of town. In Oklahoma as across the US, some theaters had galleries for nonwhite moviegoers, or midnight shows for Black spectators. Given the location and the likely layout of a theater carved out from another building, it's a safe bet that Empire's audience was entirely white.

Race and exoticism were among the attractions projected at the Empire's first moving-picture show in March 1906. For this program, the Empire featured thirteen varied short subjects including Something Good—Negro Kiss (listed as The Negro Kiss).[5] From reports of the time, it was the only film on the program that showed figures in medium close-up, amplifying the intimacy of the performance. Also on the bill were The Magician, which trained its lens on a performer enacting his tricks on stage, and The Haunted Dining Room. Audiences also saw actualities like Soldiers in the Trenches and McKinley's Last Speech, and foreign views like The Big Fountain at Versailles, Market Scene in Cairo, Egypt, and Railroad Scenes in Seoul, Korea, far-off scenes that contrasted with the closer-to-home view of Rounding up and Branding Cattle.[6]

On the same program, the Empire also screened a longer film, the five-minute drama The Deserter (dir. James Williamson, Edison, 1903), advertised as "a highly sensational picture."[7] The Deserter depicted a British soldier who slips away from camp to see his dying father one last time. Betrayed by a fellow soldier, he is arrested for desertion just as he reaches his father. A sentimental drama set in wartime, The Deserter lent gravitas to the actualities like Soldiers in the Trenches and to the comedy attractions.

How did white Ardmoreites react to these films? Would they have seen the image of Black love projected on the Empire's screen as a documented expression of actual affection? Would they have felt a closeness with the subjects of Something Good, sharing their intimacy with the help of tighter framing? Would it have been seen as a novelty exotic, rivaling in curiosity the foreign views of Cairo and Seoul? Or would they have seen it as comedy?

The Empire Moving Picture Show seems to have been successful, but it was nonetheless short-lived. The Empire only ran moving pictures a few weeks before a fire caused the theater to shut down. This in itself was not an unheard of event. With highly flammable nitrate film stock, movie theaters were susceptible to fire. The incident at the Empire was caused by a lighted cigar—probably from the projectionist or the manager—coming into contact with the nitrocellulose film. Thankfully the show had ended, and the patrons were exiting when the fire broke out.[8] Though the closure was meant to be temporary and damage apparently minimal, the theater seems to have never fully recovered. By the end of April, it had been sold to the Majestic Theatre circuit of Texas and Louisiana.[9]

Remaining in Ardmore, Charles Brown shifted focus and went on to manage the Bijou vaudeville theater in the town. He was again beset by bad luck. In one of the worst disasters Ardmore had seen since being razed by fire in 1895, the Bijou suffered from a major fire that November, costing the uninsured performers thousands in the loss of their costume trunks.[10] Fires continued to plague the town. After the discovery of oil in 1913, and the shift from a cotton to an oil economy, another fire in 1915—caused by the explosion of a train car carrying gas—destroyed all the buildings along Main Street and most of the town. This time, at long last, Ardmore established a Fire Department.

Across the tracks, farther east on Main Street in the Black business district, the Dreamland Theater began projecting moving pictures to its segregated patrons in about 1920. The Dreamland was owned and managed by a Black entrepreneur, Tobe Crisp.[11] Under Crisp's management, race films—films made with predominantly Black casts for exhibition to segregated audiences—screened locally, bringing images of Black romance to the African American citizens of Ardmore fifteen years after *Something Good* was shown at the Empire.[12]

The theater's name was common in this period, but in 1921 it took on particular significance as another Dreamland Theatre, this one in the Greenwood neighborhood of Tulsa, Oklahoma, was destroyed by marauding white mobs in the Tulsa race massacre on May 31 to June 1. Ardmore's Dreamland stood defiant, becoming a community hub for organizational meetings and events when it wasn't projecting movies.[13] Despite its own damaging fire in 1928, the Dreamland became the only surviving building from the Black business district. It was added to the National Register of Historic Places in 1984.[14]

SIX

Gertie Brown

TROUPER OF THE HARLEM RENAISSANCE

WHILE SAINT SUTTLE WAS MOVING between midwestern cities, hoofing in the circus, hocking beer, and hustling to get his various ventures off the ground, Gertie Brown found steady employment with secure companies. Her first notable stop was the newly formed all-Black Pekin Stock Company. The company was based at the Pekin Theatre, the first Black-owned theater in the United States, founded by Robert T. Motts in 1904. Suttle had tried to get an all-Black stock company off the ground just a few years earlier but seems not to have been involved in this effort. After spending the 1900s in itinerant vaudeville, Brown found a home at the Pekin in 1910. She thrived in the company's chorus and continued to develop as a performer. Over the next two decades, she partnered, offstage, onstage, and on-screen, with the celebrated comedian Tim Moore. They lived and worked together through a creative blossoming of Black art, first in Chicago and then, after time abroad and across the country, in New York, where, in the midst of the Harlem Renaissance, they settled in the cultural and intellectual mecca of Black America. With a varied career from stage to screen, chorus to solo turns, comedy bits to musical renditions, Gertie Brown was, as her obituary proclaimed, "a trouper."[1]

Outside of the theatrical world, being designated a "trouper" might evoke a kind of trudging ahead, putting up with the vicissitudes of unpredictable fortune, and willingly, if not enthusiastically, marching along. Gertie Brown, however, was a trouper in the theatrical sense, the highest praise bestowed to stage performers: she knew the show must go on. Beyond her appearance in *Something Good* relatively early in her career, Brown offers an exceptional lens onto Black performance in the early decades of the twentieth century. More typical than the outlying careers of celebrities like Florence Mills or

Aida Overton Walker, yet prominent enough to leave traces in the historical record, Brown helps us see what we might categorize as the vernacular Harlem Renaissance. Her career intersects at times with both high art and popular culture, but was largely planted in the day-to-day, season-to-season rhythms of stage life, with occasional detours to the screen.

The rediscovery of *Something Good* and the identification of Gertie Brown as the charming young actress captured by the motion-picture camera at the end of the nineteenth century laid the trail for the rediscovery of Brown herself. A trail of crumbs more than stones, it nonetheless amounts to a mapping of her life and work that allows us to envision both her and the cultural milieu of Black performance in—and just outside—the spotlight. In the peculiar operations of historical research, Brown's cinematic image in 1898 allows us to see her, even when she's no longer visible to us.

THE PEKIN STOCK COMPANY

In June 1904, saloonkeeper and gambling operator Robert T. Motts opened the Pekin Theatre at the corner of State and 27th Streets on the South Side of Chicago. Motts hired an all-Black personnel, modeled the Pekin after European cabarets, and, aiming to appeal to "respectable" South Siders, promoted the Pekin as both the "Temple of Music" and "The Home of High Class Vaudeville."[2] To produce a continuous roster of entertainments, he established a stock company of house performers led by J. Ed. Green as director of amusements. Green hired talented performers to mount a rotating bill of musical comedies, all written and composed by house writers, many of whom—including Joe Jordan, Will Marion Cook, Aubrey Lyles, and Flournoy Miller—would become internationally renowned.

Motts was tenacious. After the Pekin sustained severe damage from a fire that began in the kitchen of a neighboring Greek restaurant, he rebuilt the theater and reopened it in March 1906 as the New Pekin.[3] He also revived the stock company and eventually hired Jesse A. Shipp, lauded by African American theater critic Sylvester Russell as "America's greatest colored playwright," to, in the words of another Black newspaper, "grind out the plays and arrange the catchy music."[4] Shipp had served as stage manager of the first Black production to appear on Broadway, *A Trip to Coontown*, as well as performing in the cast, and had worked with Bert Williams and George Walker. Shipp's tenure at the Pekin was highly successful, resulting in sixteen original productions in the New Pekin's peak season of 1910–11. This was also the season when Gertie Brown joined the Pekin Stock Company.

At the Pekin, Brown participated in a reimagined minstrel show in which, as *Freeman* drama critic Cary B. Lewis put it, "not a face was blacked but plenty of make-up was used," with "the notable absence of aught that could offend the most fastidious."[5] Whereas traditional nineteenth-century white minstrel shows had been exclusively male, this up-to-date version featured men and women, a chorus of mixed voices, and a woman interlocutor (the master of ceremonies)—Pekin star Lottie Grady—to lead the troupe.

The Pekin actors might have eschewed blackface makeup, but they embraced the ethnic and race-based comedy of the age. For example, in one show, Brown sang a novelty number, "I'm a Yiddish Cowboy"—subtitled "Tough Guy Levi"—published in 1908 and popular on vaudeville stages. The cowboy of the song is set on marrying a "blue blood Indian maiden," the daughter of "Big Chief 'Cruller Legs,'" and sends for a rabbi to marry them. The cowboy declares in the chorus:

> Tough guy Levi, that's my name, and I'm a yiddish cowboy,
> I don't care for Tomahawks or Cheyenne Indians, oi, oi,
> I'm a real live "Diamond Dick," that shoots 'em till they die,
> I'll marry squaw or start a war, for I'm a fighting guy.[6]

The stereotypes on parade here were pat, and the fantasy of a Jewish immigrant participating in the violent settler-colonial project demonstrates the undergirding chauvinism of the era's comedy, but it's also the case that Brown was carving out new territory for herself as a performer. "I'm a Yiddish Cowboy" offered Brown the occasion to showcase her comedic skills and extend her tonal performance range. In the Leksvik version of *Something Good*, her repeated rebuffing of Suttle showed some obstinance, but it was tempered with feminine delicacy. Here, she must have been tough and brash, a role, it seems, in which she excelled. Lewis told readers of the *Freeman* that the song "proved to be a good minstrel song and well selected for the singer and occasion."[7] In my mind I can hear her voice assume a gruff twang inflected with a Bowery accent and see her stance widen as if mounted on a horse, fists raised in imaginary battle, as her body transforms its posture to the physique of a "Yiddish Cowboy."

With "I'm a Yiddish Cowboy," Brown was participating in a long tradition of gender burlesque and ethnic masquerade that extended from the nineteenth-century minstrel stage to the work of Aida Overton Walker, the star of the Smart Set Company and wife of George Walker, who also performed in male roles in Shipp-authored musical comedies. We might see Brown's performance, more pointedly, as an ironic response to the "coon shouting" of May Irwin, a white performer whose most famous song (as we saw in Chapter Two) had her assume the role of Black male ruffian. Now, Brown—who had already parodied Irwin in *Something Good*—was masquerading as "tough guy Levi": a different kind of bully.

Later that fall, Brown was among the "Show Girls" in the Pekin's *A Night in New York's Chinatown*, written by Shipp.[8] As with the theater's name, the show played off orientalist tropes in its negotiation of Black theatrical representation.[9] The first Black-authored and -acted play on Broadway, *A Trip to Coontown* (1898), was a spoof on the popular show *A Trip to Chinatown* (1891). It featured the song "The Wedding of the Chinee and the Coon," which likely inspired Saint Suttle's "Ma Li Hung, Chinese queen." The arrows of racialized comedy flew in all directions.

A Night in New York's Chinatown was incredibly successful for the Pekin. It also set the model for Shipp's subsequent two-act comedies, in which the second act showcased "spectacle and fantasy" building on the first act's exposition and comedic bits.[10] Brown appeared as a chorus member in these farces, including Shipp's last—and most celebrated—production at the Pekin, *The Lime Kiln Club*.

Thanks to the detailed description of theater critic Sylvester Russell, we have some idea of what *The Lime Kiln Club* was like. The title draws from white humorist Charles Bertrand Lewis's drawings of Black sociality initially published in the *Detroit Free Press* and then collected in book form as *Brother Gardner's Lime-Kiln Club* in 1882.[11] From the newspaper and book, the "Lime-Kiln Club" traveled to the minstrel stage and was featured in popular songs.[12] Shipp's play sends up the "secret order people" in imagining a men's club—the Lime Kiln Club—and a women's group, the Society for the Prevention of Extravagance, led by a character attired in "two stunning gowns," no doubt for comedic irony.[13] Brown likely played a Society member, affording her a chance to sing, clown, and peacock. The Pekin's production was immensely popular, and Shipp expanded the show into a three-act version to close out the spring 1911 season.

The Pekin Stock Company was so successful that the troupe spent part of April and May 1911 touring white Chicago theaters downtown, starting with the Globe, with the extended version of *The Lime Kiln Club*. While they did this, the Pekin opened its doors to white stock companies.[14] These arrangements constituted a kind of interracial exchange, in which performers and audiences enjoyed cross-racial entertainments and experiences in spite of de facto segregation. It was also good business. During the summer, the Pekin stage was reserved for vaudeville.[15] Before closing for the season, the Pekin Stock Company returned to the South Side and performed in a song revue.[16]

The Pekin shone as a beacon in the cultural constellation of the South Side "stroll," but its success would be short-lived. Motts died of Leukemia on July 10, 1911, thrusting the theater into a period of uncertainty and eventual decline. The building was later possessed by the City of Chicago, which eventually purchased the property in 1923.[17] As Flournoy Miller dryly recounted, "After Motts' death the Pekin reverted to a night club—Today it is a police station."[18]

Perhaps anticipating the theater's imminent closure, in the fall of 1911 Brown branched out to other vaudeville houses even as she continued to perform on the Pekin stage. At the Monogram, she partnered with musical comedian Kid Brown (no relation)—apparently under the stage name "Cheirlair," perhaps an approximation of her birth name of Chevalier—in a comedy act that included banjos and organ chimes.[19] Whether this was a recurring act or a one-off, we don't know. After the Pekin closed, she probably spent the next few years traveling between different theaters and stages, perhaps touring with companies as a chorist, perhaps on the vaudeville circuit. Then, in 1915, at age 37, she entered a personal and professional alliance with actor Tim Moore, and her fortunes changed.

GERTIE AND TIM: FROM MUSICAL THEATER TO VAUDEVILLE

In August 1915, Brown was performing at Chicago's Monogram Theatre on the same bill as Moore and the highly respected actor Lawrence Chenault.[20] She likely knew Moore before this engagement, perhaps going back to her time at the Pekin Theatre.[21] Like her, he had grown up on the stage, having gotten his start in a popular juvenile act as one of the original Gold Dust Twins. As a young man, he began boxing and competed as "Young Klondike" before returning to the stage in a series of traveling minstrel shows and vaudeville acts, where he performed in blackface. Moore was a large man with a larger-than-life personality. His charisma magnetized audiences and critics regardless of the material or cast with which he worked. Well-managed revues simply carved out time for him to do his thing on stage. He developed a repertoire of comedic bits—including a one-man *Uncle Tom's Cabin*, in which he simultaneously portrayed Simon Legree and Uncle Tom, his face divided down the middle by makeup—and audiences adored him. Generous, seasoned, and very, very funny, Moore was a comedy legend.

Moore and Brown's romance may have started when they shared the bill at the Monogram; they became inseparable afterwards. For the autumn 1915 season, with Brown in the company and by his side, Moore partnered with Sidney Perrin to lead *The Chicago Follies*, combining their two companies to perform farce.[22] The show centered on the trials of a group of stranded players, a premise that enabled individual performers to showcase a rotating roster of acts, performing multiple roles across different sketches and acts week to week or within a single program. In one act, Perrin's wife, Goldie Crosby Perrin, played a schoolgirl opposite Brown's school mistress. In another, a Western skit, Brown played "Arizona Nell."[23] As it had been at the Pekin, racial masquerade was a staple of the show. Continuing the orientalist fad, Perrin played a "Chinaman" and Crosby Perrin a "Chinese miss."[24] One bit showcased the women company members as "Girls of All Nations," with Brown in Indian costume. Versatility afforded performers more stage time, and comedic range was a desirable trait for company actors.

On September 5, 1915, early in the run of *The Chicago Follies*, while the show was in Louisville, Kentucky, Moore and Brown were married.[25] He was twenty-seven and she had just turned thirty-seven, though through the years she would adjust her age on various official documents, narrowing the gap between them. (She had only aged by a decade when she died twenty years later.) Their castmates Goldie Crosby Perrin and Edna Benbow served as witnesses. Louisville proved auspicious for the company, which reached a record five thousand spectators in its first week at the Ruby Theater, leading the manager to hold them over for another week.[26]

In the new year, Tim and Gertie left the company behind and embarked on a Midwest vaudeville tour as a duo.[27] Their partnership was relatively new, but, wrote the *Freeman*, "This team is a standard, like wine, improving with age."[28] The *Freeman*'s compliment alluded to the potentially awkward fact that, at age thirty-seven, Gertie was no longer an ingenue, but nonetheless she held her own in an unforgiving business. Age yielded to experience and the Moores were utter pros.

Their vaudeville act abounded with jokes and songs, including Tim's irreverent original composition "All Aboard for Jungle Land;" covers, including

FIGURE 28. Gertie Brown Moore in the Indianapolis *Freeman* at the time of *The Chicago Follies*. *Freeman*, October 16, 1915, 4.

"Everybody's Done Something But Me" and "I am Going Back to Louisiana"; and parodies of popular songs like Shelton Brooks's hit "Some of These Days," made popular on the Pekin stage and other South Side venues before white singer Sophie Tucker made it her signature song.[29] Talented singing combined with irreverence distinguished their style; one critic described how they infused "I am Going Back to Louisiana" with a "pleasing operatic touch although done in a playful mood."[30] The playfulness Gertie exudes with Suttle in *Something Good* must have transferred across her acts. On stage, Tim and Gertie projected an air of ease and "seeming carelessness," extolled in the Black press as key to their success.[31] The lightness and humor of their act endeared them to audiences, and their reliability ingratiated them to theater managers.

SOUTH PACIFIC TOUR

By the mid-1910s, with motion pictures ascending to a dominant cultural position and vaudeville getting more and more crowded and competitive, savvy live performers sought creative solutions to the changing times. Audiences chased novelty, so performers either reinvented their acts or staged them before fresh eyes. Tim and Gertie did both.

Like John and Maud Brewer fifteen years earlier, the Moores sought to cash in on the novelty of "authentic" blackness on foreign stages. Their radiance and success enticed Black composer and impresario Hen Wise to sign them in Chicago to headline the Pacific tour of his *Bronze Revue*, a versatile show that could supply theaters with an entire evening's entertainment or discrete vaudeville acts.[32] Wise had been a partner of Sidney Perrin at the turn of the century, and had served as Robert T. Motts's first stage manager at the Pekin, where he performed on the theater's opening night.[33] While Wise and Gertie didn't overlap at the Pekin, the theatrical world was small, and reputations were key to opportunities. Tim and Gertie took a chance on Wise and departed for what would become a three-year South Pacific tour.

The Bronze Revue began its Pacific tour in Honolulu at the Bijou Theater in October 1916, advertised as "a mélange of minstrelsy, comedy, mirth and harmony."[34] This mixture appealed to audiences' appetite for "authentic" Black music, understood narrowly as Southern plantation songs, while allowing performers to advance up-to-date musical comedy reflecting contemporary Black theater in North American cities. As one Honolulu newspaper

FIGURE 29. Advertisement, *Honolulu Star-Bulletin*, October 3, 1916, 7. Gertie might be the second woman from the right. Subsequent advertisements featured Tim Moore in blackface makeup instead of the women of the company.

described, the company presented "plantation melodies, not as usually rendered by white artists profusely decorated with burnt cork, but by genuine Afro-Americans."[35] Tim and Gertie were billed as "That Clever Colored Couple" and reprised their earlier vaudeville routine.[36]

Other members of the Honolulu press shared this focus on supposed authenticity, with the claim that many of the performers "learned those same melodies on cotton plantations of the Sunny South."[37] In fact, most learned these melodies on the South Side of Chicago. Playing to audience expectations, the troupe embedded the plantation songs in a "genuine, old-fashioned 'minstrel first part,' with a stage setting similar to that which delighted the ma's and pa's [*sic*] of the present generation of amusement seekers."[38] After "the merry jest and joke and the sweet melody that is always the piece de resistance of the opening portion of a minstrel program," the company switched to "clever musical comedy of a high class."[39] Ever chasing novelty, the revue changed programs twice a week, with the company swapping out songs and changing the contemporary playlet in the second half. The sketches centered on simple—often thin—plots "just sufficient to carry the comedy and music" selected for the show.[40] Frequent changes in the program encouraged repeat spectatorship. The company aimed at wide appeal, with a weekly children's matinee and a clean show without "the slightest taint of nastiness about it, not an evil joke or a suggestive song," as one reviewer distinguished it from other traveling companies.[41] Their pitch was perfect. For the run of the revue, the Bijou was sold out with an audience of about 1,700 per show.[42]

While in Hawaii, Tim and Gertie were signed for a forty-two-week tour in Australia and New Zealand, where they were promoted as Tim and Gertie Moore, "America's So Different Colored Comedians."[43] What made them "different" was that they were "Chocolate in color," with rare humor and fast feet.[44] The duo received accolades across the tour. In Adelaide, they provided vaudeville entertainment on an otherwise exclusively motion-picture program, and "the audience was kept in roars of laughter by the patter and songs of the colored comedians."[45] A Brisbane newspaper reported, "As entertainers they were very successful. They submitted a turn brimful of bright songs, snappy patter, and clever dancing."[46] One reviewer noted of Tim's countenance, "He has the largest mouth that we ever saw and when it is fully expanded it reminds one of the Mt. Cenis tunnel. That yawning orifice is Tim's 'strong suit.' Without uttering a word he can 'bring down the house.'"[47] This mention of a large mouth links Moore's stage persona to earlier famed minstrels like Billy Kersands and Ernest Hogan, and functions, much like it did for Saint Suttle, as a synecdoche for Black comedy.

After the season in Australia and New Zealand, the couple sailed from Sydney to Hawaii to headline a vaudeville program, first in Honolulu and then in Maui.[48] At the end of the summer, Tim and Gertie landed in California, where they performed before playing around the Midwest for the balance of the season. Their time abroad contributed to their prestige once back in the US, as their shows were advertised with the enticing explicator, "Direct From the Orient."[49] Once back in Chicago, Tim and Gertie paid a visit to the office of *The Chicago Defender*, which reported they "were looking like $1,000,000."[50]

While they were abroad, the movie industry had undergone significant changes, not least the sector focused on Black-cast films made for Black audiences, known as race films. In March 1919, novelist turned filmmaker Oscar Micheaux released his first film, an adaptation of his novel *The Conquest*, under the title *The Homesteader*. Tim and Gertie could not have failed to know the film: their act followed a screening in Detroit.[51] For stage performers, motion pictures were still complements more than competition; despite their popularity with audiences, films were not yet able to convey comedic banter or melodic song as effectively as vaudeville performers. The duo might have been stunned by the idea that in a little more than a decade, Moore would perform before Micheaux's camera and his voice—and comedic wit—would be recorded for the director's first sound short, *The Darktown Revue* (1931). Before then, however, the couple would star in their first feature-length film.

THE CHICAGO FOLLIES AND *HIS GREAT CHANCE*

The movies were transforming and so was the stage. Tim and Gertie's return to the US coincided with the establishment of the Theater Owners Booking Association (TOBA), the first Black-run vaudeville circuit. Founded by Sherman H. Dudley, the circuit enabled Black performers access to longer term contracts, and while the pay and terms were worse than those of their white counterparts, the regularity—and monopoly—rendered it necessary. Prior to TOBA, Tim and Gertie booked themselves independently, playing two to three weeks in each theater.[52] TOBA largely improved the conditions for actors, though Tim would later complain that acts needed "better routing and more money."[53] It may have been more stable employment, but the Dudley circuit was notorious for its grueling schedules. Popularly known as "Dudley Time," blues singer Gertrude "Ma" Rainey famously dubbed TOBA "Tough on Black Asses," and the nickname stuck.[54]

In 1920, Tim and Gertie gathered ten additional performers into a company under the same name as their 1915 revue, *The Chicago Follies*. Advertised as "The great Company of Joy," and "More Fun than a Circus," *The Chicago Follies* toured the Midwest on the TOBA circuit, offering ninety minutes of song and dance, "pretty girls," "nifty costumes," comedy, and "straight work."[55] Moore, the star of the show, was onstage "from the rise to the fall of the last curtain," with the rest of the company supporting him in variety bits and Gertie Moore leading "the feminine contingent."[56]

From 1921 to 1923, the Tim Moore Company traveled with their *Chicago Follies*, sometimes appearing along with another troupe, the Sandy Burns Company. This was by no means unusual. TOBA brought acts together on the same bill, enabling performers to develop with and alongside other acts. Shared bills could lead to new opportunities. While performing in Winston-Salem, North Carolina, in January 1923, the two companies were scouted by the white-run Ben Strasser film company.[57] The Strasser company specialized in Black-cast films, one of a host of companies (many white-owned) aiming to appeal to segregated Black audiences and to white audiences drawn to

Black comedy. It was common for film producers to enlist actors from the stage, and race-film companies turned to established Black theater companies for talent: William Foster hired performers from the Pekin Stock Company in the 1910s, and Robert Levy and Oscar Micheaux drew from New York's Lafayette Players in the 1920s. Strasser enlisted Moore and Burns and members of their companies to appear in his latest production. This is how Gertie Brown, twenty-five years after her screen debut, came to act in a feature film.

No trace survives of the production of the film that can tell us about Tim and Gertie's experience, how the performers related to Strasser, or what his attitudes might have been toward his exceptionally talented, yet certainly underappreciated, cast. We only know that the film was titled *His Great Chance*, a five-reel comedy-drama feature film, and the fourth race-film production of Ben Strasser, following *A Giant of His Race* (1921), *A Shot in the Night* (1922), and *The Devil's Match* (1923). All but *A Giant of His Race* starred child actor Bobby Smart, known as the "colored Jackie Coogan" after the famed white child actor of the 1920s.[58] We also know that the film was drawn from a story by Gerald Beaumont, who specialized in short sports stories for popular magazines and newspapers.[59]

None of Strasser's race films are known to survive. While films fixed stage acts on nitrocellulose stock, paradoxically film prints could be precarious objects, compounding the ephemerality of silent-era filmed performance. A touring print of *His Great Chance* met the fate feared by both producers and theater owners in the era of highly flammable nitrate stock: it burned up on route to the Star Theatre in Shreveport, Louisiana.[60] In an era when independent producers could afford to strike only a few exhibition prints, such incidents spelled disaster. Many nitrate fires destroyed entire theaters and yielded mass deaths, so it was lucky that the only casualty of this incident seems to have been *His Great Chance*. We don't know what happened to the other copies of Gertie's only feature-film performance, but this print was reduced to ashes.

Strasser released *His Great Chance* to the public in March 1923, and he also held a private screening in New York City, inviting the celebrated Black actor Leigh Whipper. While no copies of *His Great Chance* remain, Whipper's detailed review, along with the few others and commentaries, provide a sense of the film's form and its narrative. The plot is simple: A traveling theater producer discovers two country boys (played by Sandy Burns and Bobby Smart) dancing behind a stack of straw. Impressed with their talent, he hires them on the spot. A series of incidents traces the boys' development from country bumpkins to professional performers, with their bouts of acute stage fright providing fodder for the comedy. Eventually, the boys overcome their fears and find success as dancers. However, their fame makes them neglectful of their aging parents (played by Tim and Gertie). Meanwhile, a love story blossoms between the theater manager's daughter (played by Fannette Burns) and the older son. With the boys away, the parents try to enjoy Christmas despite their absent sons. Happily, the boys return in time for the holiday, having achieved success and fortune—and the older son having gained a bride—and lavish their parents with affection and gifts.[61]

Whipper's review, published in both the industry journal *Billboard* and the Baltimore *Afro-American*, declared the film "by far the best negro picture it has been my fortune to see," comparing it favorably to two of the earliest Black-directed comedies, William Foster's *The Railroad Porter* (1913) and Hunter Haynes's *One Large Evening* (1914).[62] Whipper declared the photography "excellent" with a good story and settings. He conceded, "The continuity was not of the highest, but something had to be left to the imagination, so we will pardon that." In film, continuity typically refers to editing (smooth transitions between shots and narrative coherence). Reviews suggest that the issues with continuity may have been in narrative coherence and realism more than technical insufficiencies, such as gaps in the story or unexplained ellipses. Given the emphasis on theatrical gags as the boys develop their stage act, some of the inexplicable plot elements might have surrounded the interplay between the boys as actors and the audiences in the film, who presumably tolerate their inexperience and then cheer on their success.

Pointing to an under-recognized formal component of silent cinema, Whipper offers an interesting account of the opening sequence. He writes that the actors are individually introduced, indicating perhaps that the film followed a convention in silent films (but less common in surviving race films) of introducing characters along with the name of the actor playing the role with a living headshot or portrait of either the character or the actor as him or herself. In this way, the film counters the more common elision of Black performers. Gertie—anonymous in *Something Good*—is given star treatment in *His Great Chance*.

Critics tended to praise the cast, though some had reservations about whether Burns's role involved much acting or whether looking beautiful was "about all required of her," and whether the Moores were well-cast as the "old folks."[63] Others took issue with the direction, production design, and the plot, perhaps because of the way they cycled through tropes that seemed increasingly out-of-date.[64] While reviewers consistently noted the talents of the actors, the film seems to have had difficulties in booking.[65]

Still, the film played in Black theaters: the Dunbar in Baltimore, the Globe in Cleveland, and the Lincoln in Pittsburgh.[66] At the Lincoln, the film was celebrated as a race-film production—the first to show in the city since Micheaux's popular *The Homesteader* (1919)—with the local African American paper *The Pittsburgh Courier* imploring readers: "Go out and learn something of your Theda Baras, Gloria Swansons, Mary Pickfords, Norma Talmadges, Charles Murrays, Harry Myers, Carl Laemmles and Charlie Chaplins. Compare them with your favorites and see if they do not measure up."[67] Certainly, by age forty-five, Gertie Brown Moore had proved to be an accomplished comedian, singer, dancer, ingenue, and consummate professional in the manner of some of these white stars. But as the studio star system consolidated in the mid-silent era, fame and fortune were reserved almost exclusively for white actors.

With race films struggling to compete with Hollywood films, the stage remained the primary domain where Black performers could achieve success. After filming *His Great Chance*, and after *The Chicago Follies* ended its initial run, Tim and Gertie returned to the vaudeville circuit as a duo. Tim's successful, outsized stage persona seems, at times, to have left little room for Gertie: one reviewer noted, "Mrs. Moore had little to do but prove a foil for Moore's jokes."[68] Nonetheless, the duo drew audiences whose laughter filled theaters, "without once deviating from decency."[69] *Billboard*'s dedicated African American reporter, J. A. Jackson, writing a column "in the interest of the colored actor, showman, and musician of America," provides a description of the tenor of their vaudeville act. Reporting on a gig at New York's Lafayette Theatre, Jackson noted the duo performed what amounted to two acts, the first involving banter and singing "redolent of the London music halls," which "went big" with the audience "because the musical phases and chatter were removed from the usual Negro style." Here, Jackson suggests that the Moores' comedy departed from that of other Black performers, perhaps even eschewing race-based tropes as fodder for comedy. In the second part of their time on the Lafayette stage, Tim performed his "protean and modernized" one-man *Uncle Tom's Cabin*, which Jackson praised for its "unctuous humor and novelty."[70]

As successful vaudeville entertainers in the mid 1920s, Tim and Gertie worked alongside the era's biggest stars. For example, when the famed blues entertainer Bessie Smith performed a week's engagement at the New Lincoln Theater in Pittsburgh in March 1924, Tim and Gertie were among the headline acts on the same bill. On opening night, crowds gathered early. They kept coming, filling the street, and blocking traffic. Thousands were turned away, and some even stormed the theater to gain entry. While Smith, who had recently begun her recording career with Columbia Records, was the far more famous performer, Tim and Gertie were a reported hit with the audience too. On the heels of the release of *His Great Chance*, the press identified Tim and Gertie as "of moving picture fame," something that not even Bessie Smith could claim—at least, not yet: her only film appearance would be in Dudley Murphy's 1929 sound film *St. Louis Blues*.[71]

As this episode shows, when films are lost and history is crafted from the survivors, events like Gertie's feature-film turn in *His Great Chance* slip through history's interstices. When we seek what no longer survives, however, we find her a star of stage and screen at the peak of her fame. I imagine her and Moore in love, happy with their shared opportunities, and dreaming of a future that, despite the vicissitudes of a trouper's life and the ever-present obstacles of Jim Crow, seemed capable of bringing joy and fulfillment.

HOME TO HARLEM

In the late 1920s, after headlining a series of traveling musical shows, Tim and Gertie settled in Harlem and helmed the Alhambra stock company. At 126th Street and Seventh Avenue, the Alhambra Theatre had long stood as a jewel in Harlem's elite vaudeville scene, constituting a key stop on the Keith-Albee circuit. By the mid-1920s, however, vaudeville, New York theatergoers, and the neighborhood of Harlem were all undergoing massive transformations. The Great Migration brought Black southerners to northern cities, and many of those that came to New York settled in Harlem. In 1920, Central Harlem was 32 percent Black; by the end of the decade that would more than double to reach 70 percent. As Black families moved in, whites moved out. When some local theaters closed, the entertainment industry trade journal *Billboard* sounded a racist alarm, asserting, "one of the best theater communities" in New York had become "one of the lowliest," due to the "Expansion of Black Belt."[72] *Billboard* lamented "the mushroom growth of colored and West Indian colonies in its residential districts" leading to white flight and the decline of "a class patronage" for theaters.[73] Turning to the Alhambra, *Billboard* decried, "once one of the finest two-a-day stands in the country, passed out of the Keith-Albee operation several years ago, when the flood of colored population made its first ravages on the white patronage."[74] Within a few short weeks, *Billboard*'s racist requiem for Harlem would prove to be unwarranted—indeed, completely wrong. The Alhambra was about to take off.

Billboard was correct that white shows had indeed been doing poor box office at the Harlem theater as the theatrical clientele was changing. However, *Billboard*'s racist laments about shifting demographics in Harlem failed to note the popularity of Black performers on New York stages, a fact *Variety* seized on with a front page story published a few months later celebrating "Colored Show Folks' Best Season for White Stage Jobs." While *Billboard* emphasized (white) audience decline, *Variety* celebrated—even if partly as novelty—opportunities for Black actors. Pointing to all or mostly Black cast productions like *Porgy*, *Show Boat*, *Lulu Belle*, and *Golden Dawn*, among others, *Variety* noted nearly three hundred Black performers were employed in otherwise white troupes, in addition to a large number of "All-Colored Shows."[75] Echoing *Variety*, *The Baltimore Afro-American* noted the apparent sudden shift in fortunes for Black performers who had been out of work until the fad for shows with a "Dixieland background," a euphemism for Black-cast and Black-themed productions.[76] Harlem was in vogue, so while the climate for performance shifted, there were ample opportunities for Black performers. And the Alhambra knew which way the wind was blowing.

The Alhambra developed an innovative strategy, changing tack to appeal to the predominantly Black residents of the neighborhood.[77] After several failed ventures led by white men seeking to capitalize on the vogue for Black theater but lacking sufficient financial backing, producer Milton Gosdorfer, a specialist in acquiring flagging theaters to rebuild—and rebrand—leased the theater from the Keith-Albee management and inaugurated a policy of presenting "colored revues catering to patronage of that race, which now forms the great majority of the population of Harlem."[78] The Alhambra also instituted a policy of showing high-quality movies, screened solely by African American motion-picture operators, and hired an all-Black stock company to stage a changing roster of productions. Theatrical celebrities augmented the stock actors.[79] Gosdorfer hired Al Watts, "an old favorite," who had spent twelve years as stage manager for Madame Sissieretta Jones (known as "Black Patti") and her Troubadours, to manage the stage productions.[80] Watts then turned to Tim Moore and George W. Cooper to headline the company of fifty performers, including twelve comedians, twenty "sunkist dancing dolls," and Edgar Hayes and his symphonic orchestra.[81] Moore was also enlisted to write and produce the stock players' productions.

To pay for the Alhambra's costly reinvention, Gosdorfer and the theater's new management secured financial backing from investors encouraged by the 1921 musical sensation *Shuffle Along* and the ensuing success of subsequent Black-cast musicals on Broadway.[82] Syncopated jazz rhythms, chorus girls, and catchy songs sparked a vogue for Black musical comedies and a broad appetite for Black creative culture that fueled (and partly funded) the Harlem Renaissance. From Broadway, the wave of interest in all things African American soon surged uptown, and Gosdorfer's investment paid off. Following the "stormy period" after the departure of Keith-Albee and the failed attempts at reinvention, the new Alhambra opened on August 22 with an explicit goal of catering to Harlem's changing demographic. While other Harlem theaters eschewed locals while courting white curiosity seekers, the new Alhambra warmly welcomed both Black and white patrons.[83] And its first event was all-Black: Gosdorfer rented out the entire 1,500-seat theater to the Negro Order of Elks for its annual convention, beating out the Lafayette for the lucrative business.[84] The Elks convention coincided with the debut of the Alhambra's stock company, billed as "The Troubadours"—no doubt inspired by the famed company that toured the globe with Sissieretta Jones—as part of a three-hour program including musical productions and films.[85] With the Elks filling the theater, the Alhambra opened to immediate, albeit manufactured, success.

The Elks convention kick-started the new theater and the company ran with it. The schedule was grueling. With a weekly change in shows, the company was in rehearsals when it wasn't performing. Tim Moore stayed busy performing, writing sketches, and managing the stock company. In the theater's second week, Tim led the company in its production of *The Harlem Rounders*, a musical comedy revue that also featured Gertie among the "ladies of the troupe."[86] In its third week, Tim and Gertie together led the company in *Lucky Numbers*, "a new spicy revue," drawing the largest crowd since the Alhambra shifted its programing to attract Black patrons.[87] The theater critic for *The Pittsburgh Courier*, Chappy Gardner, credited Tim's "pulling power" for the Alhambra's success.[88]

While Tim was certainly a draw, the Alhambra's new anti-segregation policy caught headlines and attracted patrons. Noting the string of previous managers who ill-treated Black patrons, segregating them in the balcony or relegating them to the edges of the theater, the *New York Age* told its readers,

"There is no longer any prejudice at this temple of the stage arts. . . . At present there are no reserved seats and a patron can get a seat wherever there is one vacant."[89] All seats, boxes, loges, and every corner of the theater were now available to Black patrons. The paper marveled that the stage hands, motion-picture operators, ushers, ticket sellers, and complete house staff "are now colored."[90] A complete change from the segregation policies of the old management, the Alhambra became a theater for Harlemites, as *The New York Amsterdam News* celebrated, "The spirit of cordial welcome accorded to all is meeting with an agreeable response and happy countenances are now the rule at this theatre."[91] Occasionally, Black theatergoers unaware of the new policy would arrive at the theater and be stunned when ushered to the best seats in the house.[92] News of the Alhambra's new policy as an "equal rights theater" quickly spread.[93] Sissieretta Jones herself wrote to the new management congratulating them on "opening this house to colored players" and encouraging Black audiences to "show their appreciation by giving their support to them."[94]

The Alhambra sought to surpass downtown theaters in creativity and innovation. One of the theater's main novelties included an illuminated runaway extending from the footlights of the stage through the center of the orchestra floor, stretching almost to the rear of the theater, augmenting the spectacle for those seated in the orchestra, especially as the "sunkist dolls" danced and promenaded among the audience.[95] The runway elevated the staging of the stock company's productions to mimic Broadway's Winter Garden and other posh venues. When it suddenly illuminated, audiences were delightfully surprised.[96] The Alhambra became a beacon for aspiring chorus girls and launched an in-house dancing school to train them.[97] At the Alhambra, like other stages in Harlem in this period, dancers embodied what performance scholar Jayna Brown describes as their "urban élan," emblematizing the Jazz Age of the 1920s.[98]

Further competing with downtown theaters, the Alhambra secured Pathé newsreels on the day they were issued so patrons could see "the news of the world on the very same day," an innovation for a Harlem theater.[99] Along with newsreels, the motion-picture offerings included the "Our Gang" comedies and first-run motion-picture features.[100] One of the most anticipated motion pictures it screened was of the September 1927 Dempsey–Tunney fight, originally intended for Madison Square Garden but canceled out of concern for the censors. While courts reviewed the legality of screening fight films, the Alhambra screened the bout without interference, likely because, as *Variety* noted, "The house plays to Negro audiences, the company also being all-colored."[101] The Black press boasted, "The Alhambra management knew the law—and the august District Attorney didn't—which he now admits," so while Madison Square Garden eschewed the pictures, the Alhambra had them.[102] Further, the management shrewdly added the films to the regular program without charging an additional fee for the fight, drawing a large crowd who would otherwise have had to pay two dollars a seat to see the fight film at the downtown theaters that dared to screen them.[103] The fight film was so popular the theater held it over for a longer engagement, screening to "very large, but perfectly orderly crowds."[104]

With its new policy in place and its eye on Harlem-based patrons, the Alhambra proudly advertised itself as "The Equal Rights Theatre."[105] The Alhambra's policy of Black stock theater may have initially been to capitalize on the changing neighborhood demographics and cater to Black Harlemites, but the theater soon drew a majority (sixty percent) white audience.[106] To meet demand, the company grew to fifty-one members under the direction of Dave Blythe.[107] Blythe told *Variety*, "so heavy is the demand for negro entertainers" of all forms that "they are being imported" from across the country "to reap the biggest season dusky performers have ever known in and about New York."[108]

White actors and "theatrical folks from Broadway to whom Harlem talent is a revelation" were especially drawn to the Alhambra's late night Wednesday "Midnight Rambles."[109] Downtown theater companies sent their entire casts: Rouben Mamoulian, for example, took the entire cast of seventy performers in *Porgy* along with members of the Theatre Guild staff to a Midnight Ramble to see the Alhambra stock company in action.[110] Such visits were ways to pay homage, but also to scout talent and steal ideas. The Alhambra cast noted an uptick in spies from downtown theaters "engaged in the gentle art of 'choosing,'" the practice of noting popular acts and attempting to copy them on their own stages. To the imitators, the confident stock company eagerly invited them to return, "Come again next week. We'll have some good stuff for you—if you can do it."[111] Reporting on the phenomenon of "choosing," *The New York Amsterdam News* pointed out the common misconception among downtown theater critics that Black companies frequently imitate white actors, when in fact the material originated in Harlem and then was "lifted" by a "chooser" with no original material "who can hold a job only by filching ideas."[112]

Each week, the stock company mounted a new production, and each week, theatrical stars came in for guest appearances. Themes were loosely drawn from Black cultural life, from playing the numbers in *Lucky Numbers* to Pullman porters in *Pullman Dandies*, about railroad men "and their charmers."[113] *Pullman Dandies* included a "School Days" playlet in which the "bronze beauties" played school girls.[114] The show also included a sketch, "Fun in a Motion Picture Studio."[115] Given Tim and Gertie's appearance in movies, they likely drew from their own experiences in crafting the comedy around moviemaking foibles. The following week, in *Dixie Magnolias*, Tim continued to send up actors and producers in a sketch called "The Assistant Manager."[116] With free rein over the content of the productions and total autonomy over his own material, Tim was clearly having a good time with the roles he cast for himself and Gertie. For example, in *Hot Dog!*, Gertie played a "hot senora" at a border army camp flirting with two American soldiers played by Tim Moore and Mantan Moreland, a comedian who was about to hit the big time in the Harlem vogue that would lead to a four-decade movie career.[117] Tim and Gertie even poked fun at their offstage partnership with the skit *Matrimonial Blues*, advertised with the caveat "All in Fun."[118] In *Lady Luck*, they played opposite each other in a sketch titled "I Want a Little Lovin'," in which "He gets it—and how!"

At the Alhambra, Gertie also performed in *Seventh Avenue Strollers*, a novelty act with seals trained to juggle, balance objects, play ball, and catch firebrands tossed by Gertie. The seals were on loan from the popular act known as Roderick's Seals, which trained Gertie for a week before *Seventh Avenue Strollers* opened.[119] In *Rodeo Girls*, a Western-themed show, Gertie played a school mistress protecting her seminary girls (played by the Alhambra chorus girls) from two male intruders.[120] From mothering seals to schoolgirls, Gertie's myriad roles at the Alhambra seem to have played up her matronly stature.

In late November 1927, three months after the Alhambra debuted its new policy, it formally affiliated with the Lincoln Theatre on 135th Street, going under the joint management of Maria C. Downs, a white theater owner with nearly twenty years' experience running the Lincoln.[121] Recognizing the success of the Alhambra, she wisely encouraged its managerial autonomy. The alliance allowed performers to appear on both stages, and Tim and Gertie, along with Moreland and the rest of the stock company, brought the Alhambra Girls to the Lincoln for a week-long residency in January 1928.[122]

In March, the New Negro Art Theatre presented Oscar Wilde's *Salome* at the Alhambra, staged by pioneering modern dancer Hemsley Winfield. The Alhambra then added a dramatic company to its roster under the name the Alhambra Players, led by former Lafayette lead actress (and star of Oscar

Micheaux's films) Evelyn Preer.[123] The Alhambra Players mounted thirty-minute dramas alongside the theater's usual bills of musical comedy revues and motion pictures in a "three-in-one program."[124] The Alhambra Players joined the Alhambra Comedians as twin stock players housed at the theater, forming a locus of "high" and "low" Black arts in one Harlem location.

Just as the Alhambra was evolving yet again, Tim was scouted for an opportunity that became the most acclaimed stage role of his career: lead comedian in the 1928 edition of Lew Leslie's popular *Blackbirds* revue that was playing on Broadway. The following year the company took the show to Paris, seizing on the French fascination for Black performance and the craze around Josephine Baker. Gertie followed Tim overseas, though she stayed behind the scenes while he performed. After the Paris run of *Blackbirds*, Tim and Gertie returned to New York to lead a company at Harlem's Lafayette Theatre, where Gertie returned to the stage.[125] Tim even appeared in Oscar Micheaux's first short sound film, *The Darktown Revue* (1931), alongside comedian Andrew Tribble. In his early 40s, Tim was at the peak of his theatrical stardom and, as George Tyler told readers of the *Afro-American*, "Wherever we find Tim we are sure to find Gertie."[126]

Back in New York in the early 1930s, the couple was able to settle down and establish roots in the community after a lifetime on the road. While Gertie performed with Tim at the Lafayette and Alhambra on occasion, in this period she shifted her energies to philanthropy and hostessing, headlining benefits and receiving guests in their Harlem home. The Moores were central to the musical theater branch of the Harlem Renaissance and their "beautiful home" became a meeting place for Harlem's theatrical world.[127] Gertie's kitchen even inspired Black drama critic Theophilus Lewis to devote a column of his "Harlem Sketch Book" to its "spacious, sunny" splendor.[128]

One of the causes to which Gertie dedicated herself was the Florence Mills Theatrical Association, named in honor of the beloved late actress. The Harlem-based Association aimed to serve unemployed actors, feeding an average of eighty-five men and women per day. Gertie's philanthropic work for the benefit of her fellow actors demonstrates the care she brought to the profession, looking after down-on-their-luck performers. Stars like Tim Moore certainly recognized the precarity of their position and many, including Bill Robinson, Flournoy Miller, Aubrey Lyles, Ethel Waters, Leigh Whipper, and Shelton Brooks supported the Florence Mills Theatrical Association by volunteering and performing at annual benefits.[129] Here, too, Gertie was a trouper, "on the scene daily to prepare the meals."[130] Every day, she dished out soup, scrubbed pans, and cheered up her fellow actors. The Black press lauded her grit and commitment, with one paper noting, "Gertie has given all of her time to the job and has been a combined cook, waitress, housekeeper and treasurer for the cause."[131] Even as she supported Tim's success, her Harlem Renaissance was one dogged by the thinning faces of the actors unable to catch a break despite the vogue for Black performance.

By 1932, the Moores had established a residence at the Adrienne Hotel on Seventh Avenue. In his "Harlem Scandals" column for *The Baltimore Afro-American*, George D. Tyler, writing as "The Rambler," gave his readers a taste of life at the center of Harlem's cultural scene. Writing as a tour guide about the hot spots where "Harlem loves to dance," he told readers, "Shove off to the Adrienne and meet the ideal couple of the stage that can make print without being involved in any sort of scandal . . . . Tim and Gertie Moore . . . thou art a jewel!"[132] Their personal and professional partnership was a model. In a 1933 article in the *Afro-American* asking "Can Artistic People Stay Married?," Tim and Gertie were singled out as "one of the unusual couples of the stage" who have managed to "stick it out" in marriage.[133]

Tragically, within six months, Tim would be a widower.

Gertie Moore contracted a case of double pneumonia and died suddenly in February 1934 at age fifty-five. Tim was also a trouper. Ten years her junior, Tim was still mid-career. That season, he appeared in *Blackbirds of 1934* and stayed with the show for several seasons. Moore went on to wider fame in the midcentury, playing George "Kingfish" Stevens on the TV series *Amos 'n' Andy* (CBS, 1951–53), opposite Alvin Childress and Spencer Williams in the titular roles. He remarried, first to Benzonia Davis in 1941 and then to Vivian Cravens in 1957 after Davis's death. He also found a new on-screen partner with Ernestine Wade, who played Kingfish's harping wife, Sapphire. When he fell ill at age seventy, he refused to see a doctor, declaring, "I know I am going to die, but the show must go on."[134]

. . .

In a 1950 column for *The Pittsburgh Courier*, Theophilus Lewis offered a lengthy assessment of fifty years of African American progress in the theater. Comparing the ephemerality of the stage to the longevity of recorded music, Lewis wrote, "Acting excellence, on the other hand, is a perishable product that dies with its creator. I regret that more names, for instance, those of Tim and Gertie Moore, cannot be included in this slightly less perishable appraisal of our progress in the theatre."[135] Lewis's nod to the duo came long after Gertie's death and on the eve of Tim's television debut, a mention that relegates the performers to the category of "also ran"—figures who are part of the constellation of key performers but not among the brightest stars in the firmament—a frustrating dismissal for the reader invested in Harlem's "troupers."

Compared with Gertie, Tim's performance persona would become indelible as his "acting excellence" was recorded by Micheaux and, later, television cameras. These recording technologies secured his legacy, however fraught it would be in the latter half of the century as consciousness around race—and racist—representation would dominate discourse around Black performance. "His [Moore's] voice will carry on," declared Freeman Gosden, the white originator of the Kingfish role on radio. "His comedy will carry on for years after he's gone."[136] Gertie, on the other hand, lives on in image only, her voice lost with her passing.

Tim's and Gertie's careers coevolved with the explosion in popularity of Black entertainment known as the Harlem Vogue. Their performance careers also coincided with the proliferation of media that disseminated popular culture, from the stage to screen to radio to television. Their colleagues would likewise follow paths in entertainment that catapulted them to national and international fame: Mantan Moreland in Hollywood; Flournoy Miller on Broadway; and Jackie "Moms" Mabley on stage, record, and television. There were others, too.

Gertie never made it to Hollywood, nor did she appear on television. But in a new century, her image went viral on social media where her audience matched, if not surpassed, that of her colleagues. The resurfacing of *Something Good* uncovers a career that would otherwise be lost to time. And with her career, we get a trouper's view of the first few decades of the twentieth century in all its pressures and promises.

EXHIBITION · MAN RAY

APRIL · 1945

JULIEN LEVY GALLERY · 42 EAST 57 N.Y.

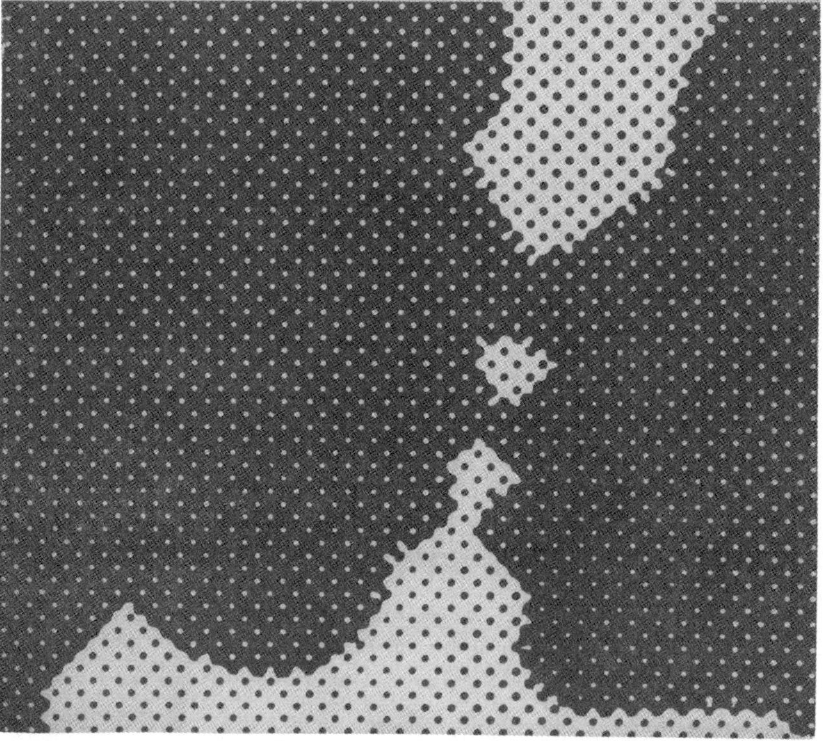

☞

Julien Levy Gallery

NEW YORK CITY, 1945

IN 1945, MARCEL DUCHAMP DESIGNED the cover for the brochure for an exhibit of Man Ray's photographs titled Objects of My Affection *at the Julien Levy Gallery in New York City.*[1] *Duchamp based his design on a film still provided by Alexander Hammid, born Hackenschmied, the experimental photographer and filmmaker who was at that time married to filmmaker Maya Deren. Hammid had a collection of "cinema-photos" showing various kisses from the history of film. Duchamp wanted to reference Man Ray's own photographs of kissing couples, such as the 1922* Rayograph *featuring multiple exposures that create an effect of superimposition of the hands and faces of an embracing couple. According to Julien Levy, the image selected by Duchamp, and then rendered in a Ben-Day dot pattern for* Objects of My Affection, *was of a frame from an early film of a Black couple kissing, "the first kiss in the annals of cinema."*[2]

Duchamp seems to have rephotographed and blown up a frame from a print. The abstracted remediation from film frame to brochure cover makes it impossible to tell whether the source material was Something Good—Negro Kiss, New Colored Kiss No. 2 *(Siegmund Lubin's knockoff of Selig's film with Saint Suttle and a different partner), or a similar film that no longer survives. How the film came into Hammid's collection, and why Duchamp chose that particular image, also remain a mystery. Yet the cover presents a distinct blip—a surfacing in 1945—in an otherwise submerged trajectory between the turn of the century and the research surrounding the early film cycle of Black couples kissing that opened this book.*

And yet the midcentury appearance of the filmic image of a Black couple kissing fits a broader pattern. In the remediation of the film frame to abstracted, uniform, light-blue Ben-Day dots, Duchamp gestures to but ultimately elides blackness.

The avant-garde of which Duchamp, Man Ray, and Hammid were a part held a long-standing fascination with ideas of race, from the primitivist attractions of African masks to the negritude that attended celebrated performer Josephine Baker. The Julien Levy Gallery exhibition catalog shows that blackness is also present within the avant-garde's direct and repeated return to early film as both material source and inspiration. The irony in Duchamp's cover is how cinema's display—here of affection—meets the effacement of the Black figures. The cover represents a mise en abyme of absence.

Duchamp was not the only one interested in Hammid's movie still collection. Nearly sixty years later, in 2004, poet, photographer, and filmmaker Gerard Malanga—who appeared in Andy Warhol's 1964 film Kiss*—published a poem, "Movie Still," in a special issue of* Conjunctions, *featuring writers responding to film. Dedicating the poem to Hammid who had died that year, Malanga pays tribute to his longtime friend. The poem reflects on loss, ephemerality, incompletion, and contingency. While completing this book, one line of the poem in particular caught my eye. Invoking Hammid, Malanga writes, "'The most important thing is to be close to what's missing,' he once said."*

In researching Something Good *and the lives of Saint Suttle and Gertie Brown, I have thought a lot about what's missing and how to get close to it: how to write history about under-documented figures and lost films, and how rediscovered artifacts can enable new histories to be written. So close to showing the thing itself, Duchamp's cover for Man Ray's exhibition brochure emblematizes the opacity of the past as well as its Rorschach test–like cipher on which we project our own needs and desires. It is fitting, then, that* Something Good *has also become a mirror for contemporary viewers when we come up against these specters from the past.*

Conclusion

THE AFTERLIVES OF ARCHIVAL REDISCOVERY

ON JANUARY 26, 2019, POET Gabrielle Daniels published a poem titled "Something Else Again" on the poetry website "Poets Reading the News."[1] The poet was responding to a story from *UChicago News* announcing the rediscovery and identification of *Something Good—Negro Kiss* and its naming to the National Film Registry.[2] Dedicating her poem to the performers Saint Suttle and Gertie Brown, Daniels celebrates the film as "Evidence of things seldom seen" and the affection between Suttle and Brown, in the midst of racial terror, as evidence of "Something else going on." The poem opens:

> Evidence of things seldom seen
> emerging from the past
> of ropes and bending boughs,
> threats that happened
> for even talking back, man or woman,
> and of black marias making mischief with
> dark room cut-ups for only thirty seconds
> to a minute or two for the nickelodeons.
> A blind over anyone's eyes
> against the truth of seeing
> real life.
> Something else going on.

From this piercing opening, the poem poses a series of questions, expressing a desire for this "evidence" to be more forthcoming, as the poet attempts to read intention and meaning in the film's fleeting images. Daniels celebrates the novelty of the film—"Negroes kissing. Imagine that"—and the relatability of Suttle and Brown's rapport: "Just enjoyment, fleeting but appealing / to anyone who could be shy / or who could be goofy at the moment / of connection." At the same time, the poem captures the film's oscillation between enactment and improvisation: Suttle and Brown's performance of affection and affection as performance. *Something else going on.*

Something else is going on in the wake of the rediscovery of this archival artifact. As I've argued in this book, the rediscovery of *Something Good* compels us to write a new history of film and theater at the turn of the century. We have a richer picture of how early cinema negotiated race and racialized representation, how this brief glimpse of Black affection on screen constituted a parodic response to white minstrelsy and asserted an image of Black joy unlike anything we've known in early cinema. The film unlocks the histories of its performers, revealing the lives and careers of Suttle and Brown, unrecognized until the rediscovery of their brief appearance before the Polyscope more than a century ago. *Something Good* adds to cultural history and upends what historians understand about early cinema and Black representation. But it does more. The cinematic depiction of joyous affection touches viewers, and its audience continues to make meaning out of the spectacle and find inspiration in its images.

Daniels's poem is part of a set of creative projects made in the aftermath of the rediscovery of *Something Good*, from 2019 to the present. Emerging from a moment when the film went viral on social media, these include a poem by Christian Campbell as well as film projects by Ina Archer, Elaine Fuentes and Jane Brown, and Kahlil Pedizisai and Kevin Jerome Everson, among others. The film's circulation across platforms from social media to contemporary independent cinema amounts to what I'm calling the afterlives of its rediscovery.

By way of conclusion, I explore the film's afterlives through two interrelated trajectories spurred by its rediscovery. The first is the response the film elicited on social media. The second strand involves artistic engagements with *Something Good*, which I consider through a close look at *Glenville* (2020), a short film by experimental filmmakers Pedizisai and Everson. The case of *Something Good*'s celebrated rediscovery, while exceptional, offers a way to account for the afterlives of rediscovered early films in the public imagination and as sources for contemporary film practices.

NO BLACKFACE, JUST #BLACKLOVE

When *Something Good—Negro Kiss* was named to the National Film Registry in December 2018, the film elicited a tremendous amount of attention. The singularity and charm of the film spurred media interest and the publicity generated even more press. The film was, quite simply, something no one had seen before. At a time of virulent, systemic, and representational racism (a statement true in 1898 as it is now), representation matters. As a social media user named Goddess of Gumbo told her Twitter followers: "artists were fighting the battle of representation ... no blackface, just #BlackLove."

The attention in the mainstream press and the viral circulation of the film on social media fortuitously led to the further rediscoveries discussed in this book. In this way, the film's novelty and popularity among contemporary audiences directly contributed to additional rediscoveries that inform our understanding of the film, its performers, and its context of production and exhibition.

Here, though, I want to look at the way in which the film's rediscovery and circulation is itself an event worth discussion. What does this moment of viral circulation and media attention contribute to the history of this media object?

In all the hype about unvarnished #BlackLove, much of the discourse took *Something Good* as an unmediated view of Black life around 1900, as if it were a home movie or a peek at historical lovers. As I've shown throughout the book, such reception overlooks the fact that Suttle and Brown were professionals, filmed in their stage attire, performing an act of love for the camera. I mention this not to correct the reactions of social media commentators, but because of a striking contrast. By and large, the artists whose work engaged with the rediscovery of *Something Good* responded not only to the film but to the context of its reemergence, and precisely to its own status as a performance.

Among the social media users who encountered *Something Good* in 2018 was Kahlil Pedizisai. Pedizisai is a filmmaker and photographer, and he is also the assistant director on many of Kevin Jerome Everson's films. A major contemporary artist working across media, Everson is best known for his filmmaking, operating at the intersection of experimental and documentary cinema. As a filmmaker, Everson is deeply invested in the lives and experiences of working-class African Americans, in the communities surrounding his hometown of Mansfield, Ohio, and in the residual media artifacts that drift forward in history.

Pedizisai shared *Something Good* with Everson and, thinking that everyone would be rushing to make a contemporary film inspired by this nineteenth-century kiss film, they immediately set out to make a version of it by

FIGURE 30. *Glenville* (dir. Kahlil Pedizisai and Kevin Jerome Everson, 2020).

restaging and resituating it in Glenville, a neighborhood on the east side of Cleveland, Ohio.

GLENVILLE

For their film inspired by *Something Good*, Pedizisai shot in HD and Everson shot on 16mm (with his beloved, damaged Bolex). They titled the resulting film *Glenville*. *Glenville* is a ninety-second film comprising six shots of a Black man and woman flirting and kissing. Set on New Year's Eve (per the filmmakers' description), the couple hold hands and repeatedly embrace outside the Red Apple Supermarket at the corner of Eddy and Oakview in the Glenville neighborhood of East Cleveland.

At first glance it might seem like a straightforward reenactment, an homage, or even playful parody of the nineteenth-century kissers. However, in its engagement with *Something Good*, *Glenville* provides us a model for film historiography: a way of approaching this rediscovered archival artifact, contextualizing it, and ascribing meaning while critically confronting the implications of these acts of recuperation. As a critically aware film, *Glenville* helps bridge the distance from 1898 to the present, not least by mapping the failures of the twentieth century while claiming Black love and Black resistance through reenactment and restaging.

Like Suttle and Brown, the lovers in *Glenville* are also hired local actors, Sabrina McPherson and Hakeem Sharif. Pedizisai and Everson showed them *Something Good* and invited them to riff on it. *Glenville*'s actors both perform intimacy *and* perform performing intimacy. In this, they capture a key aspect of Suttle and Brown's original act for Selig: the concurrence of professionalism and a studied sense of the impromptu. Both performances consist of a tension between choreography and improvisation, planning and happenstance, intimacy and construction for the benefit of the camera.

Indeed, just like Brown and Suttle, McPherson and Sharif look to the unseen camera operators for direction, then resume their embrace. More subtly, McPherson's slight caution to Sharif, in the form of a discreet sign and demure glance before their first kiss, recalls Brown's smile and coy headshake as Suttle pulls her toward him.

FROM STUDIO TO STREET CORNER

But there is more to *Glenville* than the kiss. In place of Selig's plain canvas backdrop, *Glenville* is staged against an urban background: bodega signs, cigarette promotions, and customers moving in and out of the space. In being firmly situated in a specific place, *Glenville* undoes the placelessness of *Something Good*. Filmed at a spot near Everson's daughter's home, *Glenville*'s location has not only personal meaning for the filmmaker but also deep significance in the history of race- and class-based oppression in Cleveland. *Glenville* gives us a specific location, one that reinscribes the scene with the signification carried by the place, a signification that points to a legacy of insurgence, resistance, and ensuing retribution.

This aspect is, I believe, deeply important for understanding the work *Glenville* is doing. In focusing on Black people in situations and environments shaped and circumscribed by legacies of systemic racism, *Glenville* offers an answer to the question Kyle Alex Brett posted on Twitter, asking what the twentieth century did with the happiness exuded by *Something Good*.

The encounter of this couple on New Year's Eve is filmed in the milieu of an under-resourced community, in front of a bodega in a food desert. As Pedizisai comments, "It fits into the overall dynamic of what neighborhoods are in Cleveland." The bodega is designed for foot traffic, for people who don't have access to the major thoroughfares. These small independent stores are thus stocked with basic house supplies and products from processed foods to cigarettes. This backdrop indexes the long-term, systemic disinvestment in lower-income Black and Brown communities, resulting in massive health disparities and foreclosed opportunities. But the filmmakers do not directly reference systemic underdevelopment or aestheticize ruin (in what Everson has critiqued as "that poverty or ruin porn bullshit made by those carpetbagging motherfuckers") but rather invoke a site of resistance and insurrection.[3]

To get at this, we need a bit of context. Events that were known as the Hough riots took place in the Hough neighborhood of Cleveland from July 18 to 23, 1966. Officials blamed the uprising on "communists" and "black nationalists," dismissing the systemic, economic, and environmental conditions as merely the "uneasy backdrop" to the outbreak of civil disorder.[4] Against this official narrative, local Black leaders and organizations pointed to rampant racism, police brutality, community poverty and despair, and resultant social problems.

In the aftermath of the uprising, in 1967, Cleveland elected Carl Stokes as mayor, the first African American to lead a large US city. A year later, the July 1968 incident known as the Glenville shootout took place between the Cleveland police and the Black Nationalists of New Libya, who were under police surveillance. An uprising broke out, and Stokes called in the National Guard. He ordered all white policemen out of Glenville, replacing them with African American officers.

Stokes was blamed (by many whites) for the uprising. As a result, redevelopment and revitalization plans were stymied as the police budget ballooned and its force became increasingly militarized.

To Pedizisai, the Glenville incident, compared with the more well-known Hough uprising two years earlier, was the more impactful event in Cleveland's history, especially with the consequences it had on the community. Pedizisai argues, "In a major way Glenville has had to pay for that riot, that rebellion of '68, by the level of lack of service. So, for years it has carried that stigma and because of that stigma, this place where there was this insurrection, they have long been underserved by the police and overpoliced. They've been underserved by their level of healthcare, access to commercial districts, underserved by the education system."[5] Pedizisai sees *Glenville* as a kind of "part two" of an earlier film, *Emergency Needs* (2007), Everson's film on Mayor Stokes's press conference addressing the Glenville uprising (for which Pedizisai served as assistant director).

All of this is to say that "Glenville" as a title as well as a location invokes an emplaced history of police violence, systemic racism, and oppressive state institutions. At the same time, it summons the spirit of insurrection and self-determination that marked the events, albeit with devastating consequences for the community. The name, then, calls up the legacies of antiblack and antipoor conditions, and the resilience of a community rejecting these conditions.

LOVE IN THE WAKE OF DEATH

Here we return to the questions of performance that motivate the filmmakers and the radical possibility of Black love. The political valences of Black love predate the Movement for Black Lives, of course, but I want to point to the significance of love, affection, and joy that Black writers and artists have invoked in our current moment to demonstrate, as bell hooks asserts, that "Love is profoundly political."[6] As James Baldwin's niece, Aisha Karefa-Smart, said at the premiere of Barry Jenkins's *If Beale Street Could Talk* (based on Baldwin's novel), "The act of loving while black is a revolutionary act. It's an act of resistance to love under the conditions with which we live" (a quote Kyle Alex Brett posted on Twitter in the same thread as his initial post sharing *Something Good*).[7] Adjacently, we might also think about the radical possibilities of Black *joy*, as Pedizisai invites us to do, commenting on a recent photographic project he produced: "I believe that Black Joy is one of the most precious forms of resistance."[8]

The expression of affection in this setting is an homage to resistance. As a film, *Glenville* softly but unequivocally asserts the politics of Black love as revolutionary action against state violence. Everson and Pedizisai turn toward this in *Glenville*, not to show an unmediated picture of Black love but to think about it as thoroughly imbricated in place and politics. *Glenville* reminds us of the radical possibility of Black love at the site of violence and rebellion; love is the ultimate form of resistance and resilience.

To approach *Glenville* with the lens of radical Black love is to look through a prism of refracting and multiplying loves—the New Year's Eve actors-as-lovers in their performative homage to the first known kiss between Black people recorded by a motion-picture camera. To look at it now is to look at both the radical possibility of Black love on the street (*Love is the Message*) and the actions that once seemed harmless but carry a disproportionate risk in the time of global pandemics and emboldened white supremacist attacks on Black being (*The Message is Death*). Like Arthur Jafa's 2016 masterwork, *Glenville* stages the palimpsest of love and death. This is not just because of location or post-2020 framing. The precarious margin between love and death, between celebration and threat, is echoed in *Glenville*'s soundtrack of DIY fireworks, the rat-a-tat-tats of automatic gunfire recorded in Glenville on New Year's Eve. In this way, the muffled sound of AR-15 rifles shooting into the ground is the film's chorus—part of the backdrop but also the explicator, for the spectator, of the setting of the action.

Sound is also what led *Something Good* to go viral: not the film itself, as impactful as it was, but Brett's setting of it to Nicholas Britell's "Agape" from the soundtrack of *If Beale Street Could Talk* and posting it to Twitter. *Something Good* went viral because of the interplay of sound and image, specifically the matching of archivally recovered image and contemporary sound. Thus, in its rediscovery and widespread circulation, *Something Good* was a remix, a found footage film. "Agape"—"a sound that felt like love"—replaces the ragtime music that Suttle and Brown performed and that would have accompanied most screenings of the film in its first release.[9] Barry Jenkins instructed Britell on the score, "It needs to feel like joy."[10] At the same time, the score reflects what Britell calls "the music of injustice, and the horrors of injustice."[11] Brett's marrying of *Something Good* and "Agape" invokes both the "upward looking" melodies and the "parallel universe" of injustice represented by the music, underscoring—or *scoring*—the concurrent joy and pain of the nineteenth-century performers.

Glenville's sound derives from joy—celebration—that is at the same time inexorably linked to violence and pain—gunfire. Like the soundtrack of *If Beale Street Could Talk*, the instruments used to suggest joy are the same ("though they are bent and distorted") as those used to express "the horrors of injustice."[12] In this way, Everson and Pedizisai invoke a key aspect of Brett's version of *Something Good*: what the twentieth century did with the couple's happiness.

We can see *Glenville* as a meditation on sites of residue and resistance, one that insists on joy—on love—as the defiant response to foreclosed hope. Importantly, the film does not elide the violence of the site's history but recuperates it; gunfire becomes the celebratory soundtrack to falling in love.

I want to conclude by proposing that *Glenville* performs a kind of "wake work," to invoke Black Studies scholar Christina Sharpe's evocative process modeled in her 2016 book *In the Wake: On Blackness and Being*. The multiple registers she activates on the afterlives of slavery—the wake as the consequence of something, the path behind a ship, as keeping watch with the dead, being awake as coming to (and into) consciousness—are also aspects of the afterlives of archival rediscovery that I believe are generative for thinking about the significations of *Something Good*. My invocation of archival afterlives of an artifact of Black performance of/and affection intends to carry these resonances. With *In the Wake*, Sharpe helps to map an imperative for thinking through and with archival afterlives.

With the wake, Sharpe offers an analytic that checks my impulse (as a film historian) to "correct" the (mis)readings of contemporary spectators. Thinking about social media responses to *Something Good* as a form of "Black annotation," in Sharpe's terms, is important here. These engagements offer a counter-annotation to the captioning, framing, and explanatory text furnished by producers and distributors, and elaborated on by exhibitors (as discussed in Chapter One). Descriptors such as "Darky burlesque" and "very grotesque" become the portion redacted in favor of a new annotation celebrating Black love. These annotations offer a counternarrative to racist framing while still acknowledging the general climate in which the film was made and produced—the weather, in Sharpe's term, of antiblackness.

My own annotative work here, then, is in a dynamic constellation with the voices on social media that discuss the film and Black media more generally. It is also engaged with Everson and Pedizisai's film, itself another form of "Black annotation" that alongside and from the Black annotative work of thousands of social media commentators functions as "ways of imagining otherwise."[13] *Something Good* imagines a world in which the filmic expression of Black love is one of endearing affection rather than racist ridicule. It imagines an audience for the expression of Black affection. It imagines humor deriving from interpersonal dynamics rather than racist framing. It imagines that it is not unique, that is it as ubiquitous as *The May Irwin Kiss*. It imagines a world in which it is as *un*remarkable as a home movie, or, in poet Gabrielle Daniels's words, "Special but just everyday." It imagines itself as a vernacular expression of romance and affection.

What, then, might *Glenville* be imagining otherwise? *Glenville* allows for the desires of *Something Good* to coexist with the conditions that foreclosed its aspirations. Sharpe reminds us, "In the wake, the past that is not past reappears, always, to rupture the present."[14] *Glenville* allows Suttle and Brown to be performers and lovers; it allows the performance of love to imagine the neighborhood of Glenville otherwise—as a site of love and resilience on the pavement that barely muffles its history.

Seen this way, *Glenville* is a work of love *as* resistance. This is wake work. For Pedizisai and Everson, the work is filmmaking, specifically imaginative reenactment. For me, the work of writing film history in the wake of archival rediscovery, especially of Black subjects in early cinema, is to hold the present close even as we scaffold the artifact with the contextual apparatus woven from disciplinarity and expertise. That present, then, demands an undisciplining—in Sharpe's formulation—to recognize the afterlives not just as responses but as answers to the question about what the twentieth century did to Black happiness. It's through Everson and Pedizisai that the question becomes one that turns back on *Something Good*'s act of love.

SOMETHING ELSE: A CHANCE TO FEEL "UP"

Something Else, a 2007 film by Everson, comprises a short found-footage interview with a white male reporter interviewing a young Black woman, addressed as Miss Stevens, after winning the 1971 Miss Black Roanoke Valley pageant. The interview starts off rather mundanely, with the reporter asking her if she plans to do the same talent in the upcoming Danville pageant, to which she replies, she's planning "something else, something different." Without hesitance or embarrassment, revealing the ingrained acceptance of these institutions, even in the so-called post–civil rights era of the early 1970s, the reporter then asks if she prefers to be in a segregated or an integrated pageant. She responds with shy by firm candor that it's not a matter of preference, but that she would not have a chance of winning in an integrated pageant: "I hate to say it, but it's kinda true." She clarifies, "It's not that it's segregated ... but it's necessary to segregate in order to give Blacks girls a chance to feel ... 'up.'" Everson then cuts to apparently more recent footage of a Black pageant queen on a float, waving to onlookers. Shot from a low angle looking up at the woman, slowed down, repeated, and filtered with pink, we are given both *something else* and someone *up*.

FIGURE 31. *Something Else* (dir. Kevin Jerome Everson, 2007).

Thinking of *Something Else* in dialogue with *Something Good*, and not merely because of the echoes in names, points to an aspect of *Something Good*'s appeal—the power and possible pleasures afforded by intra-racial sites of performance. Sure, the money wasn't as good, but did Suttle and Brown enjoy, say, the Milwaukee Emancipation Day performance in front of Black audiences more than their time on the vaudeville stages of Chicago's Loop? Suttle was invested in cultivating Black audiences for Black talent and dreamed of forming a stock company for an all-Black theater.[15] For her part, Brown spent her later years tending to Black actors in the center of Harlem's entertainment mecca. In the frequently demeaning milieu of the turn-of-the-century popular stage, were Suttle and Brown looking for ways to feel *up*? Selig's Polyscope contraption gave them an opportunity, a semiprivate stage for playfulness, a moment of silliness in the too serious business of entertainment. In a world that put them down, Suttle and Brown's act of kissing for the Polyscope constituted a counteraction, an insistence on being *up*.

With her coy smile and demure demeanor for Selig's camera, Gertie Brown anticipates Miss Stevens's performance before the white reporter.

What was Miss Stevens's new talent in the Danville pageant? What was her *something else*? With a sly smile holding her secret close, she doesn't reveal it to the interviewer, but her eyes tell us that it's something special. It's something that made her feel *up*.

The subtle feistiness of the fifteen-year-old Miss Stevens that we glimpse in *Something Else* carried into adulthood. Stevens became a professional singer performing under the name René Marie and committed her voice to social justice work, seeing music as a mechanism to "help us feel more deeply together."[16] In 2008, she was invited to sing the national anthem to open the Denver State of the City address. For her performance, she replaced the lyrics of "The Star Spangled Banner" with those of James Weldon Johnson's "Lift Every Voice and Sing" (1900), known as the Black National Anthem. Roundly denounced, including by then-presidential candidate Barak Obama, René Marie's act was celebrated as a bold gesture of defiance by others, including political commentator Mark Lamont Hill, who called it "black patriotism." Hill told NPR that "Lift Every Voice and Sing" celebrates progress and hope, but "it's also keenly—fundamentally, even—preoccupied with the obstacles that lay in front of us." Hill defended René Marie's adaptation, especially poignant at that political moment "where people are celebrating Barack Obama as president. People are excited that the country has moved forward—but people [are] still keenly aware that there are many, many forms of inequality, unfreedom, suffering [and] marginalization that continue to proliferate in this nation."[17]

The lyrics are unwaveringly hopeful while acknowledging the "stony road" from Emancipation to the present:

> *Sing a song full of the faith that the dark past has taught us*
> *Sing a song full of the hope that the present has brought us*

In 1900, the dark past was the previous century of enslavement and Jim Crow. The "present" of 1900 seemed hopeful enough to James Weldon Johnson, and probably to Saint Suttle and Gertie Brown as well. From this side of the twentieth century, it's heartrending to see their optimism.

SOMETHING ELSE AGAIN

Gabrielle Daniels's poem concludes, after speculating about Suttle and Brown's relationship and their ease with one another, with the lines,

At least
we know their names—
recovered but not famous.
Special but just everyday.
And now we see them
acting like
something real was going on.

Daniels captures the tension between performance and candor that makes the film so compelling. She also draws out the tension between "acting" and "something real," the performance of affection and affection as performance, which marks Suttle and Brown's rapport. Something else—as in otherwise—becomes (with vernacular inflection, that is, through living language) simultaneously *something else*—as in extraordinary. *Special but just everyday.*

The desire to know the performers across time—their story, their intentions, their feelings—echoes the desire to reclaim love in times and places of deep hostility; how do you access something from the past that only leaves incomplete traces? What's at stake in even trying? Living in the aftermath, in the wake, unmoors us when traces of the past, the causations, are silenced.

Looking at *Something Good* through the lens of *Glenville* offers a way of attending to the afterlives of archival rediscovery that is not separate from but co-constitutive of the rediscovered artifact. That's the work—and I argue the imperative—of writing history. This is research as an act of love. The result is that we are compelled to recognize that the *Something Good* we encounter is not just film history. It is a living twenty-first-century digital artifact, given to us through social media, framed through forms of generative Black annotation. The nitrate print rests preserved in a vault while the digital artifact, with all its meanings, lives on.

PLATE CAPTIONS

APPRECIATIONS

From the start of this project, I've been acutely aware of—and deeply humbled by—how much this book owes to the help of others, from the support of institutions to the generosity of colleagues.

First and foremost, this book is the product of scholar-archivist collaboration. I am grateful to Dino Everett for sharing his archival rediscovery with me and for trusting me with it. Film scholars depend on archivists' stewardship of audio-visual cultural heritage, and it has been my privilege to have benefited so greatly from Dino's work. I need, therefore, to give my deepest thanks to Dino and the USC HMH Foundation Moving Image Archive. I also want to thank the National Film Preservation Board and the Librarian of Congress, Dr. Carla Hayden, for naming *Something Good—Negro Kiss* to the National Film Registry in 2018 and thereby enabling this treasure to be shared with the world.

I was very fortunate to receive two major grants while writing this book. First, the 2020–2021 ACLS/Burkhardt Residential Fellowship enabled me to spend a year in residence at the Newberry Library and then provided a course reduction upon returning to teaching the following year. Second, the 2024–2025 National Endowment for the Humanities Public Scholar Award provided me with a yearlong fellowship to complete the manuscript.

Other institutions provided support, resources, and intellectual communities. As I embarked on this project, I had the privilege of participating in a NEH Summer Institute for College and University Faculty on Art and Public Culture in Chicago at the Newberry Library in 2018. I was, and am, deeply honored to have been named a 2019 Academy Film Scholar by the Academy of Motion Picture Arts & Sciences. Receiving an award from the Academy is a career highlight. I also want to thank the University of Chicago's Center for the Study of Race, Politics, and Culture and the Andrew W. Mellon Foundation for a Publications Support grant, and the Harvard University Department of Comparative Literature for a Schofield Fund grant. Thanks to the Franke Institute for the Humanities at the University of Chicago for a Faculty Research Grant and their support for my research project on Chicago Black Film Cultures, a project of which this book is a part.

I was fortunate to participate in the College Research Fellows Program at University of Chicago in 2017–2018, which enabled me to work with undergraduate research assistants at the early stages of this project. I want to thank the undergrad RAs whose enthusiasm fueled this research: Natasha Rodgers, Sophie Salvato, and Fikayo Walter. I also had the privilege of working with graduate student RAs whose expertise in film and media history—old and new—shaped the contours book: Tiya Bolton, Ben Kiem, Hunter Koch, Avery LaFlamme, and Aurore Spiers. Thanks as well to the students in graduate seminars at the University of Chicago, whose insights and questions challenged my readings of material I thought I already knew. These seminars were Minstrelsy–Vaudeville–Cinema: Racialized Performance and American Popular Culture (2019), The Archive of Absence: Theories and Methodologies of Evidence (2017 and 2024), and Speculation (2023).

This book would not be possible without the professional expertise of librarians and archivists. In addition to Dino Everett at the HMH Foundation Moving Image Archive at USC, I want to thank to the following people and institutions for their support: Mike Mashon and George Willeman at the Library of Congress; Ron Magliozzi at the Museum of Modern Art; Peter Bagrov, Kirk McDowell, and Beth Rennie at the George Eastman Museum; Bent Bang-Hansen, Michelle Tisdel, and Tone Føreland at the National Library of Norway; Nancy Spiegel, Susan Martin, and Scott Landvatter at the University of Chicago Library; Bridgett Pride and A.J. Muhammad at the Schomburg Center for Research in Black Culture; Alison Hinderliter, Matthew Rutherford, Maggie Cusick, Brad Hunt, Keelin Burke, Liesl Olson, and Madeline Crispell at the Newberry Library; Jonathan Hoppe at the Philadelphia Museum of Art; Valerie Stenner at the University of Delaware's Morris Library's Special Collections; Louise Hilton, Genevieve Maxwell, Kristine Krueger, and Elizabeth Cathcart at the Academy of Motion Picture Arts and Sciences Margaret Herrick Library; David M. Butler at the Music and Performing Arts Library, University of Illinois at Urbana-Champaign; Cindy Lindsay at the Columbus Metropolitan Library, Ohio; Delaney Todd at the State Fair of Texas; Ronda Sewald at the Black Film Center/Archive at Indiana University; David Kiehn at the Niles Essanay Silent Film Museum; Rick Malkames at The Malkames Collection; and Michael R. Taylor at the Virginia Museum of Fine Arts. Thanks also to the Stuart A. Rose Library, Emory University; Beinecke Rare Book and Manuscript Library, Yale University; and the indispensable Media History Digital Library and the Internet Archive.

Not all the work took place in an archive. I'm grateful to have been able to present parts of this book at many institutions and to have received such excellent ideas and questions from the audiences. These institutions include Columbia University, Ghent University, Goethe University Frankfurt, Indiana University, Northwestern

University, University of Iowa, the Center for Visual Cultures at the University of Wisconsin-Madison, and the Chaz & Roger Ebert Symposium at the University of Illinois Urbana-Champaign. At the University of Chicago, I had the pleasure of sharing my work with the Mass Culture Workshop; the Center for the Study of Race, Politics, and Culture; The Karla Scherer Center for the Study of American Culture; and through lectures organized by the Office of Civic Engagement, the Humanities Division, Media Aesthetics, and Alumni Relations and Development. Thank you to Arts & Public Life, the Reva and David Logan Center for the Arts, and the South Side Home Movie Project for giving me the opportunity to work with Reginald R. Robinson for Spinning Home Movies #19: "Rhythm and Love." I'm also grateful for the opportunity to present my work at Society for Cinema and Media Studies; Association of Moving Image Archivists; Domitor; Orphan Film Symposium; Seeing Selig at the Chicago History Museum; the Black Film Summit at the Academy Museum; Race and the Speculative at the Stanford Humanities Center; and the Newberry Library Fellows' Seminar.

Writing is a lonely enterprise but made easier by the fact I've been surrounded by incredibly supportive comrades across several writing groups. I want to thank my Newberry Fellows writing group, especially Christine Adams, Julie Fisher, Kelly Fleming, and LaDale Winling; my NEH Public Scholars writing group, especially LaDale Winling, James Romm, Andrew Huebner, and Kimberly Mack; Helen Sword and the WriteSpace community of writers; and my pandemic (and beyond) writing group: Grace An, Shannon Draucker, Ari Gass, Katerina Korola, Kate Nesbit, and Amanda Shubert. In writing and in life, Samantha Sheppard and Racquel Gates provided constant virtual companionship, and I'm grateful for their presence and friendship as we navigate academic careers, parenthood, and the ever-unsettling world.

I'm grateful for my colleagues across the University of Chicago, and especially in Cinema and Media Studies. It's been an honor to be among such extraordinary scholars over the past decade. The conversations I've had formally and informally—whether in seminars, workshops, events, meetings, or even casual gatherings—have shaped my ideas more than I can express. I thank you all. It was a privilege to work with Courtney Guerra, who provided expert support in the grant and fellowship application process. My research was also supported by two deans who went out of their way to ensure I had the time and resources to complete this project: Anne W. Robertson and Debbie Nelson.

This book would not be possible without the scholarship and generosity of two people at the University of Chicago: Tom Gunning and Jacqueline Stewart. I shared *Something Good—Negro Kiss* with Tom early in the research process, and I'm grateful for his insightful comments, astute eye, informed observations, and ongoing encouragement. Throughout the process of thinking and writing this book, I've relied on Jacqueline as a friend, colleague, and collaborator. Her feedback made this book stronger, and she has, throughout my career, provided a model for what publicly engaged scholarship could be.

Many people contributed to the research in this book, whether that was sharing expertise in conversations and correspondence, reading parts of the book and offering feedback, providing key research support, or, as so many of them did, pushing me to better hone my work. My thanks to Ina Archer, Kyle Alex Brett, Gerald Butters, Cara Caddoo, Christian Campbell, Rhea Combs, Gabrielle Daniels, Kevin Jerome Everson, Eve Ewing, Terri Francis, Jane Gaines, Racquel Gates, Michael Gillespie, Christopher Harris, Liam Kilby, Rob King, Robert J. Kiss, Amy Lippert, Shola Lynch, Ron Magliozzi, Mike Mashon, David Mayer, CK Ming, Charlie Musser, Liesl Olson, Kahlil Pedizisai, Miriam Petty, Tina Post, Thomas L. Riis, Reginald Robinson, Amina Ross, TreaAndrea Russworm, Nic Sammond, Raffeal Sears, Samantha Sheppard, Michael R. Taylor, Floyd Webb, and George Willeman.

Along the way, scholars, colleagues, and friends offered insights, wisdom, and encouragement. I'm grateful for each of them: Paula Amad, Doris Berger, Matthew Bernstein, Cynthia Blair, Larissa Brewer-García, Adrienne Brown, Madison Brown, Keelin Burke, James Cahill, Ben Caldwell, James Chandler, Ashley Clark, Liz Clarke, Kelly Conway, Susan Courtney, Sabrina Craig, Lauren Cramer, Madeline Crispell, Liz Czach, Pardis Dabashi, Dennis Doros, Erika Dudley, Chaz Ebert, Carolyn Faber, Anton Ford, Agata Frymus, Tanya Goldman, Marsha Gordon, Buckey Grimm, Katherine Groo, Saidiya Hartman, Chad Heap, Amy Heller, Maggie Hennefeld, Eric Hoyt, Patrick Jagoda, Martin Johnson, Ritika Kaushik, Sarah Keller, Jane Keranen, Amanda Ann Klein, Lies Lanckman, Patricia Leavy, Jeff Look, Agnes Lugo-Ortiz, Rochona Majumdar, Leonard Maltin, Paula Massood, Tracye Matthews, Paul McEwan, Douglas McLaren, Elizabeth Myles, Richard Neer, Arionne Nettles, Hayley O'Malley, Lakshmi Padmanabhan, Kaneesha Parsard, Alessandra Raengo, Ariel Rogers, Danielle Roper, Benjamin Ruder, Gina Samuels, Jeffrey Sconce, Ellen Scott, Elyse Singer, Saroop Singh, Amanda Shubert, Salomé Aguilera Skvirsky, Eric Smoodin, Lynn Spigel, Jeff Spitz, AE Stevenson, Wanda Strauven, Dan Streible, Werner Sollors, Julie Turnock, Lisa Uddin, Neil Verma, Greg Waller, Rebecca Wanzo, LaCharles Ward, Ken Warren, Floyd Webb, Yvonne Welbon, Mark Williams, Pam Wojcik, Josh Yumibe, Agata Zborowska, SJ Zhang, and Rebecca Zorach.

Writing about the somewhat distant past often feels like diving into another world. Reminding me of its proximity to our own times, I was fortunate to encounter living decedents of the people whose lives this book tells. I hope to do their ancestors justice and I thank them for their openness with me, their enthusiasm for this project, and their generosity with their memories and stories: Barry Moreno, the step-grandson of Tim Moore; and Cynthia Cummings and Ron Cummings, Saint Suttle's great-grandchildren—who know him as Saint Suttles. When I bemoaned the belatedness of Suttle's recognition, Ron told me "History is never late." I carry those words with me.

It has been a joy to work with Raina Polivka at the University of California Press. She helped me sharpen the ideas in this book from my initial thoughts through their development and to the point of publication. I thank her, Sam Warren, and Julie Van Pelt, who expertly shepherded this book to print, and the entire production team at UC Press. I was fortunate to have two excellent (then-anonymous) peer reviewers for this book. Thanks to Cara Caddoo and Samantha Sheppard for their careful read, thoughtful suggestions, and generous feedback. I also want to thank the anonymous first-round reader who, along with Dr. Sheppard, provided incredibly helpful suggestions. I couldn't have asked for better readers for this project. I especially want to thank the brilliant Megan Pugh for both her subject expertise and her astute editorial skill. Working with her as a developmental editor on this project was a gift. Susan Higman Larsen was a dream copy editor. Thanks also to Tere Mullin for compiling such a careful index of difficult material.

Communities matter. I wrote this book in the Hyde Park neighborhood on Chicago's South Side, surrounded by a thriving, vibrant, diverse community that offers daily reminders of love, joy, and resilience. I've also been nurtured by an amazing family of scholars and teachers whose love and support have been a constant presence in my life: my parents John Osgood Field and Nazli Choucri Field, my aunt Wasfeya Choucri, and my parents-in-law Barbara Herman and Mickey Morgan.

No one knows more what an act of love writing this book has been than Dan Morgan. His own love and care are on every page, in each tweaked turn of phrase, corrected writing tick, and improved transition; he's an incredible reader with impeccable judgment. He's also the best person I know: an unflappable moral rock whom I'm so lucky to have by my side. He expands what love means, from the love of scholarship to scholarship as an act of love. He is my love, my joy, my life. It's hard for me to separate my books from my family. *Uplift Cinema* was published shortly after our son Theo was born, while this book marks our daughter Zoe's first decade—from the day of her birth, when I first saw Dino's scans of *Something Good*, to the book's publication as she turns nine. I look forward to more of the intertwined loves. Life with Dan, Theo, and Zoe (and our smoochy pooch Milly) is full of constant discovery, exuberant joy, and steadfast love.

When *Something Good—Negro Kiss* went viral on social media, most people saw it on their phones. I'd like to think that Henry T. Sampson, as both a historian of Black cinema and an engineer whose inventions enabled modern cell phone technology, would be delighted by this convergence. This book is for him.

ACKNOWLEDGMENTS

This research was assisted by a Frederick Burkhardt Residential Fellowship for Recently Tenured Scholars from the American Council of Learned Societies.

This book was also supported by a National Endowment for the Humanities Public Scholar Fellowship. Any views, findings, conclusions, or recommendations expressed in this book do not necessarily reflect those of the National Endowment for the Humanities.

This work was also supported by a grant from the Academy Film Scholars Program of the Academy of Motion Picture Arts and Sciences.

This publication was subsidized in part by Harvard Studies in Comparative Literature.

This book was also supported by a grant from the University of Chicago's Center for the Study of Race, Politics, and Culture and the Andrew W. Mellon Foundation.

A preliminary version of Chapter One was published by Indiana University Press as "Archival Rediscovery and the Production of History: Solving the Mystery of *Something Good-Negro Kiss* (1898)," *Film History: An International Journal* 33, no. 2 (Summer 2021): 1–33. An earlier version of Chapter Two was published by Wayne State University Press as "The Cinema of Racialized Attraction(s): *The John C. Rice-May Irwin Kiss* and *Something Good—Negro Kiss*," *Discourse: Journal for Theoretical Studies in Media and Culture* 44, no. 1 (Winter 2022): 3–41.

The Introduction includes expanded ideas first published in Domitor's *Snapshots*, October 2019, and the Conclusion includes ideas first explored in *Black One Shot* 14.2, *ASAP Review*, August 27, 2020, and further developed in the chapter "In the Wake of Archival Rediscovery: The Afterlives of *Something Good—Negro Kiss* (1898)," in *The Routledge Companion to American Film History*, ed. Paula J. Masood and Pamela Robertson Wojcik (Routledge, 2025): 367–77.

NOTES

INTRODUCTION

1. Jacqueline Stewart, "Discovering Black Film History: Tracing the Tyler, Texas Black Film Collection," *Film History* 23, no. 2 (2011): 147.

2. Natalia Molina, *A Place at the Nayarit: How a Mexican Restaurant Nourished a Community* (University of California Press, 2022), 20.

3. "Gertie Moore Passes Away," *New York Amsterdam News*, February 28, 1934, 1.

4. The death certificate of infant Suttle lists the mother's name as Goldie Smith.

5. Death certificate of Saint Suttle.

6. *New York Clipper*, December 29, 1888, 675.

7. "A Black Trilby," *Purcell Register*, December 3, 1896, 1.

8. *New York Clipper*, March 15, 1890, 4.

9. The play *Trilby* was written by Paul M. Potter and based on George du Maurier's 1894 novel. "Clarksville News Items," *Freeman*, January 16, 1897, 5; advertisement, *Americus Times Recorder*, February 20, 1897, 3; "Coming Amusements," *Daily Times-Enterprise*, February 26, 1897, 1; "Theatrical Notes," *Illinois Record*, November 6, 1897, 2; *New York Clipper*, September 5, 1896, 425.

10. W. T. Lhamon Jr., *Raising Cain: Blackface Performance from Jim Crow to Hip Hop* (Harvard University Press, 1998), 136, 126. See also Eric Lott, *Love and Theft: Blackface Minstrelsy and the American Working Class* (Oxford University Press, 1993).

11. Lott, *Love and Theft*, 11.

12. Ibid., 39.

13. David Krasner, "'The Mirror Up to Nature': Modernist Aesthetics and Racial Authenticity in African American Theatre, 1895–1900," *Theatre History* Studies 16 (June 1996): 125. In his discussion of "reinscription," Krasner draws from Edward Said's reading of Frantz Fanon.

14. Alan Gevison, "Vaudeville," in *Encyclopedia of Early Cinema*, ed. Richard Abel (Routledge, 2005), 672.

15. Advertisement, *Chicago Tribune*, September 29, 1901, 38.

16. "National and Local Theatrical and Stage Notes," *Broad Ax*, September 30, 1911, 1.

17. *The Wichita Daily Eagle*, December 17, 1899, 4; *The Daily Ardmoreite*, April 1, 1906, 8; *Dallas Morning News*, August 8, 1900, 10; *Charlotte News*, April 3, 1901, 5; *Wilmington Morning Star*, June 13, 1901, 4.

18. *Moving Picture News*, January 2, 1915, 50.

19. *Motion Picture World*, May 3, 1913, 518. See also Rob King, *The Fun Factory: The Keystone Film Company and the Emergence of Mass Culture* (University of California Press, 2009), 70.

20. *Pictures and the Picturegoer*, March 11, 1916, 558.

21. The cannibal chief is played by Noble Johnson, a Hollywood character actor who was also a race filmmaker and cofounder of the Lincoln Motion Picture Company.

22. Charlene Regester offers an extended interpretation of the function of Black women in *The Navigator* and Keaton's other silent films in "Black Women Provide Divergent Representations of Blackness in Buster Keaton's Silent Pictures," *Film Criticism* 48, no. 2 (2024): 1–33.

23. See, for example, Anna Everett, *Returning the Gaze: A Genealogy of Black Film Criticism, 1909–1949* (Duke University Press, 2001).

24. Gavin James, *Stormy Weather: The Life of Lena Horne* (Atria Books, 2009), 130.

25. Ellen C. Scott, "Black Movement Impolitic: Soundies, Regulation, and Black Pleasure," *African American Review* 49, no. 3 (Fall 2016): 212. Scott notes the exception of Hollywood-produced "Soundies," three-minute films made for "Panoram" film jukeboxes between 1940 and 1947. See also Susan Courtney, *Hollywood Fantasies of Miscegenation: Spectacular Narratives of Gender and Race, 1903–1967* (Princeton University Press, 2005).

26. Harry Levette, "Gossip of the Movie Lots," *Plaindealer*, October 6, 1944, 6.

27. Harry Levette, "Gossip of the Movie Lots," *Plaindealer*, May 25, 1945, 6.

28. While *The Clock* seems to respond to Walter White and the NAACP's Hollywood bureau's call for improved Black representation in studio films, it remains an exceptional case even at a moment of increasing Hollywood liberalism in the wartime era. See, for example, Thomas Cripps, "'Walter's Thing': The NAACP's Hollywood Bureau of 1946—A Cautionary Tale," *Journal of Popular Film and Television* 33, no. 2 (Summer 2005): 116–25.

29. Ashley D. Farmer, "In Search of the Black Women's History Archive," *Modern American History* 1, no. 2 (2018): 293.

CHAPTER ONE. SOLVING THE MYSTERY OF ARCHIVAL REDISCOVERY

1. Charles Musser, *Edison Motion Pictures, 1890–1900: An Annotated Filmography* (Smithsonian Institution Press, 1997), 426.

2. Ibid., 197.

3. For a discussion of the "imitations and reworkings" of *The May Irwin Kiss*, see Charles Musser, "A Cornucopia of Images: Comparison and Judgment Across Theater, Film, and the Visual Arts During the Late Nineteenth Century," in *Moving Pictures: American Art and Early Film 1880–1910*, ed. Nancy Mowll Mathews with Charles Musser (Hudson Hills, 2005), 33–34.

4. The International Federation of Film Archives (FIAF) online database only accounts for known films held by FIAF member archives. It does not include unprocessed films, unidentified films, films held by private collectors, or nonextant films (films that no longer survive). For American film, the American Film Institute (AFI) print catalog and online catalog (in searchable database form) is more comprehensive, as it includes every film produced in the US or by American production companies. This online database (and the print catalog that preceded it) does include films thought to be nonextant and is aggregated from original producer and distributor catalog records and other sources. After using the combined AFI–BFI (British Film Institute) online catalogs and the FIAF online database to compile an initial filmography, I turned to the microfilm edition of *Motion Picture Catalogs by American Producers and Distributors, 1894–1908*, edited by Charles Musser in 1985. The catalogs are also available in PDF form online through Rutgers University Libraries.

5. Musser notes that at the time of the compilation of the microfilm edition of American motion-picture catalogs published between 1894 and 1908, "a comparatively small number of such catalogs remain. Some are fragmentary or incomplete; most are unique; and all are fragile. In a few cases only photocopies of the originals survive." Charles Musser, ed., introduction to *Thomas A. Edison Papers: A Guide to Motion Picture Catalogs by American Producers and Distributors, 1894–1908; A Microfilm Edition* (University Publications of America, 1985), 1.

6. Terry Ramsaye, *A Million and One Nights: A History of the Motion Picture* (Simon and Schuster, 1926), 308.

7. *1903 Complete Catalogue of Films and Moving Picture Machines* (Selig Polyscope Co., 1903), 27, in William Selig papers, Margaret Herrick Library, Academy of Motion Picture Arts and Sciences.

8. *1907 Catalogue of the Selig Polyscope and Library of Selig Films* (Selig Polyscope Co., 1907), 66.

9. *Catalogue of New Films for Projection and Other Projects* (F. M. Prescott, 1899). Prescott sold films made by Edison and Lubin, and he was sued by Edison in 1899, so it is possible that he was selling other producers' films.

10. *Animated Pictures* (Schneider, n.d.).

11. *AFI Catalog*, ProQuest, 2021. AFI dates the film as 1902, citing an advertisement for Lubin's films in the *New York Clipper*, October 4, 1902, 712; *Complete Catalogue of Lubin's Films* (January 1903), 36.

12. *AFI Catalog*, ProQuest, 2021; *Complete Catalogue of Lubin's Films*, 52.

13. *Complete Catalogue of Lubin's Films*, 41.

14. *1903 Complete Catalogue of Films and Moving Picture Machines*, 27.

15. Harold Brown, *Physical Characteristics of Early Films as Aids to Identification* (FIAF, 1990), 6.

16. Though partially based on the Armat-Edison model, Lumière's machine was not subject to litigation as Edison had not sought foreign patents.

17. Andrew A. Erish, *Col. William N. Selig, the Man Who Invented Hollywood* (University of Texas Press, 2012), 9–10, 226n14.

18. William Selig, interview by Charles Clarke, n.d., Charles G. Clarke collection, Margaret Herrick Library, Academy of Motion Picture Arts and Sciences; Erish, *Col. William N. Selig*, 10; Paul Spehr, *The Man Who Made Movies: W. K. L. Dickson* (John Libbey, 2008), 369.

19. Minutes of the directors' meeting of the Selig Polyscope Company, December 18, 1900, folder 527, William Selig Papers, Margaret Herrick Library, Academy of Motion Picture Arts and Sciences.

20. *Oxford English Dictionary* (July 2023), s.v. "osculatory (adj.), sense 2."

21. *Oxford English Dictionary* (March 2024), s.v. "burlesque (n.), sense 3.b."

22. *Special Catalogue of the Optigraph Moving Picture Machines: Calcium Light Outfits, Films for Moving Pictures* (Sears, Roebuck and Co., 1898).

23. A comparison of the titles for sale in the Sears catalogs and the list of films in the Selig inventory as well as other manufacturers' catalogs suggests that while Sears did indeed sell Selig films, it did not do so exclusively.

24. The University of Delaware's Morris Library's Special Collections has a copy of the first edition of *Public Exhibition Outfits: Moving Pictures, Magic Lanterns, Talking Machines* (Sears, 1900). The fifth edition of this catalog (1905) is archived in the Anthony Slide collection, Margaret Herrick Library, Academy of Motion Picture Arts and Sciences. This edition is different from the 1900 catalog at the University of Delaware.

25. The 1900 issue of *Public Exhibition Outfits* does not include no. 21287 or a film with the corpulent couple advertised in the earlier catalogs.

26. *Public Exhibition Outfits* (1900).

27. *Public Exhibition Outfits* (1905), 155.

28. In the spring 1898 catalog, both the twenty-five-foot film and the fifty-foot film are titled *Kissing Scene*. In fall 1898, both films are titled *Kiss Scene*. In the two subsequent catalogs, the twenty-five-foot film is titled *Kissing Scene* and the fifty-foot film is titled *Kiss Scene*.

29. *Catalogue of Magic Lanterns, Stereopticons, and Moving Picture Machines* (Montgomery Ward & Co., n.d.), 39. The catalog is not dated, but it includes pictures of the Trans-Mississippi and International Exposition, which was held June 1–November 1, 1898. It also includes Edison's *Wreck of Battleship "Maine,"* which went down in February 1898, and *Bombardment of Matanzas*, which occurred on April 25, 1898.

30. *Oxford English Dictionary*, 2nd ed. (1989), s.v. "grotesque."

31. "New Films for 'Screen' Machines," *Phonoscope*, January 1899, 15.

32. Erish, *Col. William N. Selig*, 7.

33. Ibid., 7–9.

34. Ibid., 11; Eugene Dengler, "Wonders of the 'Diamond-S' Plant," *Motography*, July 1911, 17; Michael Glover Smith, *Flickering Empire: How Chicago Invented the U.S. Film Industry* (Wallflower, 2015), 42.

35. Ron Magliozzi, correspondence with the author, December 15, 2017.

36. "J. B. Wilson," *National Police Gazette*, September 28, 1901, 5; advertisement for J. B. Wilson, *Billboard*, May 6, 1905, 13. Wilson's studio was at 163 State Street at Monroe.

37. Print orientation was confirmed by the emulsion side as well as the correct placement of the man's boutonniere, which would be on the left lapel.

38. Lubin catalogs also include *Darkies' Kiss*, but as discussed above, that title and *Colored Kissing Scene* are probably the same film.

39. Advertisement, *Sunday Telegraph*, April 1, 1900, 5. In this advertisement, the film is listed as *Colored Kiss No. 2*, and it is unclear if it's the same film as *New Colored Kiss No. 2* or a previous iteration.

40. Everett, with the help of his students, scanned the film frame by frame at 3K resolution with a Pacific Image PrimeFilm 7250u 35mm film scanner. A digital copy of the restored film can be viewed at https://vimeo.com/305144396.

41. Carlo Ginzburg, "Clues: Roots of an Evidential Paradigm," in *Clues, Myths, and the Historical Method*, trans. John and Anne C. Tedeschi (Johns Hopkins University Press, 1989), 113.

42. *1903 Complete Catalogue of Films and Moving Picture Machines*, 40.

43. *Public Exhibition Outfits* (1900).

44. *AFI Catalog*, ProQuest, 2021.

45. Advertisement, *Chicago Tribune*, October 30, 1898, 42.

46. 1900 US Census.

47. *1903 Complete Catalogue of Films and Moving Picture Machines*.

48. *Catalogue of New Films*; *1903 Complete Catalogue of Films and Moving Picture Machines*.

GRAND THEATER, BEDFORD, INDIANA, 1899

1. The History & Social Justice project lists Bedford as a possible sundown town based on evidence from oral tradition. See entry for Bedford, Indiana, on the History & Social Justice web site, https://justice.tougaloo.edu/sundowntown/bedford-in.

2. "The Spanish-American War Pictures," *Hancock Democrat*, March 2, 1899, 8. Hogan likely purchased the film from the distributor F. M. Prescott, who sold *Something Good* under the title *Colored Kissing Scene*.

3. "As Hogan Saw It," *Daily Mail*, February 23, 1899, 1.

4. Ibid.

5. Ibid.

6. "The Spanish-American War Pictures," *Hancock Democrat*, March 2, 1899, 8.

7. Films of Black soldiers include Edison's *Colored Troops Disembarking*, showing the US 24th Infantry Regiment leaving the steamer *Mascotte* in Tampa, Florida, on May 20, 1898.

8. The film is presumably lost, but three key frames survive in the American Mutoscope and Biograph Company exhibitor catalogs.

9. *Orleans Progress*, July 27, 1899, 7.

10. Ibid.; *Cambridge City Tribune*, August 3, 1899, 7.

CHAPTER TWO. THE ATTRACTION OF AFFECTION

1. "Hopkins' South Side Theater," *Chicago Daily Tribune*, July 5, 1896, 36.

2. Ibid.

3. Charles Musser, *Edison Motion Pictures: An Annotated Filmography* (Smithsonian Institution Press, 1997), 190.

4. Ibid., 195; "Hopkins' South Side Theater." The paper named the actress as Loïe Fuller, but Fuller was not recorded by Edison at this time. It's more likely that the film was of Amy Muller.

5. "Amusements," *Chicago Daily Tribune*, July 7, 1896, 9.

6. Charles Musser, *The Emergence of Cinema: The American Screen to 1907* (University of California Press, 1994), 290.

7. Tom Gunning, "Attractions: How They Came into the World," in *The Cinema of Attractions Reloaded*, ed. Wanda Strauven (Amsterdam University Press, 2006), 37. Gunning published his essay "The Cinema of Attraction: Early Film, Its Spectator, and the Avant-Garde" in *Wide Angle* 8, no. 3–4, in 1986. He revised it for Thomas Elsaesser's anthology *Early Cinema: Space, Frame, Narrative* (BFI, 1990), pluralizing "attractions" in the title; Gunning, "Attractions," 35–36.

8. Tom Gunning, "The Cinema of Attraction[s]: Early Film, Its Spectator, and the Avant-Garde," in *The Cinema of Attractions Reloaded*, ed. Wanda Strauven (Amsterdam University Press, 2006), 384. See also Tom Gunning, *The Attractions of the Moving Image: Essays on History, Theory, and the Avant-Garde*, ed. Daniel Morgan (University of Chicago Press, 2025).

9. From 1893 to 1895, Selig co-owned two minstrel companies composed of Black performers. See Andrew A. Erish, *Col. William N. Selig, the Man Who Invented Hollywood* (University of Texas Press, 2012).

10. Allyson Nadia Field, "The Cinema of Racialized Attraction(s): *The John C. Rice–May Irwin Kiss* and *Something Good—Negro Kiss*," *Discourse: Journal for Theoretical Studies in Media and Culture* 44, no. 1 (Winter 2022): 3–41.

11. *Special Catalogue of the Optigraph Moving Picture Machines: Calcium Light Outfits, Films for Moving Pictures* (Sears, Roebuck and Co., 1898); *Public Exhibition Outfits: Moving Pictures, Magic Lanterns, Talking Machines* (Sears, 1900); *1903 Complete Catalogue of Films and Moving Pictures* (Selig Polyscope Co., 1903), William Selig papers, Margaret Herrick Library, Academy of Motion Picture Arts and Sciences.

12. Constance Rourke, *American Humor: A Study of the National Character* (Harcourt, Brace, 1931), 82.

13. For example, *A Night in Blackville* (Selig, ca. 1898), *Prize Fight in Coon Town* (Selig, ca. 1898), *An Interrupted Crap Game* (American Mutoscope and Biograph Co., 1899), *The Tramp and the Crap Game* (Edison, 1900), and *Shooting Craps* (Selig, 1903).

14. Musser, *Edison Motion Pictures*, 197.

15. Linda Williams, "Of Kisses and Ellipses: The Long Adolescence of American Movies," *Critical Inquiry* 32 (Winter 2006): 293; Mrs. McGuirk, "The Anatomy of a Kiss," *New York World*, April 26, 1896, 21.

16. McGuirk, "Anatomy of a Kiss," 21.

17. "Edison Kinetoscopic Record of a Sneeze," *Harper's Weekly*, March 24, 1894, 280.

18. Williams, "Of Kisses and Ellipses," 293.

19. Williams suggests that the film may have elicited embarrassment and that laughter would have stemmed from "a nervous release covering over shock." See Ibid., 294.

20. "Notes," *The Chap-Book*, July 15, 1896, 240.

21. Ibid.

22. Ibid. Also quoted in Terry Ramsaye, *A Million and One Nights: A History of the Motion Picture* (Simon and Schuster, 1926), 259–60. Ramsaye attributes the review to Herbert S. Stone, publisher of *The Chap-Book*, though Linda Williams notes that John Sloan's second wife attested that he wrote the unsigned review. See Williams, "Of Kisses and Ellipses," 294n10.

23. See Adam Mack, *Sensing Chicago: Noisemakers, Strikebreakers, and Muckrakers* (University of Illinois Press, 2015); Zachary Samalin, *The Masses Are Revolting: Victorian Culture and the Aesthetics of Disgust* (Cornell University Press, 2021).

24. This aspect of the film is suggested by Terry Ramsaye's pithy remark, "this *Kiss* picture won wide attention for the Vitascope and became a fertile text for that persistent race of people who make a career of writing letters to the newspapers." Ramsaye, *A Million and One Nights*, 260.

25. F. Z. Maguire, *Catalogue* (March 1898), 31. Quoted in Musser, *Edison Motion Pictures*, 197.

26. For a thorough discussion of these films, see Amanda Ann Klein, "The Kissing Cycle, Mashers, and (White) Women in the American City," in *Cycles, Sequels, Spin-offs, Remakes, and Reboots: Multiplicities in Film and Television*, ed. Klein and R. Barton Palmer (University of Texas Press, 2016), 22–40.

27. Musser, *Edison Motion Pictures*, 580. For a discussion of Edison's remake, see J. A. Sokalski, "Performed Affection: The Spectacle of Kissing on Stage and Screen," in *Allegories of Communication: Intermedial Concerns from Cinema to the Digital*, ed. John Fullerton and Jan Olsson (John Libbey, 2005), 314–15; Edison Manufacturing Co. catalog, July 1901. Kid Foley and Sailor Lil also appeared in Edison's *The Ragtime Waltz* (1901) and *The Tough Dance* (1901), and American Mutoscope's *A*

Tough Dance (also known as *The Bowery Dance*, *Dance at McGurks*, and *"Tough Dance" at McGurks*) in 1902 and a second version of *The Bowery Kiss* (1902).

28. Alice Maurice, *The Cinema and Its Shadow* (University of Minnesota Press, 2013), 30.

29. On the cultural practice of slumming, see Chad C. Heap, *Slumming: Sexual and Racial Encounters in American Nightlife, 1885–1940* (University of Chicago Press, 2009).

30. Musser, *Emergence of Cinema*, 292.

31. Robert C. Allen, *Horrible Prettiness: Burlesque and American Culture* (University of North Carolina Press, 1991), 169.

32. Musser, *Emergence of Cinema*, 292.

33. Charles Musser, "*The May Irwin Kiss*: Performance and the Beginnings of Cinema," in *Visual Delights Two: Exhibition and Reception*, ed. Vanessa Toulmin and Simon Popple (John Libbey, 2005), 99, 104.

34. *New York Herald*, December 29, 1895, 4D. Quoted in Musser, "*May Irwin Kiss*," 99.

35. Musser, "*May Irwin Kiss*," 100.

36. Ibid., 104.

37. Giorgio Bertellini, "The Atlantic Valentino: The Inimitable Lover as Racialized and Gendered Italian," in *Intimacy and Italian Migration: Gender and Domestic Lives in a Mobile World*, ed. Loretta Baldassar and Donna R. Gabaccia (Fordham University Press, 2011), 37. Nethersole's mother was of Spanish descent; Charles Musser, "A Cornucopia of Images: Comparison and Judgment Across Theater, Film, and the Visual Arts During the Late Nineteenth Century," in *Moving Pictures: American Art and Early Film 1880–1910*, ed. Nancy Mowll Mathews with Charles Musser (Hudson Hills, 2005), 33.

38. Kiki Loveday has offered a queer reading connecting Nethersole to Irwin and reading *The May Irwin Kiss* as a lesbian kiss. Kiki Loveday, "*The Kiss*: Forgetting Film History," *Feminist Media Histories* 8, no. 3 (Summer 2022): 178–215.

39. Klein, "Kissing Cycle, Mashers, and (White) Women," 27.

40. In his important discussion of *The May Irwin Kiss*, Musser notes that Irwin's popularity as an interpreter of "Negro or 'Coon' songs" was a key selling point for *The Widow Jones*, but he does not discuss her racialized performance in relation to the play or the film. Musser, "*May Irwin Kiss*," 98.

41. "Boston's New Productions," *New York Times*, September 3, 1895, 3.

42. Sharon Ammen, *May Irwin: Singing, Shouting, and the Shadow of Minstrelsy* (University of Illinois Press, 2017), 34.

43. "Home-Made Comic Plays," *New York Times*, September 17, 1895, 5.

44. The National Jukebox collection includes a 1907 recording of Irwin singing "The Bully." See "The Bully: May Irwin's 'Bully' Song," Library of Congress, www.loc.gov/item/jukebox-124996.

45. Abbott and Seroff, *Ragged but Right: Black Traveling Shows, "Coon Songs," and the Dark Pathway to Blues and Jazz* (University Press of Mississippi, 2007), 15; Lori Lynne Brooks, "'To Be Black Is to Be Funny': 'Coon-Shouting' and the Melan-

cholic Production of the White Comedienne," *Women & Performance* 25, no. 1 (2015): 7.

46. Abbott and Seroff, *Ragged but Right*, 3; James Dormon, "Shaping the Popular Image of Post-Reconstruction American Blacks: The 'Coon Song' Phenomenon of the Gilded Age," *American Quarterly* 40 (1988): 453.

47. Abbott and Seroff, *Ragged but Right*, 4.

48. Quoted in ibid., 16.

49. Edward A. Ditchmar, "The Theatres," *New York Times*, January 17, 1897, SM6. See also Abbott and Seroff, *Ragged but Right*, 17.

50. Ammen, *May Irwin*, 108–9.

51. Khalil Gibran Muhammad, *The Condemnation of Blackness: Race, Crime, and the Making of Modern Urban America* (Harvard University Press, 2011), 4.

52. "Songs from Steel Cages," *Kansas City Journal*, January 17, 1898, 3.

53. Edison filmed three African American performers from *The Passing Show* revue in October 1894 and James Grundy's dances from *The South Before the War* revue sometime before late January 1895. See Musser, *Edison Motion Pictures*, 133–35, 174–75.

54. The song was reprised in the play *Courted into Court* the following year, as referenced by the *New York Times* in the review cited above.

55. Charles E. Trevathan, "The Bully," sheet music published as a supplement to *The Journal*, April 12, 1896.

56. Paul Oliver, "Lookin' for the Bully: An Enquiry into a Song and Its Story," in *Nobody Knows Where the Blues Come From: Lyrics and History*, ed. Robert Springer (University Press of Mississippi, 2006), 112. There are conflicting accounts of how Irwin first heard the song. See Ammen, *May Irwin*, 94. White minstrels dating back to T.D. Rice typically claimed to have learned tunes and songs from Black singers, a "theft" that resulted, as Eric Lott has traced, in "white guilt or anxiety about minstrelsy as a figure for the plundering of black culture." Eric Lott, *Love and Theft: Blackface Minstrelsy and the American Working Class* (Oxford University Press, 1993), 59.

57. "Notes from New York," *Nebraska State Journal*, January 25, 1897, 3.

58. "Boston's New Productions," *New York Times*, September 3, 1895, 3.

59. This version was published as a special supplement to *The Journal*, April 12, 1896, and signed by "Davenport."

60. "Exhibits in the Shows," *The Sun*, March 30, 1896, 5.

61. Ammen, *May Irwin*, 98.

62. I am grateful to Racquel Gates for this description.

63. Ammen, *May Irwin*, 98.

64. Ibid., 95.

65. Alan Dale, "Chilly Mme. Melba and Magnetic May Irwin," *Examiner* (San Francisco), January 17, 1897, 35.

66. Bertellini, "Atlantic Valentino," 37.

67. "Suttle and Brown," *National Police Gazette* (New York), September 9, 1899, 6.

68. Abbott and Seroff, *Ragged but Right*, 22.

69. *1907 Catalogue of the Selig Polyscope and Library of Selig Films* (Selig Polyscope, Co., 1907), 66.

70. The song was copyrighted in 1898 and published in 1899 by the S. Brainard's Sons Co. with a photo of a woman who could be Brown, given that she was his partner in the "Creole cake dance."

71. Paul Oliver notes that the term "wingin'" derived from the traditional kicking and arm-flapping dance, the "buck-and-wing." See Oliver, "Lookin' for The Bully," 109–10.

72. W. Forrest Cozart, "Important Points," *Freeman*, January 25, 1902, 2.

73. *Catalogue of New Films for Projection and Other Projects* (F. M. Prescott, 1899). 34; *Dallas Morning News*, August 8, 1900, 10; Advertisement, *Wichita Daily Eagle*, December 17, 1899, 4.

GEORGE INNES & CO. DEPARTMENT STORE, WICHITA, KANSAS, 1899

1. Advertisement, *Wichita Daily Eagle*, December 17, 1899, 4.

2. Advertisement, *Wichita Register*, December 17, 1899, 5.

3. All of these items are listed in the *Wichita Daily Eagle* advertisement.

4. *Wichita Daily Beacon*, December 19, 1899, 6.

5. Advertisement, *Wichita Register*.

6. "The Vitascope," *Wichita Daily Beacon*, December 19, 1899, 6; advertisement, *Wichita Daily Eagle*.

7. *Wichita Daily Beacon*, December 21, 1899, 8.

8. "City in Brief," *Wichita Daily Eagle*, December 21, 1899, 2.

9. *Wichita Price Current*, December 25, 1899, 5.

10. Charles Musser, *Edison Motion Pictures, 1890–1900: An Annotated Filmography* (Smithsonian Institution Press, 1997), 242.

CHAPTER THREE. TO TAKE THE CAKE

1. The details of this incident are taken from *The Chicago Chronicle*, January 2, 1897, 7. It's possible that H. C. Winn is actually Edward H. Winn, a performer with John W. Isham's famous Octoroons. Hough is likely white, given the only photographers in Chicago with that name were white. See 1900 US Federal Census.

2. *The Chicago Chronicle*.

3. No author given, "The Origins of the Cake Walk," *The Journal of Blacks in Higher Education* 35 (Spring 2002): 134.

4. Thomas L. Morgan and William Barlow, *From Cakewalks to Concert Halls: An Illustrated History of African American Popular Music from 1895 to 1930* (Elliott & Clark, 1992), 8.

5. "Origins of the Cake Walk," 134.

6. Quoted in Brooke Baldwin, "The Cakewalk: A Study in Stereotype and Reality," *Journal of Social History* 15, no. 2 (Winter 1981): 208.

7. Megan Pugh, *America Dancing: From the Cakewalk to the Moonwalk* (Yale University Press, 2015), 17.

8. Rudi Blesh, *They All Played Ragtime* (Knopf, 1950), 96.

9. Marshall W. Stearns, *Jazz Dance: The Story of American Vernacular Dance* (Macmillan, 1968), 22. Stearns conducted "numerous interviews" with Whipper in New York from 1959 to 1966 (373n17).

10. Stearns, *Jazz Dance*, 22.

11. Pugh, *America Dancing*, 18.

12. Blesh, *They All Played Ragtime*, 1971, 97.

13. *Los Angeles Times*, February 14, 1898, 5.

14. Amiri Baraka, *Blues People: Negro Music in White America* (William Morrow, 1963), 93.

15. Unmarked clipping, Harvard Theatre Collection, quoted in Daphne Brooks, *Bodies in Dissent: Spectacular Performances of Race and Freedom, 1850–1910* (Duke University Press, 2006), 234.

16. Brooks, *Bodies in Dissent*, 235.

17. "Rivals Arouse," *Boston Daily Globe*, January 17, 1898, 4.

18. Brooks, *Bodies in Dissent*, 234.

19. Pugh, *America Dancing*, 19.

20. Ibid.; "Walking for a Cake," *Chicago Daily Tribune*, March 2, 1892, 1.

21. "Walking for a Cake."

22. Ibid.

23. "Billie Farrell Victor Again," *The Sunday Chronicle*, August 8, 1897, 3; "Willie Wins in a Walk," *Chicago Tribune*, August 8, 1897, 2. The *Tribune* names Suttle's partner as "May Williams" and misidentifies John Brewer as "John Brenner" and his partner Alice Liddell; "Cake Walk in Evanston," *The Chicago Chronicle*, September 17, 1897, 4.

24. "Cake Walk in Evanston."

25. Ibid.

26. Ibid.

27. The S. W. Christian Advocate, "Are We not Drifting Backward?" *Colored American*, March 25, 1899, 6.

28. "The Best Things from Exchanges," *Illinois Record*, December 4, 1897, 2.

29. Ibid.

30. Ibid.

31. "The Emancipation Proclamation," *Wisconsin Weekly Advocate*, May 14, 1898, 1; "Celebration for Emancipation Day," *Wisconsin Weekly Advocate*, May 7, 1898, 5.

32. "Emancipation Proclamation."

33. Ibid.; "Celebration for Emancipation Day."

34. *1903 Complete Catalogue of Films and Moving Pictures* (Selig Polyscope Co., 1903), William Selig papers, Margaret Herrick Library, Academy of Motion Picture Arts and Sciences.

35. *Wisconsin Weekly Advocate*, November 4, 1898, 8.

36. See advertisements in *New York Clipper*, October 29, 1898, 4; *Chicago Tribune*, October 30, 1898, 42; *Chicago Tribune*, November 6, 1898, 46; *Chicago Tribune*, December 11, 1898, 46.

37. Advertisement, *Chicago Tribune*, October 30, 1898.

38. "At the Outlying Playhouses," *Chicago Tribune*, November 15, 1897, 5.

39. Advertisement, *Chicago Tribune*, December 11, 1898.

40. *Wisconsin Weekly Advocate*.

41. Ibid. In 1901, the Rohlfing building was destroyed by fire. In addition to pianos, original manuscripts were destroyed.

42. "Rohlfing & Sons," *The William Steinway Diary, 1861–1896*, ed. Cynthia Adams Hoover and Edwin M. Good, https://americanhistory.si.edu/steinwaydiary/annotations/?id=746.

43. *Wisconsin Weekly Advocate*.

44. The copyright catalog indicates the copies were received on May 20, 1898. *Catalog of Title Entries of Books etc.*, April 13–July 6, 1898, 15: 747.

45. "At the Play," *Duluth News-Tribune*, November 22, 1898, 4.

46. Cook maintains that Dunbar's libretto "was never used" and only "a few of the lyrics" were in the play. He recalls, "Naturally, [Hogan] had eliminated Dunbar's dialogue, for a lot of dialogue on an uncovered roof garden after eleven p.m. would have been impossible." Will Marion Cook, "Clorindy, the Origin of the Cakewalk," *Theatre Arts* 31, no. 9 (September 1947): 61, 64.

47. Cook, "Clorindy," 65.

48. Advertisement, *Chicago Daily Tribune*, December 11, 1898.

49. "Bills at Other Playhouses," *Chicago Daily Tribune*, November 21, 1898, 5.

50. Ernest Hogan performed with Black Patti the week of December 12, 1898. It's not clear whether he went between shows or if *Clorindy* replaced him with a substitute.

51. Marriage licenses, *Chicago Daily Tribune*, November 27, 1898, 6; Cook County, Illinois, U.S. Marriages Index, 1871–1920.

52. Bill Egan, *African American Entertainers in Australia and New Zealand: A History, 1788–1941* (McFarland, 2020), 70.

53. "The Georgia Minstrels," *The Wagga Advertiser*, July 18, 1899, n.p.

54. "Palace Theatre," *Evening News* (Sydney), July 3, 1899, 8.

55. Egan, *African American Entertainers*, 73.

56. Ibid.

57. Ibid., 74.

58. "Jim Harris Writes," *Topeka Plaindealer*, August 11, 1899, 4.

59. "The Georgia Minstrels," *Bendigo Independent*, August 1, 1899, 2.

60. Egan, *African American Entertainers*, 25.

61. *Broad Ax*, October 30, 1909, 2; *The Forum*, May 7, 1910, 1.

62. *Freeman*, June 20, 1900, 5.

63. Ibid.

64. Jim Harris, letter to the *Topeka Plaindealer*, August 11, 1899.

65. "The Stage," *Freeman*, November 4, 1899, 5.

66. *Recorder*, March 10, 1900, 2.

67. 1900 Census, Pueblo, Colorado, District 98. In the census, Maud's birthplace is listed as Honolulu, then crossed off and corrected to Hawaiian Islands, though her father's birthplace is given as Kentucky and her mother's as Honolulu. She's listed as an alien. John's birthdate seems to be written as 1864, though his age is given as thirty-one, so the "4" is likely a "9." They are listed as having been married one year.

68. The 1900 Census, recorded in June and transcribed in August, does not include an infant nor does it indicate if Maud had a child, living or dead.

69. "Working Together to Reduce Black Maternal Mortality," April 8, 2024, CDC, www.cdc.gov/womens-health/features/maternal-mortality.html.

70. Caleb J. Jang and Henry C. Lee, "A Review of Racial Disparities in Infant Mortality in the US," *Children* 9, no. 2 (2022), ncbi.nlm.nih.gov/pmc/articles/PMC8870826.

DALLAS STATE FAIR ADVERTISING CAR, TEXAS, 1900

1. "Will Visit the Fair," *Dallas Morning News*, July 16, 1900.

2. "Races at the State Fair," *Dallas Morning News*, August 8, 1900.

3. Ibid., which lists details of the program.

4. Ibid.

5. In 1910, "Colored People's Day" was unceremoniously discontinued, and not in a way that heralded integration. In 1923, the fair held "Ku Klux Klan Day" as a recruitment event. "Colored People's Day," on hiatus since 1910, was replaced in 1936 with the euphemistically named "Negro Achievement Day," or as Dallas civil rights leader Juanita J. Craft called it in a 1955 protest, "Negro Appeasement Day." In the 1950s, Craft led an effort to desegregate the fair. Full desegregation did not come until 1967. Details about the fair's segregated history are taken from Rebekah Morr, "'Why Can't We Go?' A Dallas Woman Remembers the Segregated State Fair of Texas," *artandseek.org*, October 15, 2021, https://artandseek.org/2021/10/15/why-cant-we-go-a-dallas-woman-remembers-the-segregated-state-fair-of-texas.

6. *San Antonio Daily Light*, September 21, 1900, 3.

CHAPTER FOUR. "THE BLACK MILLIONAIRE" AND "THE CREOLE GAL"

1. "Suttle and Brown," *The National Police Gazette*, September 9, 1899, 6.

2. Ibid.

3. *Chicago Tribune*, September 10, 1899, 42; *Chicago Tribune*, September 17, 1899, 40; *Chicago Tribune*, September 23, 1900, 44.

4. Advertisement, *Chicago Tribune*, July 15, 1900, 40; "Fair Department: Brought Bushels of Answers," *The Billboard*, August 24, 1901, 10.

5. *Chicago Tribune*, September 2, 1900, 40; *Chicago Tribune*, October 6, 1901, 44; *St. Louis Globe-Democrat*, October 9, 1899, 5; *Chicago Daily Tribune*, October 20, 1901, 44; "At the Theatre," *Kokomo Daily Tribune*, February 8, 1901, 8.

6. Constance Valis Hill, *Tap Dancing in America: A Cultural History* (Oxford University Press, 2010), 22.

7. Ibid.

8. Ibid., 33.

9. *Wisconsin Weekly Advocate*, April 5, 1900, 1.

10. "Amusements," *Joliet Daily News*, December 19, 1899, 3.

11. Tom the Tattler, *Freeman*, April 27, 1901, 6.

12. *Joliet Daily News*, December 20, 1899, 3; "Amusements," *Joliet Daily News*.

13. Advertisement, *Fort Wayne Sentinel*, January 2, 1900, 8.

14. "The Coontown 400," *Joliet Daily News*, December 22, 1899, 5. The paper names the manager as Morris, which is either a misattribution of Moore or the name of the show's manager.

15. Ibid.

16. "Coontown 400 Tonight," *Fort Wayne News*, January 3, 1900, 11.

17. "The Stage," *Freeman*, September 3, 1898, 5; "The Stage," *Freeman*, September 30, 1899, 5.

18. *Catalogue of New Films for Projection and Other Projects* (F. M. Prescott, 1899); "Coontown 400," *Toulon Stark County News*, December 29, 1899, 1.

19. "Coontown 400 Tonight."

20. "After an Erring Spouse," *Ironwood Times*, February 24, 1900, 4.

21. Michigan, U.S., Marriage Records, 1867–1952.

22. Their wedding was novel enough to be covered by the local paper and reprinted across the region. The paper identifies the husband as Lee Hung, though marriage records list him as Charles Fon or Kim (handwritten and difficult to discern). "Chinaman Marries a Negress," *South Haven Sentinel*, December 17, 1898, 4.

23. Details of this episode drawn from "After an Erring Spouse."

24. *L'Anse Sentinel*, February 17, 1900, 10.

25. *Freeman*, February 2, 1901, 5; *Lawrence Daily Journal*, April 15, 1901, 4.

26. "Amusements," *Joliet Daily News*.

27. *Freeman*, November 24, 1900, 6; *Freeman*, February 2, 1901, 5. At least Sadie Citizen had been in an earlier iteration of *Coontown 400* that toured Wisconsin and Canada in late 1899. See "Notes from the 'Coontown 400,'" *Freeman*, December 2, 1899, 5.

28. Gertie Brown's participation in the company seems inconsistent, and it's probable that she was engaged in multiple companies at this time, spending some time with her former vaudeville partners on this new circuit.

29. *Logansport Pharos Tribune*, February 12, 1901, 3.

30. Advertisement, *The Morning Record* (Traverse City), January 26, 1900, 3.

31. Advertisement, *Logansport Pharos Tribune*, February 13, 1901, 5.

32. See, for example, Eric Lott, *Love and Theft: Blackface Minstrelsy and the American Working Class* (Oxford University Press, 1993), chap. 8; Linda Williams, *Playing the Race Card: Melodramas of Black and White from Uncle Tom to O.J. Simpson* (Princeton University Press, 2001), 85.

33. "The Show," *St. Mary's Journal* (Kansas), April 19, 1901, 1.

34. *Logansport Reporter*, February 12, 1901, 5; *Weekly Journal-Miner*, June 12, 1901, 3.

35. "Minstrels in a Tent," *The Topeka State Journal*, April 23, 1901, 7.

36. *Freeman*, March 9, 1901, 5.

37. *Freeman*, April 6, 1901, 5.

38. *Knox Starke County Democrat*, January 17, 1901, 12. Watson likely engaged partners along the tour as this performance was billed as "Watson & Wills' Coon Town 400."

39. *Alma Record*, April 5, 1901, 4. The paper identifies him as the general manager but mistakes his name as "Sant Fuller."

40. *Freeman*, March 23, 1901, 5.

41. *Times-Picayune*, June 1, 1902, 16.

42. For more on these songs, see Krystyn R. Moon, *Yellowface: Creating the Chinese in American Popular Music and Performance, 1850s–1920s* (Rutgers University Press, 2005).

43. "After an Erring Spouse."

44. *Freeman*, March 2, 1901, 5.

45. *Logansport Reporter*, February 18, 1901, 5.

46. "The Jolly College Town Gets Itself Shocked by Students and Members of 'Coontown 400,'" *The Kokomo Daily Tribune*, March 5, 1901, 5; "A La 'Little Egypt,'" *Greencastle Star Press*, March 9, 1901, 3.

47. "A La 'Little Egypt.'"

48. "Plays Smash with a 'Frat,'" *Kokomo Daily Tribune*, March 8, 1901, 1.

49. Cynthia M. Blair, *I've Got to Make My Livin': Black Women's Sex Work in Turn-of-the-Century Chicago* (University of Chicago Press, 2010), 143.

50. Blair, *I've Got to Make My Livin'*, 143.

51. *Knox Starke County Democrat*, March 21, 1901, 1.

52. Detour staff, "Horror in the Heartland," *Charlotte Observer*, June 22, 2023, www.charlotteobserver.com/detour/article262129217.html.

53. *Boonville Standard*, June 15, 1900, 4.

54. "Date Cancelled," *Lawrence Daily World*, April 18, 1901, 2.

55. "A Lively Chase," *Lawrence Journal World*, April 20, 1901, 4.

56. *Freeman*, April 27, 1901, 5.

57. Ibid.; *Freeman*, March 9, 1901, 5.

58. *Freeman*, March 8, 1901, 5.

59. J. Ed. Green, "Chicago," *Freeman*, May 4, 1901, 5.

60. *Chicago Tribune*, May 8, 1901, 1; *Chicago Tribune*, May 13, 1901, 7.

61. "Chicago," *Freeman*, April 27, 1901, 5; "Coontown 400—Under Canvas," *Hereford Reporter* (Texas), May 10, 1901, 7.

62. "Coontown Out Last Night," *The Emporia Gazette*, April 30, 1901, 1.

63. *The Caldwell Advance* (Kansas), May 10, 1901, 1.

64. *Western Liberal*, May 31, 1901, 3.

65. Ibid.

66. "No Redeeming Features," *Albuquerque Citizen*, June 1, 1901, 2.

67. "The Coontown 400 Show," *Graham Guardian*, May 31, 1901, 1.

68. *Arizona Republican*, June 8, 1901, 4.

69. "Notes from 'Coontown 400,'" *Freeman*, July 13, 1901, 5.

70. "Pickings from 'Coontown 400' Co.," *Freeman*, July 20, 1901, 5; Henry T. Sampson, *The Ghost Walks: A Chronological History of Blacks in Show Business, 1896–1910* (Scarecrow Press, 1988), 106.

71. "Amusements," *The Champaign Daily Gazette*, July 11, 1901, 2.

72. Ibid.

73. "Attraction at West End Park Gives Great Satisfaction," *The Champaign Daily News*, July 16, 1901, 8.

74. Advertisement, *The Champaign Daily News*, July 15, 1901, 7.

75. "Cake Walk is Coming," *The Champaign Daily News*, July 18, 1901, 4.

76. "Show Troupe Stranded," *Herald and Review*, July 28, 1901, 5.

77. *Freeman*, August 24, 1901, 5. The show continued, though apparently the Brewers, Suttle, and Brown did not remain in the company.

78. Advertisement, *Chicago Tribune*, September 29, 1901, 38; Advertisement, *Chicago Tribune*, October 6, 1901, 44; Advertisement, *Chicago Tribune*, October 20, 1901, 44.

79. *Harald-Palladium*, July 2, 1902, 3; "The Fourth Was Hot," *Daily Palladium*, July 5, 1902, 8. Benton Harbor was predominantly white at the time.

80. "The Fourth Was Hot."

81. *Complete Catalogue of Lubin's Films* (January 1903), 41. The film was likely made in 1900 or 1901.

GRACE CHURCH, WILMINGTON, NORTH CAROLINA, 1901

1. Advertisement, *St. Louis Globe-Democrat*, November 11, 1859, 2; "Butt's Panorama," *Xenia Sentinel*, September 13, 1864, 3.

2. Roberta E. Pearson, "Biblical films," in *Encyclopedia of Early Cinema*, ed. Richard Abel (Routledge, 2005), 70.

3. "Mr. Butt's Panorama," *The Rocket*, October 11, 1888, 3.

4. Advertisement, *Charlotte Observer*, April 2, 1901, 8.

5. *Wilmington Messenger*, June 16, 1901, 10.

6. *The Devil's Amusement*, considered lost, is likely Georges Méliès's *Magie diabolique* (ca. 1897–98), released in the US as *Black Art*.

7. André Gaudreault, "Lecturer," in Abel, *Encyclopedia of Early Cinema*, 380.

8. *Charlotte News*, December 10, 1900, 8.

CHAPTER FIVE. SAINT SUTTLE AFTER THE RAG-TIME FOUR

1. With thanks to Robert J. Kiss for identifying the films on this reel.

2. *1903 Complete Catalogue of Films and Moving Picture Machines* (Selig Polyscope Co., 1903), in William Selig papers, Margaret Herrick Library, Academy of Motion Picture Arts and Sciences; *1907 Catalogue of the Selig Polyscope and Library of Selig Films* (Selig Polyscope Co., 1907).

3. See Tom Gunning, "The Cinema of Attraction: Early Film, Its Spectator, and the Avant-Garde," *Wide Angle* 8, no. 3–4 (1986): 63–70.

4. 1903 Selig Catalog.

5. See, for example, David Roediger, *The Wages of Whiteness: Race and the Making of the American Working Class* (Verso, 1991); Eric Lott, *Love and Theft: Blackface Minstrelsy and the American Working Class* (Oxford University Press, 1993); Noel Ignatiev, *How the Irish Became White* (Routledge, 1995).

6. For example, in Monongahela, Pennsylvania, the Burlington Entertainment Company screened it along with *Cake Walk*. *The Daily Republican*, February 14, 1902, 1; *Wisconsin Valley Leader*, May 18, 1905, 1; *The Wollondilly Press*, March 7, 1903, 3.

7. *Xenia Daily Gazette*, January 29, 1904, 7.

8. *Titonka Topic*, August 22, 1907, 13.

9. *Wisconsin Valley Leader*, May 18, 1905, 1.

10. *The Wollondilly Press*, March 7, 1903, 3.

11. *Edgar Post*, September 11, 1906, 4.

12. Ibid.

13. "La Belle Park," *Paducah Sun*, August 27, 1902, 16.

14. "Lynching Approved," *Paducah Sun*, August 27, 1902, 16.

15. See, for example, James Allen, ed., *Without Sanctuary: Lynching Photography in America* (Twin Palms, 2000).

16. *Osceola Polk County Democrat*, June 29, 1905, 1.

17. "No. 17, *Tracked by Bloodhounds*," Selig Polyscope Company, 1905; 1903 Selig Catalog; 1907 Selig Catalog.

18. "Colored People Want a Theater," *The Inter Ocean*, May 12, 1901, 13.

19. Ibid.

20. Motts surely knew of the plans for the Adelphi, given the tight-knit theatrical world and the newspaper coverage of Hall's plans. (If they weren't close at this moment, they became so by the time of Motts's death in 1911, when Hall was named administrator for his estate). Thomas Bauman, *The Pekin: The Rise and Fall of Chicago's First Black-Owned Theater* (University of Illinois Press, 2014), 140.

21. Sylvester Russell, "A Little Bit of Everything," *Freeman*, March 7, 1903, 5. Russell and Suttle seem to have reconciled or put aside differences. When a young comedian, William Hallback, died of pneumonia leaving a widow and four young children, Russell and Suttle were the only men assisting in the funeral and helped

arrange a benefit for the family. See Sylvester Russell, "Chicago Weekly Review," December 2, 1916, 5.

22. Henry Louis Gates, Jr., "The Trope of a New Negro and the Reconstruction of the Image of the Black," *Representations* 24 (Autumn 1988): 129.

23. "Chicago News," *Wisconsin Weekly Advocate*, May 21, 1903, 1.

24. *Wisconsin Weekly Advocate*, October 8, 1903, 1. I have yet to find further mention of this incident.

25. *Freeman*, January 30, 1904, 5; *Wisconsin Weekly Advocate*, November 4, 1898, 8. Apart from "She's Ready Money," the other songs do not appear to be extant and possibly were not published.

26. *Freeman*, March 19, 1904, 5.

27. It's possible that Gideon cheated Suttle, though Gideon was lauded as "one of the few Negroes in the show business that is not being 'worked' by some white man. He conducts his own business, pays his people, and always carries a troupe of the best performers in the business." *Topeka Plaindealer*, March 31, 1905, 5.

28. *Post-Crescent*, April 11, 1904, 2.

29. Ibid.

30. Advertisements, *Chicago Tribune*, December 26, 1905, 7; *Chicago Tribune*, December 27, 1905, 4; *Chicago Tribune*, December 28, 1905, 9.

31. *Monroe Weekly Times*, September 11, 1907; *Chicago Defender*, May 6, 1911, 4.

32. "Curious Thousands Throng Inter State Fair Grounds for Opening Day's Features," *La Crosse Tribune*, September 24, 1907, 1.

33. Advertisement, *La Crosse Tribune*, September 21, 1907, 10.

34. Ibid.

35. "Stage Notes," *Defender* May 6, 1911, 4; "Greater United Shows for November Fair," *Beaumont Journal*, June 28, 1911, 1.

36. "Wrestling Match," *Monroe Weekly Times*, September 11, 1907, 7.

37. *Freeman*, July 16, 1910, 2.

38. Quoted in David Remnick, "Struggle for His Soul," *Observer Sport Monthly*, November 2, 2003.

39. *Freeman*, July 16, 1910, 2.

40. Ibid. The *Freeman* also sold, through mail order, Jack Johnson buttons made and produced by theater and sports critic William Foster, who would turn to filmmaking in 1913.

41. "Collect with Fists," *La Crosse Tribune*, September 28, 1907, 5.

42. Ibid.

43. Christina Sharpe, *In the Wake: On Blackness and Being* (Duke University Press, 2016).

44. "Events of the Past Week," *Freeman*, May 28, 1910, 1.

45. Ibid.

46. *Freeman*, December 23, 1911, 13.

47. Death certificate of infant Suttle, May 29, 1911.

48. Advertisement, *The Bee*, April 12, 1912, 3.

49. "Gossip of the Stage," *Indianapolis Freeman*, December 23, 1911, 13.

50. Advertisement, *The Bee*, April 12, 1912, 3.

51. "Calumet Celebration," *New York Clipper*, April 6, 1912, 15.

52. "Carnival to Open Tomorrow Night," *Appleton Evening Crescent*, June 17, 1912, 5.

53. *The Bee*, April 12, 1912; "Carnival News," *Billboard*, May 11, 1912, 26.

54. "The Carnival is Getting Larger," *Appleton Evening Crescent*, June 20, 1912, 5.

55. "Negro Withdraws His Complaint and Pays Cost," *Post-Crescent* (Appleton, WI), June 19, 1912, 1.

56. "300 Officers to Guard State Street Carnival," *Defender*, August 10, 1912, 1.

57. "The Amusement Week in Chicago," *Billboard*, August 31, 1912, 5; "300 Officers to Guard State Street Carnival," *Defender*, August 10, 1912, 1.

58. "Business Men's Emancipation Celebration," *Chicago Defender*, July 26, 1913, 1.

59. "Street Fete Routs Hospital," *Chicago Tribune*, August 17, 1912, 2; "Negro Business League and the Carnival: Statement of the Local League in Regard to the Controversy," *Chicago Defender*, August 17, 1912, 5.

60. "Negro Business League and the Carnival: Statement of the Local League in Regard to the Controversy," *Chicago Defender*, August 17, 1912, 5.

61. "Negroes Object to Carnival," *Chicago Tribune*, August 12. 1912, 7.

62. Ibid.

63. "300 Officers to Guard State Street Carnival," *Defender*, August 10, 1912, 1.

64. "Blackville after dark"; words by Saint Suttle, melody by Althea [*sic*] Dickerson. C. 1 c. Aug. 11, 1926; E 645220; Consolidated music pub. House, Chicago. 14993. The Library of Congress Copyright Office destroyed the deposit record on the song as it was out of the "retention period" determined by Section 405, D of the Copyright Law. Dickerson also went by "Selma Davis" and wrote music for Ma Rainey and others. Dickerson also worked as secretary for J. Mayo Williams, the manager of the Race Records division at Paramount Records. Sandra Robin Lieb, "The Message of Ma Rainey's Blues: A Biographical and Critical Study of America's First Woman Blues Singer" (PhD diss., Stanford University, 1976).

65. 1910 US Federal Census. The 1910 census lists her as Aletha and the 1940 census lists her as Alestha.

66. *Discography of American Historical Recordings*, s.v. "OKeh matrix 9766. Blackville after dark / Hazel Meyers ; Starks' Hot Five," accessed January 23, 2025, https://adp-staging.eks.dld.library.ucsb.edu/index.php/matrix/detail/2000201902/9766-Blackville_after_dark.

67. OKeh 8364, recorded June 21, 1925, in Chicago, Illinois.

68. "'Neath the Southern Moon' at the Royal," *Afro-American*, January 15, 1927, 9.

69. "New Theater Opens at Columbus," *Indianapolis Freeman*, January 4, 1913, 6.

70. Ibid.

71. "Negro Saloons Make Their Last Sunday Harvest," *Columbus Dispatch*, September 22, 1913, 3; "Notorious Saloons are Put out of Business by New County Board of Liquor Commissioners," *Columbus Dispatch*, November 5, 1913, 1.

72. "Notorious Saloons," 12.

73. "Negro Saloons," 3.

74. "Notorious Saloons," 1.

75. "Negro Saloons," 3.

76. "Notorious Saloons," 1.

77. "Two Raids Made on Hobbs' Hotel in Twelve Hours," *Columbus Dispatch*, November 22, 1915, 9; "Westerville Mayor Gives Smoky $400 Fine," *Columbus Dispatch*, November 30, 195, 3; "Colored Lawbreaker to go to Workhouse," *Columbus Dispatch*, December 15, 1915, 3.

78. "Colored Lawbreaker to go to Workhouse," 3.

79. While the date on the sheet music for "The Ill Fate of Ohio" is 1913, no copyright records appear for Suttle's song, though there were a series of songs published in 1913 commemorating the event. Cindy Lindsay at the Columbus Metropolitan Library identified the photograph on the cover of the sheet music as Dayton rather than Columbus.

80. Suttle is listed at 4881/2 West Goodale, rooming with Emmanuel Wade. Wade's role is unknown, though he had a day job as a laborer and likely worked for the theater as a side hustle, perhaps as a custodian or caretaker. Suttle, Wade, and the Pekin are all listed as "colored" in the 1913 Columbus City Directory, with Suttle listed as an actor and Wade a laborer. The city directory lists Green, also "colored," as living at 234 North Pearl. Suttle is listed as Saint D. Suttle, actor, with "(c)" after his name, indicating "colored." R. L. Polk & Co.'s *Columbus, Ohio, City Directory*, 1913. The 1890 Sanborn map of Columbus indicates the second floor of the building contained tenements. Columbus Metropolitan Library.

81. Advertisement, *Freeman*, November 8, 1913, 5; R. L. Polk & Co.'s *Columbus, Ohio, City Directory*, 1913; 1920 US Census. In 1923 Scott was leading an orchestra in Columbus. *Columbus Dispatch*, November 4, 1923, 45.

82. "Chicago Notes and Other Comment," *Freeman* August 26, 1916, 5; Curtis Schieber, *Columbus Beer*, 95. Columbus Metropolitan Library. Suttle is credited as Saint Suttee and while William S. Parks is named on the cover, the first page of sheet music lists him as William Sparks.

83. I have not been able to locate a copyright entry for this song, though the sheet music indicates a 1916 copyright by C. C. Janes. A copy of the sheet music is held at the Columbus Metropolitan Library.

84. "Chicago Weekly Review," *Freeman*, August 26, 1916, 5.

85. Advertisement, *Billboard*, December 22, 1917; "A Note or Two," *Chicago Defender*, December 22, 1917, 9.

86. *Defender*, March 23, 1918, 7.

87. "Making Headway," *Broad Ax*, March 31, 1923, 3.

88. "New Chicago Hotel Opens its Doors July Fourth," *Chicago Defender*, June 23, 1917, 6.

89. Ibid.
90. Ibid.
91. Advertisement, *Billboard*, April 27, 1918, 2.
92. Ibid.
93. 1930 Federal Census.
94. Saint Suttle death certificate.

THE EMPIRE THEATER, ARDMORE, TERRITORY OF OKLAHOMA, 1906

1. Advertisement, *The Daily Ardmoreite*, March 5, 1906, 5. It was located on Main Street in the Whittington Hotel building.

2. Department of Commerce and Labor, Bureau of the Census, "Population of Oklahoma and Indian Territory 1907," Washington, 1907.

3. "Negro Pays Death Penalty," *The Daily Ardmoreite*, July 2, 1906, 1.

4. "President's Message," *The Daily Ardmoreite*, December 3, 1906, 9; "Roosevelt on Lynching," *The Daily Ardmoreite*, December 9, 1906, 4.

5. Advertisement, *The Daily Ardmoreite*, March 25, 1906, 8. It was the first advertised motion-picture program.

6. The program was a mix of older films, some eight or nine years old, and one subject released the year before (*The Big Fountain*). The age of most of these titles indicates that Brown likely acquired the prints on the cheap.

7. Advertisement, *The Daily Ardmoreite*, March 25, 1906, 8. The advertisement listed the film as *The Deserters*, likely an error. While the ten-minute French film *The Deserter* (dirs. André Heuzé and Lucien Nonguet, Pathé, 1906) was released in 1906, it's more likely that the Empire screened Edison's 1903 film.

8. "Fire," *The Daily Ardmoreite*, April 19, 1906, 5.

9. Advertisement, *The Daily Ardmoreite*, April 30, 1906, 5.

10. "Bijou Theater Burned," *The Daily Ardmoreite*, November 19, 1906, 5.

11. *Billboard*, August 6, 1921, 63; 1920 US Federal Census.

12. *Billboard*'s list of Colored Theaters was informed by the Comet Film Exchange of Philadelphia and the Micheaux Pictures Corporation, which supplied lists of motion-picture theaters catering to Black patrons, suggesting the Ardmore rented race films. *Billboard*, August 6, 1921, 62–63.

13. See, for example, "A Worthy Endeavor," *The Daily Ardmoreite*, January 26, 1921, 5; "Negroes to Hold Mass Meeting," *The Ardmore Daily Press*, July 23, 1925, 3; "Convention Plans Pleases Negro Leader," *The Daily Ardmoreite*, January 27, 1928, 11.

14. "Dreamland, Motion Picture Theater, Is Damaged by Fire," *The Daily Ardmoreite*, January 4, 1928, 2. The National Register of Historic Places names the building at 536 E. Main Street the Black Theater of Ardmore, yet the only "colored" theater in operation in the town in 1922 was named the Dreamland at that time.

1. "Gertie Moore Passes Away," *New York Amsterdam News*, February 28, 1934, 1.

2. Thomas Bauman, *The Pekin: The Rise and Fall of Chicago's First Black-Owned Theater* (University of Illinois Press, 2014), 25, 28.

3. Ibid., 41.

4. Sylvester Russell, "A Review of the Week," *Freeman*, January 21, 1911, 3; "The Pekin Theatre," *Broad Ax*, January 28, 1911, 2.

5. Cary B. Lewis, "The Past Week with the Negro Theaters," *Freeman*, August 6, 1910, 5.

6. "I'm a Yiddish Cowboy," words by Edgar Leslie, music by Al Piantadosi and Halsey K. Mohr, published by Ted S. Barron, New York, 1908.

7. Lewis, "Past Week," 5.

8. Joe, "The Pekin Theatre," *Defender*, November 26, 1910, 3; "Sylvester Russell's Review," *Freeman*, January 21, 1911, 5.

9. Bauman, *The Pekin*, 51; see also Josephine Lee, *Oriental, Black, and White: The Formation of Racial Habits in American Theater* (University of North Carolina Press, 2022).

10. Bauman, *The Pekin*, 118.

11. Ibid., 119. Shipp's *Lime Kiln Club* formed the basis for Bert Williams's Biograph film, *The Lime Kiln Club Field Day* (1913), an all-Black cast feature film that was never released until the Museum of Modern Art rediscovered the rushes in its vaults and created an edit in 2014. Williams's film centers on the field day of the club, providing ample scenarios to showcase his comedy. When Williams shot his film for Biograph, he did so with members of the Lafayette Players, the stock company of Harlem's Lafayette Theatre that was inspired by the Pekin's.

12. Ibid.

13. Sylvester Russell, "The Lime Kiln Club Makes a Hit at the Pekin," *Defender*, March 11, 1911, 3.

14. Lester A. Walton, "Pekinites en Tour," *New York Age*, May 4, 1911, 6; Bauman, *The Pekin*, 163.

15. Bauman, *The Pekin*, 129.

16. Sylvester Russell, "The Wolf and a Song Review at the Pekin," *Defender*, May 13, 1911, 4.

17. "City Buys Pekin," *Defender*, June 16, 1923, 10.

18. Flournoy Miller, "Bob Motts," unpublished manuscript, Flournoy Miller collection, NYPL MG599 B1 F16.

19. Sylvester Russell, "Wise and Milton and Fanny Wise at the Monogram," *Freeman*, September 16, 1911, 5.

20. Sylvester Russell, "Tim Moore as Harry Brown's Redeemer at the Monogram," *Freeman*, August 7, 1915, 5.

21. Barry Moreno, correspondence with the author, August 14, 2020.

22. "At the Crown Garden Theatre," *Freeman*, October 9, 1915, 5.

23. "The Lincoln—Moore's Chicago Follies," *Freeman*, November 13, 1915, 5.

24. Ibid.

25. Marriage certificate, Commonwealth of Kentucky. Moore's name is listed as Harry R. Moore. According to Barry Moreno, Tim was able to marry Gertie upon receiving a decree of divorce from his previous wife, Hester.

26. Joseph Clark, Jr., "The Ruby Theatre," *Freeman*, September 18, 1915, 6.

27. "A Note or Two," *Defender*, February 19, 1916, 6.

28. "At the Theaters in Indianapolis," *Freeman*, April 29, 1916, 4.

29. Bauman, *The Pekin*, 104.

30. "At the Theaters in Indianapolis," *Freeman*, April 29, 1916, 4.

31. Ibid.

32. *New York Age*, July 20, 1916, 6; *Freeman*, July 22, 1916, 5.

33. Bauman, *The Pekin*, 25.

34. Advertisement, *Honolulu Star-Bulletin*, October 3, 1916, 7.

35. "No Burnt Cork is Necessary for Minstrels at the Bijou Tonight," *Honolulu Star-Bulletin*, October 4, 1916, 12.

36. "Vaudeville is Added to Bill by Bronze Revue," *Honolulu Star-Bulletin*, October 12, 1916, 7.

37. "No Burnt Cork is Necessary."

38. Ibid.

39. Ibid.

40. "Vaudeville is Added to Bill."

41. Advertisement, *Honolulu Star-Bulletin*, October 7, 1916, 7; "'Bronze Revue' Scores Big Hit in Minstrelsy," *Honolulu Star-Bulletin*, October 5, 1916, 7.

42. "Musical Comedy Bill Changes at Bijou Tonight," *Honolulu Star-Bulletin*, October 16, 1916, 10.

43. "Musical Comedy Scores Big Hit," *Hawaii Post*, January 10, 1917, 4; Advertisement, *The Evening News* (Sydney), February 5, 1917, 6.

44. Advertisement, *Sydney Sun*, February 5, 1917, 2.

45. *Daily Herald* (Adelaide), April 12, 1916, 2.

46. *Daily Standard* (Brisbane), October 1, 1917, 3.

47. *Kalgoorlie Westralian Worker*, April 27, 1817, 1.

48. "New Bijou Bill Produces Laughs," *Honolulu Star-Bulletin*, January 3, 1918, 10; *The Honolulu Advertiser*, February 2, 1918, 5.

49. Advertisement, *St. Louis Argus*, May 16, 1919, 4.

50. "Moores Back," *Chicago Defender*, April 5, 1919, 9.

51. "Tim Moore Says," *Chicago Defender*, May 3, 1919, 8.

52. "Tim Moore's Letter," *Chicago Defender*, February 23, 1924, 7.

53. Ibid.

54. For more on TOBA, see Michelle R. Scott, *T.O.B.A. Time: Black Vaudeville and the Theater Owners' Booking Association in Jazz-Age America* (University of Illinois Press, 2023).

55. Tony Langston, "The Monogram," *Chicago Defender*, March 3, 1923, 6.

56. "Rainbow: Tim Moore's Chicago Follies," *Afro-American*, March 24, 1922, 4; "Lincoln: 'Tim Moore's Follies,'" *Afro-American*, October 13, 1922, 7; "Rainbow:

Tim Moore's Chicago Follies," *Afro-American*, March 24, 1922, 4; Tony Langston, "Avenue has Vaudeville and Movies; Tim Moore's Chicago Follies at the Monogram," *Chicago Defender*, May 20, 1922, 6; "Wesley Varnell's Review," *Billboard*, July 29, 1922, 42; "Lincoln: 'Tim Moore's Follies,'" *Afro-American*, October 13, 1922, 7.

57. *Billboard*, January 13, 1923, 51. Strasser subsequently moved his offices to Norfolk, Virginia.

58. Advertisement, *Billboard*, July 1, 1922, 42; "At the New Douglas Theatre," *New York Age*, May 12, 1923, 6.

59. I have not located the source story for *His Great Chance*.

60. "Here and There Among the Folks," *Billboard*, October 13, 1923, 57.

61. Plot summary taken from "His Great Chance," *Afro-American*, June 15, 1923, 2, and Leigh Whipper's synopsis, *Billboard*, May 19, 1923, 52.

62. "His Great Chance" is Newest Film," *Afro-American*, May 18, 1923, 4; "His Great Chance," *Billboard*, May 19, 1923, 52. Whipper's review was published by entertainment correspondent J. A. Jackson.

63. "'His Great Chance' a Big Hit at Lincoln," *Pittsburgh Courier*, December 29, 1923, 11; D. Ireland Thomas, "Motion Picture News," *Chicago Defender*, November 17, 1923, 6; *Billboard*, May 19, 1923, 52.

64. Thomas, "Motion Picture News"; "His Great Chance," *Afro-American*.

65. "'His Great Chance' a Big Hit."

66. Advertisement, *Afro-American*, June 15, 1923; "At the Globe," *Cleveland Gazette*, September 15, 1923, 2; "'His Great Chance' a Big Hit."

67. "At the Lincoln," *Pittsburgh Courier*, December 22, 1923, 8.

68. "Douglass: Vaudeville and Pictures," *Afro-American*, October 26, 1923, 4.

69. J. A. Jackson, "In Old New York," *Afro-American*, January 11, 1924, 13.

70. J. A. Jackson, "Vaude. at Lafayette," *Billboard*, June 6, 1925, 48.

71. "'Blues' Queen Goes Big at New Lincoln," *Pittsburgh Courier*, March 22, 1924, 10.

72. "Harlem, Once One of New York's Best Vaudeville Neighborhoods, Fading Out," *Billboard*, August 20, 1927, 11.

73. Ibid.

74. Ibid.

75. "Colored Show Folks' Best Season for White Stage Jobs," *Variety*, October 12, 1927, 1.

76. "Actors See Most Prosperous Theatre Season Ahead," *Afro-American*, October 22, 1927, 9.

77. "Mutual Off Alhambra," *Variety*, August 17, 1927, 41.

78. "Musical Comedy at the Alhambra Next Week," *New York Age*, June 11, 1927, 6; "Another Alhambra Theatre Debacle," *New York Amsterdam News*, June 29, 1927, 11; "Gusdhofer [*sic*] Acquires Alhambra from Keith," *Billboard*, August 20, 1927, 11.

79. "Alhambra Theatre Will Open Under New Policy Monday, August 22," *New York Amsterdam News*, August 17, 1927, 10.

80. Ibid.

81. Advertisement, *New York Amsterdam News*, August 22, 1927, 7.

82. "Alhambra Theatre Shows Progress After 2 Months Under New Management," *New York Age*, October 29, 1927, 6.

83. "Alhambra Theatre Will Open Under New Policy."

84. "Negro Convention Buys out Alhambra for Week," *Variety*, August 24, 1927, 36.

85. Advertisement, *New York Age*, August 20, 1927, 6.

86. "Alhambra to Present New Revue Monday," *New York Amsterdam News*, August 26, 1927, 7.

87. Advertisement, *New York Age*, September 3, 1927, 6; "'Lucky Numbers' at the Alhambra," *New York Amsterdam News*, August 31, 1927, 13.

88. Chappy Gardner, "Tim Moore's Popularity," *Pittsburgh Courier*, September 3, 1927, 3.

89. "All Negro Staff at the Alhambra Theatre," *New York Age*, September 3, 1927, 6.

90. Ibid.

91. "Alhambra Revue Went Over Fine," *New York Amsterdam News*, September 7, 1927, 13.

92. "Alhambra Theatre Shows Progress."

93. "De Bidgell Making Good," *New York Amsterdam News*, September 14, 1927, 12.

94. "Once Famous Singer Sure Alhambra Will Succeed," *New York Amsterdam News*, September 14, 1927, 12.

95. "All Negro Staff at the Alhambra Theatre," 6.

96. "Alhambra Revue Went Over Fine."

97. Chappy Gardner, "Color Line 'Taboo' At New York Theatre," *Pittsburgh Courier*, October 15, 1927, 14.

98. Jayna Brown, *Babylon Girls: Black Women Performers and the Shaping of the Modern* (Duke University Press, 2008), 190.

99. "Alhambra Has Splendid Bill," *New York Amsterdam News*, September 14, 1927, 12.

100. "'Dixie Magnolias' at the Alhambra Theatre Next Week," *New York Age*, September 17, 1927, 6.

101. "Judge Goddard's 3 'No's' Clear Up Angles on Fight Films," *Variety*, October 26, 1927, 11.

102. "Fight Pictures Drew Well Here," *New York Amsterdam News*, October 19, 1927, 9.

103. "Harlemites Can See Fight," *New York Amsterdam News*, October 12, 1927, 10.

104. "Dempsey-Tunney Fight Pictures Being Shown at Alhambra Theatre This Week," *New York Amsterdam News*, October 12, 1927, 12.

105. Advertisement, *New York Amsterdam News*, September 28, 1927, 8.

106. "Inside Stuff on Vaude," *Variety*, October 19, 1927, 39.

107. Ibid.

108. Ibid.

109. *New York Age*, October 1, 1927, 6.

110. "Brunettes Are Really in Order," *New York Amsterdam News*, October 5, 1927, 10; "'Porgy' Cast in Harlem," *New York Amsterdam News*, November 30, 1927, 13.

111. "'Choosers' at the Alhambra," *New York Amsterdam News*, January 4, 1928, 10.

112. Ibid.

113. "'Pullman Dandies' at Alhambra Next Week," *New York Amsterdam News*, September 7, 1927, 12.

114. "Alhambra Has Splendid Bill," *New York Amsterdam News*, September 14, 1927, 12.

115. "'Dixie Magnolias' at the Alhambra."

116. "Henderson and Brown with 'Dixie Magnolias,'" *New York Amsterdam News*, September 21, 1927, 12.

117. "Tim Moore and Eddie Hunter," *New York Amsterdam News*, November 16, 1927, 8.

118. Advertisement, *New York Amsterdam News*, September 28, 1927, 8.

119. "Novelties at the Alhambra," *New York Amsterdam News*, October 19, 1927, 8.

120. "A Touch of the 'Wild and Wooly,'" *New York Amsterdam News*, November 2, 1927, 9.

121. "Two Harlem Theatres Catering to Colored People Have Formed Merger," *New York Amsterdam News*, November 23, 1927, 13.

122. "Tim Moore and Company at the Lincoln Theatre," *New York Amsterdam News*, January 25, 1928, 9.

123. "'Circus Day' the Revue at the Alhambra Theatre," *New York Amsterdam News*, March 28, 1928, 8.

124. *New York Age*, March 31, 1928, 6; "Alhambra Idea Meets Success," *New York Amsterdam News*, April 11, 1928, 9.

125. "At the Lafayette Theatre," *New York Age*, March 1, 1930, 5.

126. George Tyler, "Harlem Rambles," *Afro-American*, February 28, 1931, 9.

127. "Baby Moore Gilbert," *Chicago Defender*, August 18, 1928, 6.

128. Theophilus Lewis, "The Harlem Sketch Book," *New York Amsterdam News*, June 25, 1930, 11.

129. "Harlem Rambles," *Afro-American*, February 14, 1931, 8; George D. Tyler, "Benefit Shows in N.Y., Balto., D.C., for Actors," *Afro-American*, April 4, 1931, 8.

130. Tyler, "Benefit Shows."

131. W. Rollo Wilson, "Many Cities Will See Big-Time Stage Stars in Series of Benefits," *Pittsburgh Courier*, March 28, 1931, 8.

132. The Rambler, "Harlem Scandals," *Afro-American*, May 7, 1932, 20.

133. Ralph Matthews, "Can Artistic People Stay Married?," *Afro-American*, October 7, 1933, 18.

134. "Hundreds View 'Kingfish's' Body," *Los Angeles Sentinel*, December 18, 1958, 1.

135. Theophilus Lewis, "Fifty Years of Progress in the Theatre," *Pittsburgh Courier*, July 15, 1950, 8.

136. "Harry Moore, TV 'King Fish,' is Dead at 70," *Chicago Daily Tribune*, December 14, 1958, 49.

JULIEN LEVY GALLERY, NEW YORK CITY, 1945

1. I'm deeply grateful to Michael R. Taylor for bringing this exhibition catalog to my attention.

2. Julien Levy, *Memoir of an Art Gallery* (Putnam, 1977), 28.

CONCLUSION

1. Gabrielle Daniels, "Something Else Again," *Poets Reading the News*, January 27, 2019, www.poetsreadingthenews.com/2019/01/something-else-again. Daniels published the poem, with slight differences, in *Something Else Again: Poetry & Prose, 19752019* (Dogpark, 2020), 98–99.

2. Jack Wang, "Silent Film of Black Couple's Kiss Discovered, Added to National Film Registry," *UChicago News*, December 12, 2018.

3. Michael Boyce Gillespie, "B.A.D. (Black Abstraction Dreaming): A Conversation with Kevin Jerome Everson," *Black Camera* 8, no. 1 (Fall 2016): 158.

4. Walter Rugaber, "Cleveland Riots Linked to Reds," *New York Times*, August 10, 1966, 1, 30.

5. Kahlil Pedizisai, interview by the author, July 13, 2020.

6. bell hooks, *Salvation: Black People and Love* (Perennial, 2001), 16.

7. Hannah Giorgis, "*If Beale Street Could Talk* and the Urgency of Black Love," *The Atlantic*, December 25, 2018, www.theatlantic.com/entertainment/archive/2018/12/if-beale-street-could-talk-channels-baldwins-vision-of-black-love/576751.

8. Michael Loderstedt, "Holding Pattern: Michael Loderstedt Interviews Kahlil Pedizisai About Collinwood Now," *CAN Journal* 9, no. 2 (Summer 2020), canjournal.org/holding-pattern-michael-loderstedt-interviews-kahlil-pedizisai-about-collinwood-now.

9. Mat Grobar, "In the Right Combination Of Brass & Strings, 'Beale Street' Composer Nicholas Britell Finds the Sound of Love," *Deadline*, December 21, 2018.

10. Jenkins, quoted in ibid.

11. Britell, quoted in ibid.

12. Ibid.

13. Christina Sharpe, *In the Wake: On Blackness and Being* (Duke University Press, 2016), 124.

14. Ibid., 9.

15. "Chicago to Have a Colored Theater," *Freeman*, August 3, 1901, 5.

16. Web site of René Marie, https://renemarie.com/about.

17. Lara Pellegrinelli, "Poetic License Raises a Star-Spangled Debate," July 3, 2009, www.npr.org/2009/07/03/106257394/poetic-license-raises-a-star-spangled-debate.

INDEX

Page numbers followed by *fig.* indicate illustrations, and notes are indicated by "n" followed by the note number.

Founded in 1893,
UNIVERSITY OF CALIFORNIA PRESS
publishes bold, progressive books and journals on topics in the arts, humanities, social sciences, and natural sciences—with a focus on social justice issues—that inspire thought and action among readers worldwide.

The UC PRESS FOUNDATION
raises funds to uphold the press's vital role as an independent, nonprofit publisher, and receives philanthropic support from a wide range of individuals and institutions—and from committed readers like you. To learn more, visit ucpress.edu/supportus.